AF765056

'Monsters and other figures of the inhuman have become an ethical and political task that this book tackles with excellence and originality. Drawing on the strangeness that inhabits us and the very specific type of anguish it causes, Rodrigo Gonsalves paints a portrait of the monstrosities of our time, showing how every monster is always a re-edition of a previously forgotten monster, that returns to remind us that the past has not passed yet, even when they present themselves as a future to come.'

Christian Ingo Lenz Dunker, *University of São Paulo*

'Rodrigo Gonsalves book is a landmark in the politics of negativity. In our subjective economy, negativity has to be read through the lenses of the Freudian notion of the uncanny – in this way, a new perspective opens up to investigate recent figures of monstrosity and to further our understanding of angst, fears and desires in the face of the ideological predicaments of nowadays. Gonsalves monstrosity suggests another look at Lacan's ethics of psychoanalysis, one pertinent for today's dimension of subjective suffering which derives from our capitalist global structure. An essential book for anyone interested in where we stand today!'

Slavoj Žižek, *Birkbeck Institute for the Humanities, University of London*

'As an author who more than three decades ago happens to have written one of the seminal texts on the uncanny, I now rejoice at this new book which takes the multifarious clue of the uncanny much further and wider, using it systematically as a red thread leading from Freud's initial insights through Lacan's complex ramifications to Marx's logic of commodity universe, the horror in popular culture and to the monstrous logic of the present-day capitalism – finally proposing the prospect of a monstrous materialism that could be a match for the monstrosity of late capitalism. A very necessary reading.'

Mladen Dolar, *University of Ljubljana*

MONSTROSITY AND THE PSYCHOANALYTIC DIMENSIONS OF THE UNCANNY

This accessible and meticulously researched book is a philosophical study dedicated to the psychoanalytic dimension of the uncanny and the discussions on monstrosity as fundamental concepts to address contemporary experiences of anguish, desire, suffering and alienation.

Examining the uncanny in Freud and Lacan, the book explores its emergence through psychoanalysis and aesthetics, as well as its meta-psychological implications. Chapters explore the history and connection between the uncanny and monstrosity in both philosophy and psychoanalysis, following on from the construction of Freud's 'The Uncanny' in 1919, and focusing on these concepts through different perspectives, such as Marxism. Finally, the book argues towards the importance of a monstrous grammar (re)introduced to psychoanalysis, in order to sustain a specific clinical listening of our times.

Offering new insights and arguments on these fascinating concepts, this book will be of interest to philosophers, psychoanalysts and psychologists, as well as also appealing to professionals and students in the worlds of arts, film and history.

Rodrigo Gonsalves is a practicing psychoanalyst, with a PhD in Philosophy, Critical Theory and the Arts at European Graduate School and is a PhD candidate in Clinical Psychology at the University of São Paulo. He authored numerous chapters and articles about Lacanian psychoanalysis and new directions in Marxist theory. He is currently a researcher for Latesfip (Interdepartmental Laboratory of Social Theory, Philosophy and Psychoanalysis/USP), member of GPOL/PSOPOL (USP), member of the editorial committee of the journal CT&T: Continental Thought and Theory and an editor-member of Lavra Palavra, an independent publishing house from Brazil.

Philosophy and Psychoanalysis
Series Editor Jon Mills

Philosophy and Psychoanalysis is dedicated to current developments and cutting-edge research in the philosophical sciences, phenomenology, hermeneutics, existentialism, logic, semiotics, cultural studies, social criticism and the humanities that engage and enrich psychoanalytic thought through philosophical rigor. With the philosophical turn in psychoanalysis comes a new era of theoretical research that revisits past paradigms while invigorating new approaches to theoretical, historical, contemporary and applied psychoanalysis. No subject or discipline is immune from psychoanalytic reflection within a philosophical context including psychology, sociology, anthropology, politics, the arts, religion, science, culture, physics, and the nature of morality. Philosophical approaches to psychoanalysis may stimulate new areas of knowledge that have conceptual and applied value beyond the consulting room reflective of greater society at large. In the spirit of pluralism, *Philosophy and Psychoanalysis* is open to any theoretical school in philosophy and psychoanalysis that offers novel, scholarly, and important insights in the way we come to understand our world.

Titles in this series:

Philosophy Meets the Infant: How New Research Transforms the Understanding of Human Existence
Stephen Langfur

R. D. Laing in the Twenty-First Century: Sanity, Therapy, Love
Michael Guy Thompson, Fritjof Capra and Douglas Kirsner

Monstrosity and the Psychoanalytic Dimensions of the Uncanny
Rodrigo Gonsalves

MONSTROSITY AND THE PSYCHOANALYTIC DIMENSIONS OF THE UNCANNY

Rodrigo Gonsalves

Routledge
Taylor & Francis Group
LONDON AND NEW YORK

Designed cover image: Getty Images

First published 2026
by Routledge
4 Park Square, Milton Park, Abingdon, Oxon OX14 4RN

and by Routledge
605 Third Avenue, New York, NY 10158

Routledge is an imprint of the Taylor & Francis Group, an informa business

British Library Cataloguing-in-Publication Data
A catalogue record for this book is available from the British Library

ISBN: 978-1-032-56890-4 (hbk)
ISBN: 978-1-032-56888-1 (pbk)
ISBN: 978-1-003-43754-3 (ebk)

DOI: 10.4324/9781003437543

Typeset in Times New Roman
by SPi Technologies India Pvt Ltd (Straive)

CONTENTS

ACKNOWLEDGEMENTS

This book is dedicated to Maria Eugênya Pacioni Gomes for all her loving support.

This book is a result of my PhD dissertation at the European Graduate School. It consolidates the result of years of study dedicated to Freud's uncanny and its echoes. First, I would like to thank my supervisor Alenka Zupančič for all the support and lessons from which I will dearly carry out for the rest of my life. I wish to thank Slavoj Žižek for his insightful research, his thought provoking classes and for all the exchanges during my T.A. years in EGS. I would also like to thank Mladen Dolar for all his support, kindness and crucial conversations during the development of this project. I wish to also thank other EGS professors who had a significant impact in my way of thinking and ultimately my own life: Alain Badiou, Jacques Rancière, Giorgio Agamben, Elie During and Christopher Fynsk. Thank you all.

I would like to especially thank Cindy Zeiher for her honest friendship, intense engagement, critical commentary and all the support throughout the laborious development of the present book. On the same note, I wish to thank Christian Dunker and Ivan Estevão for all their support, guidance, supervision, trust and inspiring exchanges throughout these years. I'd like to thank Vladimir Safatle for his critical remarks and Clarissa Metzger for her close listening throughout the years.

This thesis would not have seen the light of day without the collaboration, conversations and support of some dear friends of mine: Federico Ruberto, Victor Marques, Daniel Tutt, Reza Naderi, Fernanda Magallanes, Lydia Magyar, Marcelo Checchia, Marilia Pisani, Gregor Moder, Samo Tomšič, María Angélica Madero, Rebecca Sanchez, Roland Bolz, James Batcho, Grace Euna Kim, Manuela Koelke, Maíra Marcondes, JP Caron, Gabriel

Tupinamba and Dennis Yao. I really wish to thank my fellow comrades Gabriel Landi, Daniel Fabre, Douglas Barros, Bruno Santana and Giovana Aranda, for their dedicated militant efforts towards collective work. I also would like to thank my fellow travellers in the studies of monstrosities: Jorge Adeodato, Cian Barbosa, Mariana Haddad, Luciano Nuzzo, Manuella Mucury and Cassia Figueiredo (*in memoriam*), your continued efforts provided a much-needed push towards the end of this research. I would also like to thank my friends from the University of Sao Paulo: Rodrigo Alencar, Lucas Bulamah, Rafael Alves Lima, Mário Senhorini, Paulo Beer, Augusto Coaracy, Priscilla Santos, João Felipe Domiciano, Patricia Ferreira, Bruno Belém, Sophie Bergheimer, Hugo Lana, Luciana Guarreschi, Rafael Cossi, Gabriel Binkowski and Aline Martins, whose continued discussions can be noticed throughout each page of this work.

I'd like to thank Dr. Jon Mills, Cindy Zeiher, Alice Maher and Katie Randall for accepting this project and materializing years of dedication into a book. Thank you!

I also would like to thank all the love and support from my family during the development of this research.

INTRODUCTION

We need to talk about monsters. It is undeniable that monsters populate our culture nowadays, present in films, TV shows and literature. Monsters have become "normalized" in our everyday culture. This book is not dedicated to the historical account of monsters *per se*, historians like Jean Delumeau (1978) in *La Peur en Occident (XIVe–XVIIIe siècles)*, as well as other have already established a solid account for the history behind monsters in Western societies. Instead, the key objective of this book is to provide theoretical dignity to monsters as an ideological *symptom* (in the psychoanalytic sense) of late capitalist societies, and how their presence invites a better look to our own constitutive *strangeness*.

As Jacque Lacan argues, we are all born into language, we all emerge as beings into and through it. This fundamental remark sustains that what happens in language has effects over us. In this specific sense, the presence of monsters has consistency to a certain degree within our imaginary and symbolic exchanges. The presence of monsters provokes our imaginative and critical thinking and to discuss abstractions, we must make room to discuss that which is not in the world outside, but something which makes itself present as an idea through language. Monsters have a certain degree of philosophical consistency which shouldn't be dismissed as juvenile. Their presence in our culture may transmit something about our own lives if we allow ourselves to pay attention to them. There is a certain wisdom behind horror films, they invite us to pay more attention to things which we *don't want to see*. So, what if instead of dismissing the immediate impression of the realm of horror, we paid more attention to what bothers us in it? Could monsters teach us something about ourselves? Could we learn something about our fears through them? This book

DOI: 10.4324/9781003437543-1

aims at providing dignity to monstrosity as a field, considering what we can learn about our humanity from what we fear. Even if these horrific fictional creatures aren't out there, their invisible presence expresses something about our fears and anxieties. So, more than a simple exercise of abstraction, this book discusses how the cultural creatures we create and embrace, manage to formulate a specific symbolic and imaginary fabric that translates our feelings, fears and desires.

Horror literature mobilizes feelings, invades our affection and can provoke a reaction. We can feel frightened, scared and so on, but most of all, monsters allow for a particular investigative direction about our own (in)humanity. We live in a world where fear has become a fundamental affect to organize social and political narratives. Thus, understanding what we fear allows us to comprehend what we are subjected to, and it provides a better understanding of what imprisons us. Certainly, there are real-life frightening fears and imaginary fears – but the border between them is not always as clear as we would like to think. Our imaginary fears, which are also accommodated in language and can be traced back to social context and to our own lives, can inform us about our subjectivization process. Considering how the psychoanalytic apparatus allows someone to take a step towards subjective emancipation – a transformation which may take place through the subjective dissolution of what dominates the subject – psychoanalysis can be a crucial ally in the investigation of our fears, systems of domination and oppression. There is something that only through the discussion about monsters and monstrosity can fully express our own angst. Such creatures populate language and imagination, they push the boundaries of our traditional pairs of opposites, that is, dead and alive, body and mind, normal and abnormal and so on. To provide philosophical dignity to monsters means pursuing the critical questions they allow us to ask about ourselves and the ideological elements guiding our contemporary society; these lines of questioning are what this book aims to defend when it establishes *monstrosity* as an aesthetic-political category.

The theoretical realm of philosophy and psychoanalysis has historically engaged with tragedy and comedy to sustain their investigations, this book defends that the horror is also deserving of attention. There are aesthetic-political consequences which can only be critically examined and reached through the investigation of monstrosity. The book argues how monstrosity encapsulates and expresses aspects of the subjective suffering fruit of the technologies of exploitation under neoliberal capitalist societies. In short, there are narratives expressed through horror, in all its strangeness, which translate subjective dimensions of contemporary suffering as valid as tragic and comic ones and therefore also, deserving our attention.

The realm of horror as a genre can prove itself pertinent to further critical thought for today's sensibilities (or lack thereof). This is why we should take a closer look at our sociability nowadays, especially considering the following question: what is our stand concerning *strangeness*? The underlying premise here is that anguish nowadays has developed monstrous contours. This certainly does not mean that everybody should go through an analysis, nor does this work ascribe a universal desire to psychoanalysis; this book is one amongst other attempts to (re)introduce the *uncanny* and its internal dialectical configurations as *aesthetical* grounds to articulate *monstrosity*. Much like aesthetics is the philosophical realm of studies dedicated to sensibilities, affections and to the Arts; it is also the realm which can indicate how we can organize our thinking from another standpoint regarding our own feelings. If the Arts can indicate how our lives could have been, then aesthetics is the philosophical field that learns from its transformative teachings. This is why the uncanny as a psychoanalytic operator can be pertinent to consider today's sensibilities. The aesthetic-political dimension of the uncanny under Lacan's dialectical materialistic perspective, provides grounds to suggest a *monstrous grammar*, that is, a linguistic logical structure which deals with negativity in its most radical form. This is what the book defends as groundwork towards *monstrous materialism*.

Reference

Delumeau, Jean. *La Peur en Occident (XIVe–XVIIIe siècles)*. Paris: Fayard Édition, 1978.

1

ON PHILOSOPHY AND PSYCHOANALYSIS

An (uncanny) compossibility

1.1 Compossibility

The present section discusses the contours and impasses of the *short circuit* between psychoanalysis and philosophy. It is true that both fields are *vast* and that within themselves lie more internal conflicts and battles that one could care to enumerate..., this brief section has no intention of ultimately *setting the score* between the fields. What it does is to investigate this *non-encounter* inspired by Jacques Lacan's psychoanalysis and some of the consequences which derive from it.

Lacan investigated Freud's psychoanalytic method through many years of his life. It was his clinical practice that paved the way to his theoretical developments in the field and not the opposite. Lacan's formalizations are the result of his clinical endeavours, and his teachings are the consolidation of these attempts. Instead of severing Lacan's thinking into parts, his teachings should be considered as a constant construction, where his early lessons are as significant as his later ones. Nonetheless, a constant element in Lacan's efforts is his integration and discussion with different fields of knowledge to improve his clinical reasoning. This formalization left marks for branches of both psychoanalysis and philosophy.

Alenka Zupančič addresses such tensions in her book *What is sex?* (2017). The author defends how *sex* is an element that lies between both fields and not the one or the other. The lesson to take from this point was elegantly summarized by her in an interview in 2019. When asked about philosophy *or* psychoanalysis, her response was: *yes, please!* In a way, the thinker encapsulates how productive it can be to think about such tension (2017, 1), but she also addresses impasses for both *philosophy* and *psychoanalysis* as a result. On the

DOI: 10.4324/9781003437543-2

one hand, philosophy has benefited from this encounter by reconnecting to concepts that were being abandoned (aiming at pure philosophy and ontology) and then, inventing new ontologies; on the other hand, (Lacanian) psychoanalysis got busy "rediscovering" the experimental clinic to sustain their "exclusive" access to the Real (2017, 3). Facing this scenario, Zupančič aims at a *third* direction, a non-given alternative, to construct her Freudo–Lacanian philosophical investigation of the *concept* of sex for psychoanalysis as an inherent contradiction of being. Thus, Zupančič's gesture of *not abandoning this site* invites productive consequences to be thinking. Or to better put it, what follows is an uptake of this position of not abandoning this site and moreover listening to it properly.

Prior to Zupančič, the philosopher Alain Badiou dealt with the (non)articulations between *philosophy* and *psychoanalysis*. Although his philosophical project is somewhat instigated by Lacan, at the very end of *Being and Event* (2005), Badiou sets distinctions between his philosophy and psychoanalysis (e.g., his theory of the subject (2009) differs from Lacan's unconscious subject and so on). For now, let's consider a common ground according to Badiou's thoughts. In his book *Conditions* (2008), Badiou argues that *love* and *mathematics* are external borders shared between both fields. Thus, he addresses a *compossibility* between them:

> Philosophy and psychoanalysis can be *compossible*, since the double paradoxical condition of mathematics and love cross over at the point where the void is localized in the disjunction of an un-known truth and a knowledge of that truth. This point, I maintain, is that of the Idea. Psychoanalysis and philosophy both ultimately demand that we adhere to Spinoza's unfounded and unfoundable maxim: '*Habemus enim ideam veram*', we in effect have, but as an effect of nothing, as localization of the void, a true idea. One, at least.
>
> *(Badiou 2008, 208)*

Much could be said about the encounter between philosophy and psychoanalysis. And Badiou here provides some indications on another meaningful aspect about this encounter, he points towards *what cannot be said*. From this argument we can understand two main things: (1) Badiou's discussion about *compossibilities* through external shared borders between the fields (i.e., *double paradoxical condition*) and (2) a delimitation (or denunciation) of *limits* between both fields. If, at the first level, we notice an open invitation towards theoretical endeavours, it is at the second level that a vital procedure is required simultaneously: to be aware of *limitations* within both fields. The consequences to this very point are detrimental to adequately discuss what is at stake in this encounter; nonetheless, this is a line of argumentation which usually bothers some (mostly psychoanalysts more than philosophers…). It is true that both fields are constantly growing within themselves, but to *bridge* them is simply not an *automatic* or obvious procedure (some more fragile articulations tend to miss this critical point). Another essential aspect of understanding limitations between both fields is that it prevents naive troubling confusions, (mis)appropriations and (mis)usage. Mladen Dolar in *Freud and the Political* (2008) provides an understanding concerning such *limitations*:

> The difference is not that between "theory" and "practice," for psychoanalysis involves a practice of its own, a practice that is always also a social practice, although on the basis of one-by-one, not of collectivity; and politics always involves a theory. One could put it this way: if psychoanalysis refrains from making a step, from deciding the ambivalence, filling the crack, proposing a new tie for the untied, if there is a missing step where a step would have to be made, then politics makes a step too much. It decides the ambiguity; it proposes a new tie; it engages what Badiou calls fidelity to the event, a subjective stance, a process of truth without a guarantee, a transformation. It turns the negative condition into a positive project, a movement, a party, a militancy. It proposes a new master signifier, although it may well be aware of its contingency. No doubt it thereby obfuscates the crack; it eludes the contingency and the ambiguity; it represents the unrepresentable – that is, it misrepresents it – but this is the price of taking the step. On the other side, psychoanalysis is not simply apolitical; rather, its circumscribing the site of the political is something that calls for politics, for an engagement in that site, for a step too far, although one can only do it at the price of entering into another logic than the one that sustains psychoanalysis. The circumscription of the site is no neutral description; it requires a step, although it itself doesn't prescribe what this step should be.
>
> *(Dolar 2008, 28)*

Dolar neatly explains this rather usual (mis)usage that psychoanalysis imposes onto itself, for simply confusing its own coordinates with social reality coordinates as the same. Psychoanalysis is not *apolitical* but it has a politics of its own, which is not *the* shared social politics. The (social) practice of psychoanalysis *is* that of one-on-one, small groups, local intervention and it cannot pretend that a transposition of its operational logics works *automatically* towards large social impasses, to follow this path means to obliterate psychoanalysis itself and missing what could be its more meaningful contribution towards radical emancipatory understandings towards impasses of reality. As Dolar describes, psychoanalysis' importance of "circumscribing the site of politics" (Dolar 2008, 28) means it can locally provide all the required *thinking* prior to taking an actual political step (therefore, it is not a neutral procedure, but an *immanent* and dialectical one), but it cannot prescribe which step *must* be taken. It is for *seriously assuming* these limitations that Dolar manages to draw consequences from this *encounter*.

Here, Dolar does not refrain from Badiou's own engagement with both limits and potentials from this encounter. Dolar defends the role of psychoanalysis providing context to someone's suffering and its validity drawn from within its limitations, and he also presents this non-bridgeable, fundamental aspect concerning its practice. In a way, Dolar has the impasses from compossibilities in mind, improving valid consequences drawn to both sides of this encounter. This point becomes even clearer when Dolar engages with Freud's "Group Psychology and the Analysis of the Ego" [1921]:

> …psychoanalysis does engage with the mass, but only at its core – that is, at the point of *Masse zu zweit*, the mass of two, the point of the vanishing mediator of hypnosis, the missing link that Freud interposes between the phenomena of love and the mass formation. The vanishing mediator returns with a vengeance, for psychoanalysis itself can be described precisely as the reenactment of the mass of two. This is its home ground, but the whole point is precisely to undo what has been tied together in hypnosis – that is, to unravel the amalgamation of the ego ideal and the object that has been put into its place.
>
> *(Dolar 2008, 28–29)*

Psychoanalysis does not engage with the masses,[1] only with the "masses" from within the "I" (i.e., the masses of symptoms which make up the "I"), specifically for those who engage in the psychoanalytical clinic. This is a valid argument for Freud, but is a lesson understood (and further clarified) by Jacques Lacan. Following Dolar's argumentation, the psychoanalytic treatment is a process of undoing an "amalgamation between the ego ideal and the object that has been put into its place" (Dolar 2008, 29). Thus, psychoanalytic practice operates on the one-on-one bases, establishing a *reenactment of the mass of two*, only to untie the knotting of masses at its core, then moving on until it unties itself. Dolar certainly translates an important feature of psychoanalysis as a practice, which is to understand its own limits, and by doing so, it builds the conditions for the analysand to find its way out of the process he got himself into. But Dolar's central interpretation concerns the internal dialectical movement of the psychoanalytic process: for psychoanalysis to still operate, it must understand its limitations and set grounds towards proper alternatives. Or to paraphrase Lacan's quote repeated by Dolar: an "analysis prepares us, but leaves us at its door…" and Lacan is clear about what this means, "the ethical limits of analysis coincide with the limits of its practice. Its practice is but a prelude to moral action as such…" (Dolar 2008, 29); it provides a prelude, it takes us to radically different positions and introduces grounds towards a *new* direction but never takes this final step for us (or the first one for that matter…).

For Vladimir Safatle (2017), the Lacanian process of analytical *cure* has *emancipatory validity* because it revolves around the *liquidation* (dissipation) of transference (Lacan 2015) between analyst and analysand. For the psychoanalytic process to work, the analysand must believe the analyst knows something about himself or about his desire that he himself does not know (what Lacan would later explain as the object a placed to the side of the analyst). After establishing this relationship of power, the analysis turns into an emancipatory process because it allows for the removal of domination by the side of the analysand, through exhaustively talking the analysand gets rid of the *identifications* he used to hold on to in the first place and finds ways to subsume the analysis itself. Safatle defends, along the lines as Dolar has argued (and Zupančič as well), that a certain subjective destitution can be accomplished through the engagement of (dis)orienting one's experience of *knowledge* through a psychoanalysis; but in order for that very process to fully *operate* in an emancipatory direction, it must necessarily build its own *conditions* to be "traversed" or to be *liquefied*.

Another interesting point made by Safatle concerns how the psychoanalytic process, through its very own mechanisms of functioning, sustains an instability to the established relationships of power and provides means to either make or unmake them (Safatle 2017, 212). Thus, this double movement provides grounds for the subject to operate power beyond domination (Safatle 2017, 213). In a way, it provides grounds to *deal* with the fact that:

> the anxiety of freedom does come from the transcendental possibility of doing and desiring it all, but from the very own realization that we are acted by an exterior causality to which, as Lacan puts it, is something in us more than ourselves.
>
> *(Safatle 2017, 212)*

Another way of understanding this impasse comes from Dolar's affirming that between the two, there is a *non-relation* at stake, that is, a *parallax gap*. And Dolar explains Žižek's parallax as:

> ...a shifting perspective between two points of view, between which no synthesis or mediation is possible. One can only see the one way or the other, although one is looking at the same thing. The two may be two sides of the same thing, but they can never meet at the same level; there is no neutral common space; there is a non-relation, but this ties them together.
>
> *(2008, 29)*

Far from being a lateral discussion (or backtracking) from the engagement between psychoanalysis and philosophy, this is a central element about this discussion. Žižek's *parallax view*, understood as an (im)possible *in-between* two points of view, without any synthesis or mediation, clearly re-introduces *negativity* from within the gap to all the attempts to address this very own encounter. And Dolar affirms that *there is* a non-relation which ties them together; he is clearly arguing that there is something of the Real at stake at this (dis)junction. In a way, to affirm this core of negativity justifies the necessity to pay better attention to the figures of negativity which define our existence. When Dolar addresses these impasses between ego and the I and its relationship with the Other, he is talking about this realm of negativity. Not only in our subjectivity, but how negativity materializes in our beliefs, our exchanges and our imaginary and symbolic ties, in our relationship with the Other. The psychoanalytic method permits a better understanding of *ontological inconsistencies* present in our everyday life.

Zupančič explains the Lacanian definition of *non-relation* as follows: "...[a] non-relation is not simply an absence of relation, but is itself a real, even the Real" (2017, 18). And in a much more precise sense, she argues that for Lacan:

> ...it is only the inexistence of the relation that opens up the space for relationships and ties as we know them...The non-relation gives, dictates the conditions of, what ties us, which is to say that it is not a simple, indifferent absence, but an absence that curves and determines the structure with which it appears. The non-relation is not the opposite of the relationship, it is *the inherent (il)logic (a fundamental "antagonism") of the relationships* that are possible.
>
> *(2017, 24)*

This clearly does not even start to cover what are all the depths of the encounter between philosophy and psychoanalysis, but it surely provides grounds to discuss how both fields deal with the impasses of our encounters with the Lacanian Real and its role in our inherent negativity in our *(in)humanity* (Zupančič 2000). Up until now, we could cover aspects of understanding the importance behind setting boundaries between philosophy and psychoanalysis, how this provides our framework and what does it mean to move on from this point on, we will cover in our next steps. Here, it is important to highlight some of these impasses which set the scene to our main discussion, mostly covering how the impasses derived from the Real instead of providing a fixity, it provides limitations to which subjects are subjected and responded to. The compossibility of the Real between both fields opens the discussion for its examination. And the overall justification of (re)articulating the *uncanny* lies not only with some interesting remarkable features of its internal conceptualization, but also for understanding that it is an open engagement with the encounter with the *unknown*, a certain fleeting feeling where the gap in knowledge and the gap in being overwhelmingly infiltrate reality and provide the utmost (dis)orientation possible for our (in)human experiences: it is an examination of the Real. The plan behind providing a monstrous grammar lies in accepting the uncanny as a concept still useful for dealing with impasses of our living(-dead) experiences and making a case for its rendition within the fruitful tension between psychoanalysis and philosophy.

1.2 Freud and *The Uncanny*: a prelude

Sigmund Freud's *The Uncanny* (2003b) [1919] has a bit more than one hundred years and yet, still seems to be one of the most curious and productive texts in psychoanalysis. Although surfacing from psychoanalysis, this text branched out towards different fields (Literature, Film Theory, The Arts, Psychology…) and some even claim that it could sustain it deserves a field for itself.[2] The present section does not aim at an exhaustive cartography of the conceptual developments of the *uncanny* through time. The objective lies in (1) presenting a certain *shift* in Freudian psychoanalysis sustained by this investigation and (2) presenting a consequence of this very own shift for psychoanalysis to be thought of. The perspective adopted here is affiliated with Freudo–Lacanian and that it does not concern a step-by-step reconstruction of Freud's text. Here, it is important to take a closer look at what the investigation of the uncanny brought upon the psychoanalytic field. Although taking also into consideration that the investigations surrounding the *uncanny* gained much attention to itself from other fields such as philosophy, literature and so on, our main concern here is the philosophical appraisal of the uncanny raised as a *concept* consisting of inherent contradictions.[3] Thus, the *uncanny* could be a productive concept to address philosophical impasses of *inhumanity* (Zupančič 2017; Žižek 2008 [1991], 2009, 2012).

Before reading or even being in "direct" contact with Freud's *The Uncanny* (2003b) [1919], one must acknowledge how popular this Freudian theme is. It is not hard to find TV shows, scenes from films that "invoke" the Freudian uncanny. Perhaps, one could argue that the same goes for some other psychoanalytic notions and its concepts, which after a centennial of existence got integrated into culture. Or, there is something to do with how the *uncanny* has an intrinsically fascinating emotional dimension, which simultaneously captures those who try to capture it. Something about how it lures and lurks upon us, it is always there as a destabilizing influence and yet we are drawn to its esoteric intrigue. Under the academic scope, the uncanny is one of those notions with an insurmountable number of articles, texts, books and interpretations, inspired either directly or indirectly by it. Although a heroic attempt of summarizing and structuring the many directions of Freudian unfolding would have an immense research value, this is not the direction which we want to take for this section. Rather, this section has a far more modest intention, it wants to *briefly* retrace Freud's original text, presenting some of its key articulations, to illustrate how the uncanny could interestingly provide philosophical insights towards an understanding of the structures of *impasses* and *paradoxes*.

Taking into consideration that, first there is the historical context in which Freud is inserted into and second, there is the metapsychological intricacies surrounding this text. About the first point, we could consider Jacques Le Rider contextualization of "Modernité Viennoise et crises de l'identité" (1992), emphasizing the blossoming of Vienna's Modernity as a certain historical "catching up" to European *avant garde* intellectual movements that had already taken place in Germany and France (1992, 21). For Le Rider, Viennese Modernity concerns a historical period from 1890 to 1910 in which philosophical, literary and artistic were creatively progressing towards establishing their own steps as a result of "political, social and cultural transformations that started in 1848, and which sensibly progressed in Vienna up until 1938, where the coincidence of new movements amongst many different fields can be noticed..." (1992, 24). Concerning philosophical thought of the time, Le Rider points out how Johann Friedrich Herbart (1776–1841) and Bernard Bolzano (1781–1848), the first one an anti-Kantian philosopher and the second one an anti-German Idealism philosopher (specifically against Hegelianism) were very influential. And that it was Franz Brentano (1853–1917) who took on Austrian philosophical tradition from its predecessors and approached with the English post-Kantian thought of John Stuart Mill that was very popular at the time.

Le Rider points out how Freud is inserted into a certain cultural crisis of identity and the impasses of "man without qualities" (referring to the context of the First World War in 1913) solidified in Romantic tendencies, but it also translates an effort to localize viable symbolic-imaginary coordinates to deal with an extreme scenario of social implosion. Thus, Le Rider argues that the most distinct aspect of Viennese Modernity is its "identity crises" and how thinkers like Ernst Mach and Sigmund Freud (1992, 74) had a role in providing answers. Le Rider posits that

> Freud introduced inquietude to notions of permanence, continuity and cohesion, traditionally tied to the idea of identity of the subject... After Freud, what does it even mean to still talk about the identity of the subject, if not only to confirm its illusory character? Or even, from it, it makes sense to substitute the notion of identity for *identification*...
>
> *(1992, 75)*

This brief discussion provides some historical context to Freud's developments but it also provides background to a point raised by Dolar (1991) concerning the uncanny as intrinsically related to the advent of *modernity* from a "historical rupture brought about by the Enlightenment" (Dolar 1991, 7). It goes without saying that there are some historically dated examples used by Freud, but Dolar's point towards an insightful aspect at the core of the notion of the uncanny, which is to assume a certain paradoxical attempt to apprehend a non-apprehensibility of a given historical moment.

The second important point to consider before a direct interaction with Freud's *The Uncanny*, concerns the *metapsychological*[4] intricacies and impasses surrounding the formulations of the psychoanalyst at that time. *The Uncanny* was published in 1919 one year prior to what is considered a significant *shift* within psychoanalysis itself, that is, the formalization of the *death drive* (*Todestrieb*) (2003a). Freud's impasses at the time concerned the question which led to his split with Karl Gustav Jung, summarized by Zupančič (2017) as follows:

> In a brief reference to Jung that Freud makes at this point, he seems to be reminded of the following fact: the dualism of the drives ("life drives" and "death drives") is actually the other side of conceiving libido as a "neutral," desexualized substance. Jung, he says, "making a hasty judgment, has used the word libido to mean 'instinctual/drive force' (*Triebkraft*) in general." This is precisely what was at stake in his split with Jung, this desexualization of the libido in terms of a neutral primary substance, subsequently divided between different drives which are all part of this "great whole" called the libido, and basically constituting two (complementary) principles....Freud's fundamental move, on the other hand, was to desubstantialize sexuality...
>
> *(99–100)*

This fundamental discussion between Freud and Jung that led towards their splitting up, concerns Freud's inclination towards a "monism (singularity) of antagonism, contradiction, or split" (2017, 100) against the Jungian "monism of the substance-libido" (2017, 100). For Zupančič:

> Freud recognizes this antagonism and split on the ground of sexual drives themselves, and not of "his" death drive, which, as we have seen, is pretty monolithic... Freud now restates his conviction that all that science can tell us here would amount to the fact that there are only sexual drives. More exactly, that only sexual drives possibly impel us elsewhere than to a return to an earlier (homeostatic) stage. This can be further focused by saying that only sexual drives "*drive*" us in any meaningful sense of the word (differently from the "magnetism of the inanimate," which seems to be of the modality of the *fatigue*, and not of the drive proper – *Trieb*).
>
> *(2017, 100)*

Zupančič emphasizes the shift in Freud's perspective, where sexual drives cannot be simplified as life drive, since within themselves "they repeat or reproduce the very split between life and death; with sexual drives death is *inherent* to life, conditioning its perpetuation" (2017, 101). In this clarification, we can localize Freud's impasses which required a metapsychological *shift* and, we can approach Freud's "solution" which is to introduce a paradoxical trait of "negativity" inherent to life at "the very site of *psychic* life – insofar as the latter is coextensive with the unconscious" (2017, 101).

Freud's reformulation of his theory drives can be understood as a recentring of negativity to the core of psychoanalysis. Freud was faced with the clinical impasse of war neurosis, with the recurrent nightmares of traumatic events, as an *unconscious compulsion to repeat* – as a proper mystery, when patients presented the tendency to re-live in their dreams a traumatic experience. Since his *traumdeutung* investigated core desires taking place in dream-form through operations of condensation and displacement, what could it mean to find someone "stuck," repeating in an oniric form that very own traumatic moment – repeatedly? What could this have to do with unconscious desires? Freud's answer is death drive and a shift in his theory of drives in 1920.

And Žižek summarizes death drive as:

> …the most radical tendency of a living organism is to maintain a state of tension, to avoid final "relaxation" in obtaining a state of full homeostasis. "Death drive" as "beyond the pleasure principle" is the very insistence of an organism on endlessly repeating the state of tension.
>
> *(Žižek 2004, 24)*

The metapsychological shift, which Freud was formulating at that time, comes to another light if articulated in terms of the negativity and paradoxical instances argued by Žižek and Zupančič. The articulation that sexuality operates *within* death drive, as this fundamental paradoxical marker of (in)humanity, defended by the thinkers, comes from Lacan's discussions between death drive and sexuality (Žižek 2004, 101). Zupančič argues how,

> Lacan often returns to and reaffirms this implication of death at the very heart of sexuation; sometimes in the very terms of "death," and sometimes in the more formal language of "reduction" or "loss" involved in sexual reproduction (for example, when he refers to the joining of two sets of chromosomes).
>
> *(Žižek 2004, 101)*

Indeed, Lacan does not abandon this point throughout his *teachings*, carrying out that death drive is the *only* drive there is.

Nonetheless, after taking a closer look at the intricacies of this Freudian impasse, we do not aim at solving the discussion between monism and psychoanalysis, but to affirm along with the Slovenian thinkers what were the clinical and theoretical impasses which led Freud to come up with this reformulation. And by doing so, we can understand the metapsychological movement in which the text of 1919 relates to. But to the extent the uncanny is concerned, Masschelein (2011) prudently reminds us how: "[a] careful examination of the word uncanny in Freud's oeuvre reveals that while the essay appeared at a turning point in Freud's thinking, it by no means occupied a central position [...] in Freud's theory." (Masschelein, 2011, 11). The fundamental turning point to Freud's psychoanalysis relates to setting *negativity* at its core and how this metapsychological transformation could better inform us about the uncanny.

So, considering the metapsychological circumstances in which Freud faced at the time of both publications (which are just one year apart from one another), this opens room for some speculative investigations. Nicholas Royle notes that in the 1920s, Freud simply forgets about *The Uncanny*. But Royle ties them together:

> Freud doesn't explicitly name the death drive in 'The Uncanny'... But the death drive lurks, as if forbidden to speak its name, everywhere in the 1919 essay. This silence is at once appropriate and strange, for it is a crucial attribute of Freud's theory of the death drive that it works in silence, imperceptibly, without being noticed.
>
> *(2003, 86)*

This is a rather valid speculative point form Royle, the uncanny gains full potency once we consider its metapsychological context, even if Freud doesn't mention it in his 1920s text. The idea of articulating *uncanny* and *death drive* makes sense, since both notions try to set the record straight with a difficulty of judgement and *repetitions*[5] (2003, 86). The commonalities between both texts could be understood as different responses to the deadlocks deriving from the *same* metapsychological shift. But the textual disappearance of the *uncanny* in "Beyond Pleasure Principle" [1920] (2003a) is a point that cannot be ignored. Nonetheless, to speculate about this common ancestry between both texts, could be a valid way not to *reinvent* death drive, but to ponder upon what death drive could inform us about some "mysterious" traits of the uncanny. For once, both notions deal with paradoxical impasses of returning to the *inanimate* and with the *compulsion to repeat* in their own terms.

1.3 A brief examination of Freud's "The Uncanny"

Freud's *The Uncanny* [1919] is composed of three different sections that could be *pedagogically* separated into main points of *investigation*: (1) *Linguistics*; (2) *E.T.A. Hoffmann's short tale The Sandman and psychoanalysis*; (3) *uncanniness and its paradoxical (non-)relation to other psychoanalytic concepts*. Let's briefly recapitulate Freud's *The Uncanny* avoiding a painstaking, *line per line*, commentary of the text. Although a certain hermeneutics of the text is in order, the overall idea is not to satisfy ourselves with it. The ultimate purpose here is to understand the particularities of the *uncanny* within Freud's psychoanalysis. From this appreciation, benefiting from the internal construction of the uncanny, we could sustain key points towards a certain *shift* that the uncanny (we can think of the uncanny as a strange opaque unfamiliarity which one simply struggles pinpoint with logic) promotes within psychoanalysis and psychoanalytic thinking. The uncanny sustains a methodological operator that organizes negativity and impasses for the psychoanalytic clinic.

The first section of the text mainly concerns a peculiar *linguistic* investigation about the uncanny.

And as Mladen Dolar (1991) summarizes the main point behind this section of the text:

> It was fortunate for Freud that such a paradoxical word existed in the German language, and perhaps it gave him the idea for the paper in the first place. The word is the standard German negation of *heimlich* and is thus supposed to be its opposite. But it turns out that it is actually directly implied by *heimlich*, which means familiar, homely, cozy, intimate, "arousing a sense of agreeable restfulness and security as in one within the four walls of his house"; by extension, what is familiar and securely tucked away is also hidden, concealed from the outside, secret, "kept from sight… withheld from others"; and by a further extension, what is hidden and secret is also threatening, fearful, occult, "uncomfortable, uneasy, gloomy, dismal… ghastly – that is, *unheimlich*, uncanny. There is a point where the two meanings directly coincide and become undistinguishable, and the negation does not count – as indeed it does not count in the unconscious."
>
> *(1991, 5)*

Dolar reads Freud's uncanny through Lacanian lenses, noticing how it is influenced by another one Freud's texts *Negation* [1925] (the unconscious knows no contradiction), he notices how Freud starts his investigation almost as if puzzled by the paradoxical linguistic dimension of the word *unheimlich*. Freud goes through different languages, dictionaries and definitions, in order to explain his perplexity. The linguistic element, which mainly characterizes this section, derives from this peculiar attitude behind Freud's investigation. Nonetheless, the main point already announced by Dolar concerns this *paradoxical trait* present in the uncanny.

Freud's starts by addressing that it is a peculiar thing for a psychoanalyst to engage with aesthetics investigations (2003a, 298) and as Royle states, this does not stop Freud from doing it anyways (2003, 7). Royle dives deep into the realm of the uncanny presenting it as a marginalized aspect of specialized literature on aesthetics. Freud establishes that:

> There is no doubt that this belongs to the realm of the frightening, of what evokes fear and dread. It is equally beyond doubt that the word is not always

> used in a clearly definable sense, and so it commonly merges with what arouses fear in general.
>
> *(Freud 2003a, 298–299)*

Clearly, Freud noticed a peculiarity within the uncanny and he tries to pinpoint it amongst different fields (aesthetics, philosophy, literature, psychiatry, psychoanalysis, just to name a few…). Freud's *linguistic* endeavour comes from the fact that he dives into dictionaries and meanings of *das unheimliche*, debating the German antonyms starting with the neutral prefix *Un*, for example, in: "*unbehagliches, banges Grauen erregend*" ['arousing uneasy, fearful horror']" (2003a, 312), then moving towards nine different languages, trying to find if this paradoxical element was somehow preserved in other languages as well. From this laborious endeavour, Freud moves towards this first finding:

> For us the most interesting fact to emerge from this long excerpt is that among the various shades of meaning that are recorded for the word *heimlich* there is one in which it merges with its formal antonym, *unheimlich*, so that what is called *heimlich* becomes *unheimlich*… our attention is seized by Schelling's remark, which says something quite new – something we certainly did not expect – about the meaning of *unheimlich*, namely, that the term 'uncanny' (*unheimlich*) applies to everything that was intended to remain secret, hidden away, and has come into the open.
>
> *(2003a, 314)*

Freud clearly tries to encapsulate an explanation towards his perplexity concerning the uncanny, especially from the puzzling *silence* about the paradoxical nature of the prefix *un* in language and the lack of discussion of the inherent ambivalence present in *unheimliche* ("unhomely" as a denied or betrayed *homely* by the negative particle which precedes it). In the second section, Freud will dispute Ernst Jentsch's interpretation of the term, Jentsch is a psychiatrist who had established prior literature about the uncanny and who's responsible for introducing E.T.A. Hoffmann's text[6] to the discussion in the first place. Jentsch makes a case for the uncanny resulting of "intellectual uncertainty" and Freud's psychoanalytic interpretation opposes this view as simplistic. Rather, Freud tries to establish a psychoanalytic perspective of the uncanny as "directly attached to the figure of the Sandman, that is, to the idea of being robbed of one's eyes" (Royle 2003, 40). So, Freud (2003a) does not directly oppose the "uncertainty" at stake, he opposes what could have been provoking it (Freud, 2003a, 319). While Jentsch places the uncanny based upon his interpretation of Hoffmann's short tale on Olympia (an automaton, a living-doll that "fools" Nathaniel, thus provoking "intellectual uncertainty"), Freud will make his case revolving around the "traumatic" repressed memories in Nathaniel's backstory (the main character of the tale). Following the tale, in Nathaniel's childhood his nanny told him a "horror story" which was associated with the non-elaborated traumatic event of his father's death. For Freud, the uncanny appears intertwined with all of Nathaniel's life's experiences when the fear of death or thoughts about finitude are revealed to the character.

Freud's psychoanalytic render of the uncanny introduces how this *feeling* requires another *grammar*, it requires an openness towards a different *logic* to fully engage with the arrival of *new signifiers* it produces. Freud examines how E.T.A. Hoffmann's narrative throughout the tale does not lead to uncertainty as Jentsch defends. Freud emphasizes *how* Hoffmann writes the tale:

> It is true that the author initially creates a kind of uncertainty by preventing us – certainly not unintentionally – from guessing whether he is going to take us into the real world or into some fantastic world of his own choosing.
>
> *(2003a, 324–325)*

Here, Royle (2003) defends that Freud's approach to the text is exactly this: *Freud's* approach. For Royle, there is not *a* single approach to text: "…what is bizarre is that Freud seems completely oblivious to the fact that his 'short summary' is fundamentally his own 'short story': he recounts the story as if it were an objective, disinterested, merely 'factual' summing u…" (Royle 2003, 40), the English author defends that by doing so, Freud tends to forget how interpretative any text actually is and how to retell a tale is actually to tell a new tale (Royle 2003, 40). Indeed, Royle's criticism is on point, but he disregards the impacts of Freud's argument *inside* psychoanalysis – the openness that the uncanny introduces to clinic interventions and to thinking about psychoanalytic cure – Royle disregards how amongst many possible interpretations, Freud's interpretation can be pertinent to psychoanalysis. Avoiding the vicious circle of hyper-speculation or relativism, Freud's openness towards multiplicity through the uncanny can be found here.

Freud disputes that the origins of the uncanny is *uncertainty* (Royle 2003, 325–326), he agrees that Hoffmann's narrative *propels* uncertainty, not like in fantastic literature or with the introduction of fantastic elements (e.g., Shakespeare' "spirits, demons and ghosts" (Royle 2003, 325)), but because he blurs the lines between reality and the fantastic. For Freud there is a *certainty* at stake:

> … in the course of Hoffmann's tale this uncertainty disappears; it becomes clear that the author wants us too to look through the spectacles or the spy-glass of the demon optician, and even, perhaps, that he has looked through such an instrument himself. For, after all, the conclusion of the tale makes it clear that the optician Coppola really is the lawyer Coppelius and so also the Sand-Man.

> ...There is no longer any question of 'intellectual uncertainty': we know now that what we are presented with are not figments of a madman's imagination, behind which we, with our superior rationality, can recognize the sober truth – yet this clear knowledge in no way diminishes the impression of the uncanny. The notion of intellectual uncertainty in no way helps us to understand this uncanny effect.
>
> *(Royle 2003, 325–326)*

The uncanny, according to Freud, derives from the unconscious. This is what he means by stating that "[t]he notion of intellectual uncertainty in no way helps us to understand this uncanny effect" (Royle 2003, 326). The uncanny is a formidable emissary of the unconscious, where certainty and uncertainty confuse themselves in an (un)translatable composition over reality for the subject, but the angst that it produces is undeniable. The subject of the unconscious is immersed in negativity, therefore, any human experience is necessarily decentralized, because the I is not in charge. This is why all human experience is fundamentally (in)human, because it cannot be fully consciously experienced. Freud's appreciation of Hoffmann's tale is concerned with the psychoanalytic comprehension of the uncanny.

Later, Freud connects the uncanny to the infantile fear of losing one's eyes, as a re-edition of the castration complex under new terms; the "mitigated form of the penalty of castration" (Royle 2003, 326) derived from the Oedipal complex. The subjective introjection of law to live in a society, which evokes the symbolic reminders of the *lex tallionis* ossified in our past and passed on generationally through culture and language. Here, Freud sets in motion his theory of substitutive representants for the fear of castration, that is, how the symbolic revitalizes neurotic structures (Royle 2003, 327). The logic of how childhood fears can be present in adults, denotes how apparent oppositions are not as clear as we would like to think. This is why Freud uses Otto Rank's (2011) emblematic research on the Double[7] in this text (Royle 2003, 327). There is something uncanny about this redoubling we experience in situations such as this.

Moreover, the uncanny and the theme of the double are completely bound to each other. Not only our own redoubling can be profoundly uncanny but otherness as such, is also profoundly uncanny. When we think about how a person relates with another, how semblance and difference can blur itself, there are many uncanny elements to be considered. Or as Freud puts it: "[t]his relationship is intensified by the spontaneous transmission of mental processes from one of these persons to the other – what we would call telepathy – so that the one becomes co-owner of the other's knowledge, emotions and experience" (Royle 2003, 330). Certainly, Freud is not taking telepathy seriously, what seems to be the case here is the neurotic mechanism of omnipotence of thought (a certain mechanism of defence against hopelessness [*hilflosigkeit*], presupposing a control – not agency, but control over one's reality). A primordial narcissistic mechanism of defence against the discontent caused by other's uncontrollable nature. Freud clearly states how between one person and another there is uncanniness at stake. He also asserts that "[t]he self may thus be duplicated, divided and interchanged," (Royle 2003, 330) defending the (dis)centralized aspect of the I and shattering any attempt at a normalized I, a self without inherent contradictions.

Freud continues his intervention of Hoffmann's tale defending how Nathaniel shows that an infantile fear of castration can be revitalized, and the feeling produced is uncanniness, a certain strangeness. Another uncanny element discussed by Freud is Olympia, the animated doll, that differently than Jentsch (who sustains the uncanny as an intellectual confusion) understands the uncanny as a childhood reminder which resurfaces in adult life. For Freud, children "...make no sharp distinction between the animate and the inanimate..." (Royle 2003, 328), but when it comes to Olympia, it is not necessarily *angst* which is at stake, there is a certain *wish* that takes place. Many children would adore having their dolls coming to life to play with them (Royle 2003, 329). Freud borrows from Rank's studies on the double that

> [t]he double was originally an insurance against the extinction of the self or, as Rank puts it, 'an energetic denial of the power of death', and it seems likely that the 'immortal' soul was the first double of the body.
>
> *(Royle 2003, 330)*

Freud argues that the double concerns an *inversion*: what was once a defence against the annihilation of self becomes a constant reminder of it, or as Freud puts it: "having once been an assurance of immortality, it becomes the uncanny harbinger of death" (Royle 2003, 331). More than a mere forgotten mechanism which disappears with primitive narcissism, it manages to "acquire new content "from later stages in the evolution of the ego" (Royle 2003, 331). Over time, a special authority within the ego manages to objectify it and confront it with "self-observation and self-criticism," building a "kind of censorship, and so becomes what we know as the 'conscience'" (Royle 2003, 331). Freud also attributes to the double the feature of carrying all possibilities of what could have been but never was, all counterfactualities of reality and speculations our imaginations cling on and "all the strivings of the ego that were frustrated by adverse circumstances, all the suppressed acts of volition that fostered the illusion of free will" (Royle 2003, 332). The uncanny is an emissary of unconscious reminders through many different actualizations.

A bit further in Freud's appreciation of the uncanny in Hoffmann's tale, he approaches another quintessential element of uncanniness: *repetition*. As he claims:

> The factor of the repetition of the same thing will perhaps not be acknowledged by everyone as a source of the sense of the uncanny. According to my

> own observations it undoubtedly evokes such a feeling under particular conditions, and in combination with circumstances – a feeling, moreover, that recalls the helplessness we experience in certain dream-states.
>
> *(Royle 2003, 333)*

All of the sudden, Freud comes up with an interesting set of examples from ordinary experiences of everyday life which he deems uncanny: trying to prevent walking into a certain part of town and ending up there (an example about Freud himself, getting lost in an Italian *piazza*) (Royle 2003, 333); getting lost in the woods trying to find its path, only to reach the same spot (Royle 2003, 334); stumbling in the dark into the same piece of furniture while trying to find a light-switch (Royle 2003, 334); other examples driven by their unintended repetition spark uncanniness, like seeing the number 62 many times during the course of the same day (Royle 2003, 334), or the (re)occurrence of the same name appearing in letters or texts in a short period of time (Royle 2003, 334–335); the uncanniness of 'presentments' that 'comes' true (Royle 2003, 338); the 'evil eye' (Royle 2003, 338); and this list goes even further... Nonetheless, two elements standout in Freud's list: first, there is *compulsion to repeat* as related to the uncanny:

> It is strong enough to override the pleasure principle and lend a demonic character to certain aspects of mental life; it is still clearly manifest in the impulses of small children and dominates part of the course taken by the psychoanalysis of victims of neurosis.
>
> *(Royle 2003, 336)*

and second, an episode from "Notes upon a Case of Obsessional Neurosis"; his famous case of obsessional neurosis (*the Rat Man*) (Royle 2003, 339). These stands representing the uncanny at the level of psychoanalytic practice, but also, this is where a clear connection between the uncanny and Freud's death drive can be established.

Another element of the uncanny concerns "omnipotence of thought," the attempt to control reality through thought revolves around *animism*, as Freud states "...everything we now find 'uncanny' meets the criterion that it is linked with these remnants of animistic mental activity and prompts them to express themselves" (Royle 2003, 340). So, two points can be understood about the emergence of the uncanny: (a) the return of the repressed and (b) inversion to its opposite:

> ...every affect arising from an emotional impulse – of whatever kind – is converted into fear by being repressed, it follows that among those things that are felt to be frightening there must be one group in which it can be shown that the frightening element is something that has been repressed and

> now returns. This species of the frightening would then constitute the uncanny, and it would be immaterial whether it was itself originally frightening or arose from another affect.
>
> *(Royle 2003, 340)*

And Freud then goes on to say that…

> …if this really is the secret nature of the uncanny, we can understand why German usage allows the familiar (das Heimliche, the 'homely') to switch to its opposite, the uncanny (das Unheimliche, the 'unhomely') (134), for this uncanny element is actually nothing new or strange, but something that was long familiar to the psyche and was estranged from it only through being repressed.
>
> *(Royle 2003, 341)*

After establishing these more general assertions from his own examples, Freud establishes how the uncanny is intimately connected with the blurred lines between life and death (a blurred line categorized in the consciousness vis-à-vis a Kantian logic of time). He makes a case that even being the most certain thing, it still gets us all by surprise:

> It is true that in textbooks on logic the statement that 'all men must die' passes for an exemplary general proposition, but it is obvious to no one; our unconscious is still as unreceptive as ever to the idea of our own mortality.
>
> *(Royle 2003, 342)*

Certainly, Freud is here addressing the impasses of finitude (and infinitude) at the level of the unconscious, especially considering that at that level, it does not know *negation* [1925] (Dolar 1991). Or perhaps, that the unconscious *is* negation. And the analyst emphasizes the centrality of dealing with death as a core element, that is intimately connected with the uncanny. To summarize his findings, Freud states that:

> [o]nly a few remarks need now be added to complete the picture, for, having considered animism, magic, sorcery, the omnipotence of thoughts, unintended repetition and the castration complex, we have covered virtually all the factors that turn the frightening into the uncanny.
>
> *(Royle 2003, 343)*

The next additional elements introduced by Freud reintroduce how animistic traits and superannuated elements of our childhood are still very much present, even after being "educated," "cultured" and/or "civilized," which for Freud could work as an attenuating factor, nonetheless, not preventing uncanniness to take place, especially when the intricacies of (in)finitude which are an inherently mobilizer of anguish is at stake. Thus,

> animism and the superannuated workings of our mental apparatus, but seems to call for special emphasis. This is the fact that an uncanny effect often arises when the boundary between fantasy and reality is blurred, when we are faced with the reality of something that we have until now considered imaginary, when a symbol takes on the full function and significance of what it symbolizes, and so forth. This is at the root of much that is uncanny about magical practices.
>
> *(Royle 2003, 345)*

The magical, demonic, illusory and all its in-betweens are interconnected according to Freud with animism and the superannuated, this goes hand in hand with other thesis previously defended by Freud in *Totem and taboo* [1913] (1955) and after this peculiar, but not exhaustive section with many different examples, Freud finally rescues that the uncanny relates to sexuality: "It often happens that neurotic men state that to them there is something uncanny about the female genitals" (2003b, 347). So, the uncanny is also an emissary of sexuality, perhaps more in line with the Lacanian affirmation of *absence*, that there is no sexual relationship (and yet the fantasy of it is so incredibly familiar!).

In the final section of the text, Freud provides a more clinical examination of the uncanny for psychoanalysis. He admits his dissatisfaction to, up until this point, adequately solve: how does one come to recognize that which is familiar but not graspable within the logic of the consciousness? As he states: "It may be that the uncanny ['the unhomely'] is something familiar ['homely', 'homey'] that has been repressed and then reappears, and that everything uncanny satisfies this condition" ([1919] 2003b, 348). *But he also notices that not all repressed desires or superannuated modes of thought will provoke uncanniness.* So, what makes the uncanny, uncanny for Freud? To sustain his position, Freud suggests that:

> Nearly all the examples that are at variance from our expectations are taken from the realm of fiction and imaginative writing. This suggests that we should distinguish between the uncanny one knows from experience and the uncanny one only fancies or reads about.
>
> *(Royle 2003, 351)*

Freud will then divide the: (1) "uncanny effects associated with the omnipotence of thoughts, instantaneous wish-fulfilment, secret harmful forces and the return of the dead…" (Royle 2003, 352) which is where a fear of the "uncanny" surfaces and requires a testing of reality (Royle 2003, 353) and (2) "the uncanny [which] derives from repressed childhood complexes…" (Royle 2003, 353) a more rare kind of uncanny to find in real-life. To Freud this distinction is crucial from a theoretical point of view, while the vast majority of uncanny examples fit the first kind, the second one is intertwined with psychical reality, or as he states: "Here we are dealing with the actual repression of a particular content and the return of what has been repressed, not with the suspension of *belief in its reality*" (Royle 2003, 353). And Freud here defends that repression must be "stretched" beyond its legitimate bounds, so to make sense of the uncanniness at stake, the animistic perspective of what was *deemed surmounted* enabling this feeling *must* be considered. Thus, Freud elaborates:

> …the uncanny element we know from experience arises either when repressed childhood complexes are revived by some impression, or when primitive beliefs that have been surmounted appear to be once again confirmed. Finally, we must not let our preference for tidy solutions and lucid presentation prevent us from acknowledging that in real life it is sometimes impossible to distinguish between the two species of the uncanny that we have posited. As primitive convictions are closely linked with childhood complexes, indeed rooted in them, this blurring of the boundaries will come as no great surprise.
>
> *(Royle 2003, 34–35)*

In a sense, it is not so much that the uncanny is a childish thing and that, over time, when you get older and become an adult the uncanny dissolves within our process of "civilizing" ourselves. Rather, the good point is understanding how adults are *not separated* from their childhood, especially when it comes to the *unheimlich*. The process of being "civilized" does not settle the score of solidifying our emotions through the domination of sensibilities (Safatle 2017). What the uncanny demonstrates is how objectivity can be problematic without accounting for individual history and local context, the pulsional circuits of the subject must always be accounted for. Thus, the uncanny portrays a certain blurring of lines between external-internal, between different temporalities, present in our interpretation reality itself. For example, the process of internalizing laws to participate in society is an uncanny redoubling process for the subject, the renunciation of satisfactions and endurance of dissatisfactions become economic modes of existence shaping how we live our lives. This peculiar unconscious (dis)agreement with the Other can easily invite someone to the couch.

As Freud states, the uncanny signals repression "…we are dealing with the actual repression of a particular content and the return of what has been repressed, not with the *suspension of belief in its reality*" (Safatle 2017, 353). There is an (un)certainty at stake with the uncanny, an invitation to review the coordinates of reality, characteristic to this unhomely sentiment. And Freud's uncanny is somewhat unique in his psychoanalytic development, the interpretation of blurred lines between (literary) fiction and reality getting a bit distinguishable, as different terms attempt to plug a fundamental crack in knowledge (these *are* tied back with primitive complexes, as Freud states, mostly because the introduction of this *unknown* element in the child, is introduced by the *unknown* from the adult herself/himself). Freud sustains how there are different kinds of the uncanny, one derived from literature and another occurs in reality, but both arising "from superannuated modes of thought" (Safatle 2017, 357), those bound with repressed complexes are more resistant in their active illusions in everyday life, maintaining their belief within reality, while the openly fictitious dissolves the uncanny.

Freud concludes suggesting a certain passiveness towards reality which "succumb to the influence of our material environment" (Safatle 2017, 358), which is a certainly intriguing aspect to defend, especially since he (reinserts into reality itself unsurmounted features of animism *present in* our symbolic fabric through our (unconscious) subjectivity. Moreover, when fiction is declared openly fiction (or fictitious) there is no uncanniness at stake, while the imaginary reliability and protections posited by our (neurotic) *belief* in reality can be quite uncanny. Finally, Freud carves out what the uncanny is for psychoanalysis: anxiety [*angst*]. Thus, "[a]s for solitude, silence and darkness, all we can say is that these are factors connected with infantile anxiety, something that most of us never wholly overcome. Psychoanalytic research has dealt elsewhere with the problem of such anxiety…" (Safatle 2017, 359), sealing this bridge between uncanny and anxiety, as the proper analytic element at stake. The uncanny experience of angst affirms the (dis)orientation of the unconscious subject. As an emissary of the negative ontology of the subject interpreting an open reality to Real's invasions. The uncanny makes a good case for the (in)humanity derived from unconscious logic, where assumptions of "pure" subjectivity and objectivity will always fall short.

1.4 An uncertain uncanny aesthetics

Reading Freud's, *The Uncanny* (2003b) [1919], it becomes clear that (1) a certain strategic *shift* in Freudian psychoanalysis sustained by this investigation. Here, by *shift*, we are understanding how Freud introduces a *different perspective* from his usual strategy behind his "aesthetical" works. And (2) how this shift sustains consequences for *thinking about the psychoanalytic praxis*. Comparing *The Uncanny* (2003b) [1919] with Freud's previous aesthetic works shows us that only *The Uncanny* holds a different strategy: instead of Freud "*psychoanalyzing*" the aesthetics or an aesthetic object, it is *the aesthetics that comes to articulate psychoanalysis*. This could sound rather esoteric and polemic, especially since this text itself is not considered a *central* text in Freud's work. But as Masschelein (2011) remembers: "…this rather short treatise had outgrown 'its marginal position in the Freudian canon' (Ellison 2001, 52) and is now regarded as a central text for Freudian aesthetics" (Masschelein 2011, 3). Indeed, *The Uncanny* is an overshadowed text, especially given the new light casted by the release of *Beyond Pleasure Principle*' [1920] and here we defend his atypical position in comparison to his other aesthetic texts.

The philosopher Ernani Chaves (2015) mentions how Freud's aesthetical contributions leave a lot of controversies along the way (Chaves 2015, 9). And Chaves' "O paradigma estético de Freud" [Freud's aesthetical paradigm] Chaves (2015) considers the exceptionality of *The Uncanny* simply absurd. For him, the text does not sustain any significant change to Freud's psychoanalysis as a whole and it makes no sense to sustain such a claim. As he argues, *Dostoevsky and Parricide* [1928] (1961a) is the antidote to anyone who has drank from the uncanny's Kool-Aid, he defends that Freud skips the strategy used in *The Uncanny* and goes back to his usual strategy: psychoanalyzing the aesthetics. So, Chaves does not see in his text "what this fuss is all about" a bit like Masschelein (2011) has had previously mentioned. But still, to ignore the role of the uncanny is also turning a blind eye to the impacts it provoked later (in and outside psychoanalysis). Indeed, Freud does not pursue aesthetics in the same way he did with the uncanny, but is this enough to affirm or to assume that the uncanny is a minor subject for psychoanalysis? One thing is certain, Freud's *The Uncanny* does not fit and yet, it belongs, as a mark in psychoanalysis.

For the sake of Chaves' argument and in order to better present this polemic, let's introduce some elements from Freud's *The Moses of Michelangelo* (1961b) [1914] and *Dostoevsky and Parricide* (1961a) [1928]. In Freud's *The Moses of Michelangelo*, his analysis starts very apologetic, perhaps even defensive, about the field of aesthetics. Freud considers himself a layman in his analysis (1961b, 211), resonating a lot with the reservations he does to himself at the first paragraph of The Uncanny (2003b, 298). Freud's overall strategy is to submit an artistic object to his psychoanalysis, looking for "...an effective expression of the intentions and emotional activities of the artist" (1961b, 212). Thus, to establish an artist's *intention*, Freud must first,

> ...find out the meaning and content of what is represented in his work; I must, in other words, be able to *interpret* it. It is possible, therefore, that a work of art of this kind needs interpretation, and that until I have accomplished that interpretation I cannot come to know why I have been so powerfully affected. I even venture to hope that the effect of the work will undergo no diminution after we have succeeded in thus analysing it.
>
> *(1961b, 212)*

This is Freud's overall strategy behind his *interpretation*, he emphasizes the mysterious effect that Shakespeare's masterpiece, *Hamlet* had on him, and how after psychoanalysis unraveled the Oedipal nature of the tragedy, he could finally explain it. Shakespeare inspires us towards the impressive aspect of language and its splendour magic appeal, but for Freud, this is a rather curious point, the "source of power beyond them…" (1961b, 213). This is the usual strategy Freud uses to approach psychoanalysis to cultural and aesthetic objects.

The marble statue of *Moses by Michelangelo* in the Church of S. Pietro in Vincoli in Rome is another object of Freud's analysis. He discusses with many different scholar interpretations, he sustains Henry Thode's explanations,[8] but notices something is missing: "Perhaps it is the need to discover a closer parallel between the state of mind of the hero as expressed in his attitude, and the contrast above-mentioned between his 'outward' calm and 'inward' emotion" (1961b, 221). Then, Freud moves on towards investigating the movement expressed by the statue (it is a static object which has the uncanny ability to convey movement and emotion), Moses' hands and hair movements, all to try to notice the forces behind this work. And in the third section, Freud presents his case concerning Moses' statue not as a vengeful moment of wrath, as he states: "What we see before us is not the inception of a violent action but the remains of a movement that has already taken place" (1961b, 229). So, we can clearly notice how Freud's examination concerns interpreting through psychoanalysis the artwork.

In *Dostoevsky and Parricide* (1961a) [1928], Freud is not as careful as his previous approaches. Freud is much more incisive, stating how, "[f]our facets may be distinguished in the rich personality of Dostoevsky: the creative artist, the neurotic, the moralist and the sinner" (1961a, 177) right from the beginning. The overall strategy behind this text and Freud's 1914 text is similar. Both analyses aim to find hidden aspects of the authors or the author's intentions, operating through the object of art. Freud has no concern against dealing with different mediums, he just jumps right at his appraisal of Dostoevsky's (who is not far behind Shakespeare, according to Freud) (1961a, 177).

Comparing the strategy behind The Uncanny [1919] to his other investigations (texts from 1914 and 1928) the strategies are very much different. For Chaves' Freud's *consistency* lies in the similar strategy behind *Moses' of Michelangelo* and *Dostoevsky and Parricide* skipping the strategy used in *The Uncanny* as Chaves states (2016). Freud does not use the strategy he did in *The Uncanny* to *Dostoevsky and Parricide* [1928] but is this enough to consider it insignificant? In other words, is the fact that Freud did not "apply" or "use" elements from his investigation of the uncanny in his later examinations enough to consider it insignificant to his aesthetic appraisals? Perhaps, it could be precisely the opposite. Couldn't it be that *The Uncanny* (2003b) *precisely* for its particularity, for its shifting nature, for its inverted stance, operates not as a tool towards aesthetics, but as an indication of aesthetics infiltrating psychoanalysis? Not so much as an aesthetic appreciation, but as a dialectical strategy for the psychoanalytic clinic itself? Not assuming *The Uncanny* (2003b) as another *aesthetic* text and placing it close to the metapsychological movement it belongs to, as a pre-conceptualization of Freud's death drive could answer Chaves' critique. Obviously, this does not mean that *The Uncanny* (2003b) is automatically rendered as a *clinical* text for Freud, but it has clinical relevance. Freud is not psychoanalysing the uncanny, is the uncanny that is used by Freud to investigate clinical impasses, to organize some of his clinical troubles. And Freud, surely benefits from this aesthetical (uncanny) infiltrations, not only on the in-between the animate and inanimate, but also to understand the compulsion to repeat.

Curiously enough, Chaves translated Freud's *Das Medusenhaupt*[9] (Medusa's head) (2013) to Portuguese. He explains how amid 1922, right after setting death drive to the psychoanalytic field, Freud and their disciples turned their interest towards mythical creatures and symbolic narratives concerning castration (2013, 91). Perhaps more interesting than that, it concerns how Freud articulates horror [Grauen] and castration, "the fear of the Medusa is fear of castration" [*Der Schreck der Meduse ist also Kastrationsschreck*], or why the Medusa provokes horror. Although this point is not further elaborated by the analyst, it is yet, speculatively consonant with a perspective derived from the uncanny after death drive.[10] Unfortunately, this is a point Freud left to be further developed and not one he himself established. Nonetheless, the horror seems to be rightfully associated with the uncanny, the anxiety [angst] emerging from uncanniness and the horror [*grauen*] articulated in 1922, provide interesting grounds to further developments.

This brief excerpt goes along the lines of the *shift* present in the 1919s text, rather than the other aesthetic articulations attempted by Freud. For Freud, castration and fear of castration relate with the sights of women genitalia or becoming aware of its imaginary operation (2013) [1922] (under Freud's psychoanalytic understanding) but, instead of falling into the revisionist perspective of Freud, one should focus on the aspect of sexuality as curiously integrated with horror. To consider how this articulation takes place right after Freud's death drive is formulated and how it *resonates* with the uncanny, certainly makes one wonder, but it is also important to remember how this text was not supposed to have seen the light of day. But making room for speculative considerations: could it be that Freud was interested in furthering yet another emissary of *angst*? Or could it be that Freud would try to articulate a paradoxical stance concerning sexuality and further add to the discussions on the (im)possibility (of the sexual relation) translated under the mythical figure of the Gorgón? Could it be that the petrifying horrors, the irresistible gazing at the uncannily sublime would have been Freud's direction? One could only speculate…

Concerning sexuality as integral to psychoanalysis, Zupančič (2017) explains how psychoanalysis rouses sexuality beyond its moral restraints, dignifying it through epistemological grounds as the crux of psychoanalysis. Not to sustain yet another normativity, but rather for articulating it as a *problem*, as a difficulty, with relevant immanent ontological consequences (Zupančič 2017, 35). As Zupančič defends sexuality is a complex aspect of being that disorient us and such complexity push us towards traits of human social bond (politics, art, science, love, religion…) (Zupančič 2017, 35). Thus, the Slovenian remarks how at first Freud: "…still played with the simple idea of casting sexuality as the hidden motive: repressed sexuality resurfaces as the driving force behind all kinds of highly spiritual human creations, as well as horrors" (Zupančič 2017, 35). Following Zupančič, sexuality is controversial not because of morals *per se*, but because it is rooted in the unconscious and to mechanisms of repression, which denotes its paradoxical ontological intricacies, "manifesting itself as an epistemological problem, or an epistemological *limit*" (Zupančič 2017, 35). This is how Zupančič summarizes one of the classic troubles between *ontology* and *psychoanalysis*, since its incompatibility was (and still is) consistently argued (and defended) by psychoanalysts against any kind of sexual essentialism or why "the desexualization of reality that occurred with the Galilean revolution in science" (Zupančič 2017, 38) was welcomed with open arms by Freudian–Lacanian psychoanalysis.

Hopefully it became clear that to think about this particular combination between the *uncanny and sexual difference* (i.e., sex is always already situated within the Real) invited by Freud through means of *horror* from Medusa's head keeps on haunting the field, not for *what* does it say, but from what persists to inscribes itself as an *impasse* at the core of the field of Lacanian psychoanalytic thinking. This leads towards the second point which we previously addressed, how this very own *shift* sustains consequences for *thinking* psychoanalysis and how raising it as a methodological concept brings fruitful implications (in and outside the field). This case becomes clearer with Lacan's efforts concerning the uncanny (as his render on object a); nonetheless, this is a paradigmatic point of *short circuit* (between philosophy and psychoanalysis) introduced by Freud himself was deeply appreciated by Lacan. Thus, the very own idea of sustaining the uncanny as a articulation informed about the troubles of the field, does not only translates a different approach towards practice of analytic cure in terms of different *narratives* that could be considered in terms of the articulation of suffering, but it seems more than just valid – it seems crucial to approach it under psychoanalytic (unconscious) logic and in clear interiority of its own terms – to (re)integrate the uncanny not as a foreign operator but as this (un)familiar one. To understand the uncanny as a homogenous operator of negativity, which signals towards the impasses of given *limits* of narratives and forcing towards new signifiers. In a way, to *listen* and to *organize* under the limits of tragic and comic narratives are in a way, *framed by the uncanny*, but its traversal makes space for further narratives, providing space the synthesis of contradiction which produce *new* signifiers in the face of our anguish and our fears.

1.5 Lacan's uncanny and its further derivations

Jacques Lacan was no stranger to Freud's *unheimlich* (uncanny), and there are significant clinical and theoretical consequences from this realization. Quickly recovering Henry Krutzen's *Jacques Lacan Séminaire 1952–1980 Index Référentiel* (2009) entry of the term *uncanny* (2009, 712), we learn that the uncanny traversed almost the complete entirety of Lacan's teachings. Lacan's psychoanalysis *propelled* the uncanny into its full potential. Throughout his teachings' Lacan engaged with the *sentiment d'étrangeté* [sentiment of unfamiliarity], for the first time in 13 of July of 1956 (in his third Seminar on Psychoses) and continue to do so, all the way until 16 of December of 1975 (in his twentieth third Seminar on the *Sinthome* (2016)). In this 20 years period, Lacan had articulated the *uncanny* in additional fifteen other occasions. Certainly, we won't visit here the entirety of this journey, but some of its more prominent articulations are to sustain this argument. Thus, it is significant to declare our commitment *with* Lacan and not *against* him (or psychoanalysis for that matter), this section is dedicated to capture a moment of his teachings and not its entirety, understanding his elaborations as fruits of a constant labour of (re) articulating his own analytic practice towards psychoanalytic cure and the dissolution of suffering.

To find in Lacan's return to Freud such an attention towards the *uncanny* speaks volumes, it is certainly one of those articulations that *move* psychoanalysis further into the consequences of its discursivity in the world. As previously stated, Lacan engages more significantly with this notion on three main moments of his teachings (which are only pedagogically separated as follows): (a) the architecture of *anxiety* and the development of the *object a*; (b) the "extimité" space and (c) the truth of the unconscious for the subject. These are constructions intrinsically bound to one another, but their confection as Lacan knew and propagated, circulates around the paradoxical force of the uncanny. This is rather significant, not only for the fact that Lacan gave a formidable amount of attention to a sort of forgotten element for psychoanalysis of his time, but also because of *how* he did it, the presence of this element lies at the very fabric of some crucial elements of his psychoanalysis.

Concerning the architecture of *anxiety* and the development of the *object a*, Lacan in his tenth Seminar *L'angoisse* [Anxiety] [1962] (2004), he establishes his *object cause of desire* articulated with *angst*, however, he directly connects it with the uncanny. Far from being a "discovery," it is more of a *fact* that within *object a*'s "dna" lies the Freudian *unheimlich*. Lacan heavily engages with two key points from Freud's *Inhibitions, Symptoms and Anxiety* (2014) [1962], helplessness [*hilflosigkeit*] and the *object-loss*. For Freud anxiety derives from an investment towards an object which the subject has lost and is desperate to encounter. Lacan invites his students to read Freud's *The Uncanny* [1919] (2014, 29–54) as a presentation of his own understanding of anxiety which sustains that *anxiety is not without an object* (he is referring to his *object a*). As he states:

> Before next time, I would ask you to take the trouble to reread – with this introduction I'm giving you here – Freud's article on the Unheimliche. It's an article that I've never heard anyone comment on and no one seems to have noticed that it's indispensable for broaching the question of anxiety. Just as I broached the unconscious with the *Witz*, this year I'm going to be broaching anxiety with the *Unheimliche*.
>
> (2014, 41)

Certainly, Lacan approach of the *unheimliche* is quintessential to his construction of the anxiety and its articulation with the *object a*. And not without some "excitement" involved in Lacan's part, he declares his articulation between the *unheimliche* with anxiety with a surprise over the fact that nobody had arrived at this point before:

> Anxiety, I've told you, is linked to anything that might appear at the place (-φ). What assures us of this is a phenomenon for which the too scant attention that's been paid to it has mean that nobody has arrived at the formulation that would be satisfactory and unified for the functions of anxiety in their entirety in the field of our experience. This phenomenon is the Unheimliche.
>
> (2014, 47)

So, Lacan incorporates the *unheimliche* into his incursions on anxiety to designate his object a. The analyst explains how the experience of the uncanny as a disfiguration of the neurotic's fantasy, relates to the unveiling of the pulsional object, revealing the object a. As Lacan further elaborates, the experience of uncanny relates from the position of (-φ) which is *heim* ("canny"), but that anything occupying such position (-φ) is *unheimliche* (2014, 47). The *unheimliche* provides the insight of Lacan's paradoxical *framing* of the *object a*, it enforces a (negative) *causal* setting into motion of desire (towards its dialectics) which operates over something intimate (*Heim*) that was always already there (2014, 76).[11] So, the pulsional object enacting the role of desired object, only does so by sustaining the i(a) in its imaginary stance, but once this is stripped away, once it falls apart, what appears is anguish (the object a). Certainly, the Freudian *unheimlich* provides a necessary paradoxical feature for Lacan; this cannot be ignored when it understands of the overall structure of object and Lacan's argument of the (dis)orientation towards objects of the subject of the unconscious.

Taking a closer look at the three crucial attributes of Lacan's articulation of anguish, we can understand its importance in terms of analytic cure (and its intrinsic articulation with the uncanny). The first passage is the famous "anxiety is not without an object":

> I should like to manage today to tell you a certain number of things about what I've taught you to designate as the *object a*,[12] to which the aphorism I put forward last time concerning anxiety steers you, namely, that it is not without object.
>
> *(2014, 100)*

the second passage concerns how anxiety (as an affect) does not deceive:

> Things can branch off in every direction starting off from anxiety. What we were waiting for, when all's said and done, and which is the true substance of anxiety, is that which deceives not, that which is entirely free of doubt.
>
> *(2014, 76)*

or likewise in, "I told you that anxiety has to be defined as that which deceives not, precisely in so far as every object eludes it. The certainty of anxiety is a grounded certainty. It is unambiguous" (2014, 218) and finally the third (a bit less known, but far more crucial) that ties the *object a* with the *real* through the *passage à l'acte*:

> ...where the function of the *a* is in a way so prevalent, that it even went to the point of passing over into the real, a passage à l'acts, whose symbolic relation he nonetheless comprehends so well – Freud gives in. I won't manage anything, he tells himself, and he passes her on to a female colleague.
>
> *(2014, 113)*

These passages do not fully capture the entirety of anguish, even less the intricacies of Lacan's object a, but these are *key* passages that "encapsulate," *grosso modo*, the more complex movements within this Lacanian construction. Lacan does not mistake *Erwartung* (expectation) with *Hilflosigkeit* (helplessness), when discussing anxiety (2014, 75). Anxiety is *not without an object*, which means that there *is* an object: the *object a*, which *frames* any possibility of (non)relating to any other objects in reality. Thus, the distinction between *object a* to any other objects is that the object *cause* of desire is not *the* object of desire, the object a operates *with* and *within* any other object that manages to occupy its *negative framing*. This connects directly with the second Lacanian affirmation concerning anxiety (*an affect which deceives not*), which explain how *certainty* lies to the side of affirming it through its (negative) consequences, the certainty of its existence through its impacts, when the object of a drive is covering it up the subject has no grand troubles with it, but if the pulsional cover gets undone, the *object a* invades, makes itself negatively present and anxiety is the expression of *this* certainty. Or as Lacan says: "[t]he phenomenon of anxiety is the sudden appearance of the *Heimlich* within the frame, and this is why it's wrong to say that anxiety is without object" (2014, 76), and Zupančič further clarifies:

> Now, as with respect in Kantian theory, in Lacanian theory anxiety is not a 'subjective' but, rather, an 'objective feeling'. It is a '*feeling which does not deceive*' (Lacan), one which indicates that we have come near to the 'object' (designating the extimate place of our *jouissance*).
>
> *(2000, 145)*

Yet, another paradoxical feature of the uncanny, as Lacan explores, surfaces when the *hôte* ("host") is considered to capture the topological torsion inherent to Freud's internal-external opposition. But the notion of "host" is not enough, so he slips towards the *hostile* to translate its tensions (2000,75), setting this inherent *struggle* into the very core of this torsion, imprinting a fundamental mobility to the subject of the unconscious and explaining how anxiety simply cannot be without object (a). Clearly, anxiety for Lacan lies at the surfacing of the *framing* of *Heim* (canny), of that which was kept in secret [*geheimnis*] (not yet subjected to recognition) (2000, 76) hidden over the covers of the *unheimliche*, only up until when the *unheimliche* surfaces since when it does, it simply cannot be unseen, simply cannot be unfelted. This articulation of Lacan exhausting Freud's *The Uncanny* pushes it even further. There is no Lacanian consideration of the anxiety without a proper consideration of Freud's *unheimliche* and certainly its most intricate movements count with it to function.

Certainly, this does not exhaust the entirety of the complex architecture of the *object a* and its relation with anxiety, but it does inform its central movements. Lacan's articulation of the *uncanny* concerns an agreement with Freud in terms of the aesthetic quality of the *narrative* present in the unheimlich. Lacan will say it concerns the *dreadful, the shady* and *the disturbing* (2014, 75), this does go right alongside with Freud's set of examples that illustrate the uncanny, and it also gets a further (logical) twist since, for Lacan "[t]he field of anxiety is situated as something framed" (2014, 74). This is the central aspect Lacan needs to consolidate in his explanation and appropriation of Freud's uncanny, in order to designate any possible "relationship between the stage and the world" (2014, 75). And yet, Lacan is blunt, *this* is the central feature of this (dis)orientation:

> Suddenly, all at once, you'll always find this term the moment the phenomenon of the *Unheimliche* enters. You'll always find the stage that presents itself in its own specific dimension and which allows for the emergence in the world of that which may not be said.
>
> *(2014, 75)*

Here it is, there is coastal blurriness of the lines for the subject (of the unconscious), but even more than that, it informs the limit between the Real and the Symbolic, concerning the "the emergence in the world of that which may not be said" (2014, 75).

Another approximation with the uncanny can be found in Lacan's (b) designation of *extimité*.[13] To briefly summarize, this notion concerns a *neologism* coined by Lacan for the first time in his seventh Seminar (1992) [1959–60] to address "the intimate exteriority or "extimacy," that is the Thing" (2014, 139). In *Ethics of psychoanalysis* (1992), Lacan engages with his ethics (of desire) articulating with the Kantian *Das Ding* (the Thing) and his theory between the subject (of the unconscious). Here we can notice another interesting *similar* feature of the Freudian *unheimlich* (although not *textually* referenced by Lacan), as a speculative approximation. And this is not an empty approximation, we can clearly notice how for Freud the designation of the uncanny as a (non)reconciliation between oppositions (inside and outside) and Lacan (under his own terms) conceptualizes *extimacy*. At the final moments of his lecture about *identification* (1961–62) the *extimité* dimension appears to designate certain dialectics between the inside and the outside for the subject (one oriented by the troubles with the Other), an operation of *totality* which takes place within narcissism. So, not so much about the mother's body as a host, is what Lacan debates here is at the level of the "lost envelopes" which conditions any operation of "*totality*" for the subject[14] (even if it means a cracked, non-total "totality" for the barred subject ($)). And finally, Lacan brings forward his final argument on *extimate* in his sixteenth Seminar, recuperating his coinage and discussion from 1959, arguing that Freud distinguishes between *das Ding* and *Sachen* (1992, 109), forcefully placing a different realm towards objects, but even further, Lacan defends the paradoxical aspect of *extimate*, since it implicates that what is more external of the Other *is* the most inner aspect of the subject (of the unconscious) (1992, 109). This reinvents the ethics of psychoanalysis and forces a much more crucial understanding of the role of politics within the field.

The *extimité* is a torsion that sets an uncanny dialectic into motion. At the core of the subject of the unconscious lies central a void prohibited to be directly reached, and this inner aspect is simultaneously external. This is another way of saying how the Other operates within the subject for Lacan and also, how *troubles with neighbours*, how living in society and dealing with the troubles of our small differences and similarities can turn into a horrific troubling dimension (Lacan's engagement with Freud's *Nebenmensch* ["fellow men"] touches precisely this paradoxical dimension: other's unbearable similarities with ourselves and so on) (1992, 109). At the level of excesses at stake, an ethical implication drawn from this discussion can be found in Zupančič's "Ethics of the Real" (2000). The philosopher explains the importance of ethics being informed by this operation, especially concerning pathological affections:

> One of the main reasons for the irreducibility of the pathological thus resides in the fact that the ultimate point of the subject's pathology 'lodges' in the Other, and that consequently, a 'successful' act is never without consequences for the Other. In relation to this, we should point out that this is a problem for every ethics, not only for Kant. The crucial question is whether we are aware of this 'extimate' and essentially empty point of our being, or whether we try to hide it behind the façade of a Good larger than the good of those affected by our actions. An ethics that identifies duty with the good of one's neighbour cannot avoid this problem. In fact redoubles it, since it is forced to confront both these questions: (1) Does what we hold to be the good of the other also function as such in his/her own judgement, or are we trying to impose on the other our idea of his/her good? (2) Whose good are we talking about, for there might be several different 'neighbours' to take into account?
>
> *(Zupančič 2000, 57)*

Thus, the limits of the *Nebenmensch* impasse, laid out and (re)introduced by Zupančič's *Ethics of the Real* (2000), explain the consequences of the Lacanian *torsion* of the "extimate" as a central ethical prerogative (for any further philosophical debate on the matter), since the empty point of our being concerning the (non)relationship established by subject between the Other to others (from social narratives to individuals). But the dimension of the Lacanian "extimate" (intrinsically bounded with *unheimliche*) is also sustained by Žižek, who argues that the:

> Abject is definitely external to subject, but it is also more radically external to the very space within which the subject can distinguish itself from reality 'out there'. Maybe we can apply here Lacan's neologism 'extimate': the abject is so thoroughly internal to the subject that this very overintimacy makes it external, uncanny, inadmissible. For this reason, the status of the abject with regard to the pleasure principle is profoundly ambiguous: it is repulsive, provoking horror and disgust, but at the same time exerting an irresistible fascination and attracting our gaze to its very horror: 'One thus understands why so many victims of the abject are its fascinated victims – if not its submissive and willing ones.' Such a mixture of horror and pleasure points towards a domain beyond the pleasure principle, the domain of jouissance: 'One does not know it, one does not desire it, one enjoys in it [*on en jouit*]. Violently and painfully. A passion'
>
> *(Žižek 2016, 261–262)*

Along the lines of Zupančič's organization of the implications of the "extimate" to thinking ethical impasses, Žižek provides additional treatment to its paradoxical torsion. Žižek borrows from Julia Kristeva's[15] derivation of Freud's uncanny, the "abject" as her translation of experiences of disintegration "of the very ontological coordinates which enable me to locate an object into external reality 'out there'," (Žižek 2016, 261) when faced with radical situations beyond disgust or to any given grammar, it is the dissolution of the given grammar, its limit and also, a convocation towards it. So, the treatment Žižek provides to the "abject" as a radically external and simultaneously the innermost core of the subject, places it at the "extimate" place of *jouissance*.[16] This explains the ambiguous trait of the admiration with horrors, the *stunningness*, which propels our gazes into an odd admiration. This ambiguity concerns the domains of *jouissance* and the space of "passion," as Žižek claims. The capture of fright is articulated by the abject, and it sets the radical experience of interiority exteriority which paradoxically explains the most intimate impasses with the neighbours: our similarities disguised as big differences.

Žižek (2016) articulates the most central feature of the "extimacy": the jouissance which is unbearable is not the inapprehensible jouissance of the other but *our own*. Extimacy describes this constant reminder of our own inability to relate to our own jouissance (even if projected to others). And as Žižek sustains along the lines of Lacan's explanation (1992), the Other "planishes" jouissance to protect his own jouissance, the subject projects its jouissance towards the Other (which is where the object lies) and provides full imaginary consistent access to it. Following Žižek (2016, 280) this is the birthplace of jealousy: one's very own jouissance that is incongruous to ourselves gets projected onto the Other and the Other has access to jouissance (after this "extimate" projection performed by the subject), than the "fear of missing out" or of being excluded from this utopia of jouissance becomes a commandment and its obverse is jealousy, as Žižek states.

But before we digress any further into the ethical stance of the Lacanian "extimacy" and its uncanny horrors, it seems substantiated that Lacan articulates the uncanny and how the "extimate" is one of its integral dimensions. Here we can turn to Lacan's last central point concerning the uncanny (c) relates to the truth of the unconscious subject. In his seventeenth Seminar, Lacan makes a rather significant argument that holds all this discussion together:

> Around all this there is a play of litotes whose weight and emphasis I've tried to show you in what I am calling the "not-without." Anxiety is *not* 'without an object. We are *not without* a relationship with truth.
>
> But is it certain that we should find intus, within? Why not to one side? *Heimlich, unheimlich – each* of us, from our reading of Freud, has been able to recall what shelters in the ambiguity of this word which, through not being within and yet evokes it, accentuates precisely everything that is strange.

> On this point languages themselves vary strangely. Have you noticed that "homeliness" in English means *sans façon*, without standing on ceremony? It is, however, just the same word as *Heimlich*, but that doesn't have the same tone at all.
>
> This is why *sinnlos* translates into English as "meaningless," that is, the same word which, in translating *Unsinn*, "nonsense," will give us *non-sensé*.
>
> We all know that the ambiguity of the roots in English lend themselves to unusual avoidances. On the other hand, and in a way that is almost unique. English will call "without" the *sans-avec étant dehors*.
>
> Truth does in effect seem to be foreign to us, I mean our own truth. It is no doubt with us, but without concerning us to the point that one really wants to speak it.
>
> All that can be said, and this is what I was saying before, is that we are *not without it*. A litotes, in short, of the fact that when we are within its reach we would happily do without it. We go from "without" to "not-without," and from there to "without-past."
>
> *(2017, 58)*

Following this journey of the Lacanian appreciation of the *uncanny*, it is plausible to assume how crucial is the uncanny to Lacanian theory, it is the central operation connecting the certainty of the *object a*, and even further, it sustains a foreignness, an uncanniness of the subject (of the unconscious). For Vladimir Safatle (2017), Freud's uncanny deals with the unexpected surface of anxiety in the face of familiar objects, going against regular procedures of identification or identity. Thus, in situations where the distinction between subject and object is instigated, the result is uncanniness (Safatle 2017, 182). So, the torsions inherent to the uncanny become an integral part of the Lacanian thinking of anxiety, since it also obeys this obliteration of common procedures of identification and identity, there are simply no safer "distinctions between subject and object, self and otherness, identity and difference" (Safatle 2017, 182). Nonetheless, Safatle reminds us that Lacan articulates two sides to the dimension of anxiety: (a) anxiety is a shattering experience, it dissolves given symbolic coordinates and the manifestation of such apparitions manage to "vacillate the relationship between the subject and structures of knowledge" (Safatle 2017, 182), the general principles of understanding fail at the presence of anxiety, and (b) "those very own objects may manage to interrogate general principles of understanding, because those are objects which carry within themselves a negation of its submission to identity" (Safatle 2017, 182). This means that the anxiety which immobilizes can also be an anxiety which transforms. And Safatle rescues a crucial argument from Lacan:

> ...these objects with the fulfillment of (death) drive, as uncanny objects of enjoyment traversed by anxiety, it is because the negativity of death drive

> can fulfill itself with the *jouissance* of an object that bears within itself its own negation, the destruction of itself, the torsion of its own identity protocols (protocols, which for Lacan, are fundamentally bound to the Imaginary).
>
> (*Safatle 2017, 182*)

But this is not a matter of *nihil negativum*, as Safatle reminds us, beyond a contradictory object, the centrality of death drive informs a "notion of object which does not reduce the figure of selfnegation of the identity to a statute of an empty object demoted of a concept" (Safatle 2017, 183), and this is where Lacan's (Hegelian inspired) negativity transpire. The surfacing of this object fragilizes the organization of reality and it also fragilizes the subject itself (Safatle 2017, 183). This is why, if there is any possible "ontology" behind Lacan's psychoanalytic developments, it must be a *negative one*. Hopefully, the argument placed here managed not only to demonstrate the importance of the uncanny for psychoanalysis, not only from the retroactive apprehension of what its articulation achieved on *external* fields over the years (Masschelein 2011) but internally to the psychoanalytic field. Certainly, Lacan took the *encounter* between philosophy and psychoanalysis inherent to the uncanny and gave it a more central *role*, (re)animating its instigating debate for psychoanalysis, but even more, propelling its (re)introduction to *unconscious thinking*, going beyond the usual grounds already sustained by Freud and inspiring its appropriation for other fields.[17]

1.6 The uncanny though Lacanian lenses: consequences of a non-encounter

It is more than obvious that Freud's designation of the uncanny is essential for Lacan in very important moments of his thinking. The Lacanian psychoanalyst Christian Dunker (2019) advocates for an inherent *openness* for the uncanny, explaining how its manifestation always operates through pairs of opposites and finds alternatives to its impasses. For Dunker, uncanny experiences are a resultant of (a) negating a mortal reality or finitude itself ("life and death") (2019, 211); (b) the denial of the opposition between inanimate and animated (2019, 212); (c) the breach of the pact between reality and fantasy (the surfacing of the affect of horror) (2019, 212) and finally, (d) the uncanny derived from uncertainty and fear towards an object (2019, 213). Dunker (2019) sustains how the uncanny (articulated under Lacanian terms) organizes contemporary experiences of anxiety, castration and subsequent suffering, if (re)articulated with its "original" Freudian contours.

For Žižek (1992), the *unheimliche* and its paradoxical torsions render different implications to the understanding of castration (as differences between the modern and postmodern). Considering the difference between *modern* and *postmodern* as a radical shift on paternal authority (Žižek 1992, 124), Žižek provides a clear pathway to explain how contemporary troubles with *enjoyment* relate to this confusion between the paternal figure sublated [*aufgehoben*] into the Name (of the Father), turning into a dead-symbolic father, a "phantom-like object" that "hinders a" normal "sexual relationship" (Žižek 1992, 124) a way to not relate with reality itself; and the troubling postmodern alternative which mistakes the dead-symbolic father with the father who is *still alive* (a *personification* of a Symbolic function or an ordinary embodiment of the Law). And while the modern render sustains the incompatibility between the symbolic order and enjoyment, the postmodern alternative fills this gap of incompatibility, ignores it or falsifies it (Žižek 1992, 124). More than a simple dispute, this concerns a paradigm shift, and Žižek posits how such distinction over the phantom-like "living-dead" of Symbolic father placed either under the terms of the Name of the Father or in its "reversal" as the "anal father" *as the one who enjoys*, determines consequences on how one determines its own position and relation with reality itself. This reversal occupies a crucial position to the subject:

> ...the obscene little man who is the clearest embodiment of the phenomenon of the "uncanny" (Unheimliche). He is the subject's double who accompanies him like a shadow and gives body to a certain surplus, to what is "in the subject more than subject himself"; this surplus represents what the subject must renounce, sacrifice even, the part in himself that the subject must murder in order to start to live as a "normal" member of the community.
>
> *(Žižek 1992, 124)*

So, Žižek (1992, 125) explains how the *uncanny* encapsulates this paradoxical feature, it operates as (a) an emissary of the limits of symbolic Law, as well as (b) an embodiment of the excess (as Father-enjoyment) as a part of what the subject must renounce to have a "normal" life in society. Further than this, Žižek articulates how the *uncanny* can be a valuable operator to investigate *modernity* and *postmodernity*. The logic derived from the uncanny points towards different logical operations. This not only supports what was already presented up until now concerning the importance of sustaining this concept, but it also defends how its psychoanalytic cunningness reaches much further once adequately articulated. Žižek defends how *sexuality* depends on the uncanny to take place (Žižek 1992, 125). Žižek furthers Lacan's rendering of the uncanny, providing an augmentation to the theme of the double in the mirror stage:

> ...the double embodies the phantom-like Thing in me; that is to say, the dissymmetry between me and my double is ultimately that between the (ordinary) object and the (sublime) Thing. "In my double, I don't simply

> encounter myself (my mirror image), but first of all what is "in me more than myself": the double is "myself," yet – to put it in Spinozian terms – conceived under another modality, under the modality of the other, sublime, ethereal body, a pure substance of enjoyment exempted from the circuit of generation and corruption. Prior to his being "sublated" in his Name, "father" designates such a Thing which is "in me more than myself.
>
> *(Žižek 1992, 125)*

This perspective (re)inserts the depths of what Lacan's uncanny can find in its most radical of possibilities. And Žižek clarifies that it is *wrong* to assume that "the relationship to the double *qua* Thing has nothing whatsoever to do with the imaginary relationship between ego and ideal ego, its mirror image, i.e., with the axis m – i(a)..." (Žižek 1992, 125), which becomes clear in Lacan's "scheme L" (a-a') (with its imaginary axis) and even more crucial, the thinker notices how the troubles with the mirror relationship lies at the *apostrophe*, or basically, how Lacan "...distinguishes the image of a double (*a'*) from 'myself' (*a*): this apostrophe later (i.e., when a is no longer conceived as an imaginary other, but as the real object-cause of desire) becomes the *objet petit a*" (Žižek 1992, 125). Žižek argues that the:

> ...*objet petit a* is the *unheimliche* surplus forever missing in the mirror image, i.e., "unspecularizable," yet precisely as such present in it in the shape of that unfathomable X on account of which the mirror image obtains its *unheimliches* character – the double is "the same as me," yet totally strange; his sameness all the more accentuates his uncanniness.
>
> *(Žižek 1992, 125)*

So, the apostrophe placed by Lacan is explained by Žižek as the formalization of a torsion (unheimlich and the heimlich), explaining the paradoxical feature of the mirror stage relationship in the formation of ourselves. Furthermore, the implications from the complexification of the double through Lacanian lenses, follow the contours of the "extimate" to the subject (of unconscious), but remembering a quintessential lesson concerning the Real: it not only lies at the heart of the Symbolic, *it is also lies at the heart of the Imaginary*. Or as Žižek elegantly explains with his joke *on vampires* that have read (and understood) Lacan, cannot have their image reflected in the mirror:

> This is why the image of a double so easily turns into its opposite, so that, instead of experiencing the radical otherness of his similar, the subject recognizes himself in the image of radical otherness, i.e., he recognizes his equivalent in the amorphous mass of the Real whose literary and cinematic versions reach from Maupassant's Horla to the "alien" from Scott Ridley's film of the same name. In this sense, one could say that the

> Lacanian formula of fantasy, $◇a, the confrontation of the empty subject with the amorphous presence of the real, displays the "truth" of the mirror relationship a – a', i.e., what confers on this relationship its antagonistic tension – another confirmation of how the Real persists in the very heart of the Imaginary. It is therefore clear why vampires are invisible in the mirror: because they have read Lacan and, consequently, know how to behave – they materialize *objet a* which, by definition, cannot be mirrored.
>
> *(Žižek 1992, 126)*

Far from a subtle or minor articulation, the discordance between eye and gaze, sustained here by the Slovenian thinker, shows that beyond the usual "someone-is-watching me" motif, which is somewhat *creepy*, it does not capture where horror truly lies, which is in the *gaze itself*. Žižek articulates how this *horror* (of the excess surplus) is a price to be paid, it is a *condition* to sustain a coherent self-image. The *unheimliche* dimension is forever inserted to the subject (of the unconscious) going through the mirror stage and facing the impasses of the *apostrophe* (the torsion of the *object a*) (Žižek 1992, 128). And Žižek repeats, the Symbolic operation of the Name of the Father, does not materialize or allows sexual relationship, it only provides a stepping stone to logically affirm that there is no sexual relationship, it only provides the "phantom" of "normal" sexual relationship, "the 'ghostly' *qua* object does nothing but materialize the inherent hindrance, the 'original' impossibility that pertains to the sexual relationship (Žižek 1992, 128). Thus, the ambiguity of the 'object-impediment' means that "at the same time, guarantees phantasmatic consistency, [and] enables us to delineate the logic of the sublime reversal" (Žižek 1992, 127), which provides

> ...the very experience of this reversal of the "condition of impossibility" into a "condition of possibility" – the experience of how "only the spear that smote you/can heal your wound" (to quote from Wagner's Parsifal) – which constitutes the core of what we call "dialectics."
>
> *(Žižek 1992, 127)*

Žižek explains Lacan's paradox of the "dialectics of desire" through Hegel's "self-relating negation," exemplifying that "the way effectively to negate and surmount frigidity is not to supplant it by its external opposite (passion), but to make it designate this opposite..." (Žižek 1992, 128). Therefore, to renounce a desire means to enact "the very form of appearance of its fulfillment – the paradox which gets lost as soon as the phallus begins to "appear" (Žižek 1992, 128). The uncanny is a fundamental operation of the object (dis)oriented ontology (as Zupančič coined Lacan's negative "ontology"). The first point is a distinction between "phallic identification" and the "revelation of the phallus":

> What Lacan calls "phallic identification" is, on the contrary, the exact opposite of this "revelation of the phallus": it is the identification with the phallus *qua* signifier of desire, i.e., the paradox of identification with *nonidentity*, with the gap which maintains the desire. In the phallic identification proper, we identify with the element which functions as the signifier of its own opposite (in short, as signifier *tout court*).
>
> *(Žižek 1992, 129)*

While the "revelation of the phallus" is the "not yet "sublated" (*aufgehoben*) in the signifier… the phallic-anamorphic distortion of the face, is a kind of brand attesting that the subject is caught in the desire of the other (mother's desire, for example) (Žižek 1992, 129). There is also the "phallic identification," operating at the paradox of identification with *non-identity*, where identification with an element operates as the signifier of its own opposite. Although both operations implicate different structural movements which can co-exist, they are not codependent, the "revelation of the phallus" operates in the suspension of the paternal function follow by the subsequent invasion of the Real, its surfacing is unbearable for anyone to survive; and the "phallic identification," as the opposite, sustains a certain "glue" between the phallus *qua* signifier of desire. This informs the emergence of the (Lacanian) Real, which is always right at the corner of the operations of "subjectivization" of the subject (of the unconscious), but that also sustains the depths and intricacies of such circuits of the (dis)orientation.

Mladen Dolar (1991) introduces a clarification of this redoubling processes of subjectivization. Basically, the *double* is actually a *quadruple* (Dolar 1991, 8). Dolar applies the Lacanian L scheme[18] to Hoffmann's short tale, portraying the tension between the imaginary and the symbolic axis within the plot for the main character, but more importantly how "both diagonals become troubled and presage a disaster…" (1991, 8), facing the invasion of what was always there in the first place: the real. Dolar agrees with Hélène Cixous'[19] point on *La Fiction et ses Fantames: Une lecture de I'Unheimliche de Freud* in *Prénoms des Personne* [1974], who states that Freud has *a* reading filled with interpretative cuts to the story which benefit his psychoanalytic view, nonetheless, that does not demolish Freud's theory of the uncanny (Dolar 1991, 8). As Dolar clarifies, the crucial point is figuring out where the uncanny lies in this tale:

> There is a strange reversal in this situation: the problem is not simply that Olympia turns out to be an automaton (contrived by the Sand-Man figure Coppola, who contributed the eyes, and Spalanzani, who took care of the mechanism) and is thus in the uncanny area between the living and the dead; it is that Nathaniel strangely reacts in a mechanical way. His love for an automaton is itself automatic; his fiery feelings are mechanically

> produced ("his senseless obsessive *[zwanghafte*, compulsory] love for Olympia," says Freud.
>
> *(Dolar 1991, 9)*

Dolar addresses how the *unheimliche* comes from this *reversal*, this inversion where it is not entirely clear who is the automaton anymore in the situation (Dolar 1991, 9). Dolar notices yet another reversal vis-a-vis his Lacanian approach, one particularly inspired by Hoffmann's social parody concerning socially assigned roles of women (e.g., when Olympia utilizes language and utters "Oh!" or "Good night, love!"). For Dolar, Olympia holds for Nathaniel a "specter of The Woman, that figure of the Other" (1991, 9), similarly as the position of the analyst for the analysand, who

> ...makes himself an automaton in order to give rise to the dimension of the Other, the real interlocutor of the patient's 'monologue,' and also in order to produce that strange kind of love, perhaps a love in its strictest and purest sense, which is transferential love.
>
> *(Dolar 1991, 9)*

Albeit in a more complicated fashion,

> ...Olympia is both the Other to whom Nathaniel addresses his love and his amatory discourse (like the Lady of courtly love) and his narcissistic supplement (love can after all be seen as the attempt to make the Other the same, to reconcile it with one's narcissism).
>
> *(Dolar 1991, 9)*

So, there is this additional layer, this overidentification between Olympia and Nathaniel, where they are both torn between two father figures. In a sense, Olympia epitomizes Nathaniel's ambivalence

> towards the father figure [as an] attempt to identify with the father on one hand, and to make oneself an object for him, to offer oneself as the object of his love on the other (what Freud calls the "feminine attitude").
>
> *(Dolar 1991, 9)*

Here, Dolar argues that Olympia is understood by Nathaniel as "the missing-half that could make him whole, but which turns out to be the materialized, emancipated death drive. She presents the point where the narcissistic complement turns lethal, where the imaginary stumbles on the real"[20] (Dolar 1991, 10). Thus, we can understand how Olympia's position of tension *is* Nathaniel's position of tension, the overidentification removes the ability of separating or inviting any symbolic grounds towards an alternative to this predicament.

In Dolar's analysis, Hoffmann's tale evokes the complex relationship of father figures, which revolve around the relationship of the *function* for the subject. Here Dolar is heavily agreeing with Freud's uncanniness from the castration process reconfigured by the fear of losing sight (Dolar 1991, 10). The way Hoffmann translates this rather complex process is under the classic didactic separation of ambiguity, splitting it into two separate figures: the good father (bearer and protector of the Law) and the bad father (castrater and "linked with terrible *jouissance*") (Dolar 1991, 10).

Dolar summarizes a central point of this tension: it is *irresolvable* (but still *livable…*). Perhaps, one could defend that the lack of conciliation to face this impasse, sets into motion the tragic features of the tale, but also, within this very own impasse where the unsurmountable traits of uncanniness surface, a viable *monstrous* direction indicates a way out of overidentification.

Dolar's investigation explains how castration is the knotting point between the two diagonals (imaginary and symbolic) in Lacan's L scheme, setting up the (non)relation to the object. Dolar argues how inside the tale, the surviving father (The Sand-Man) portrays the figure of "jouissance" *par excellence* (recovering Freud's mythical Primitive Father) as "the disturber of love [Storer der Liebe]" (Dolar 1991, 10). The aspect of this disturbance is crucial for the proper understanding behind the uncanniness and its intimate relation with castration, reminding that sexuality is the founding event of psychoanalysis (Zupančič 2017), what lies here is one of its implications. Dolar remarks this invasion of the father whenever Nathaniel is about to embark on a love encounter but is prevented from fulfilling a "sexual relation," of "trying" to find solace through an imaginary supplement, by filling in the gap. It is this appearance at the symbolic level, which prevents imaginary completion (Dolar 1991, 10). Thus, Dolar argues:

> One could say that in this first approach, the uncanny is precisely what bars the sexual relation; it is the dimension that prevents us from finding our Platonian missing halves and hence imaginary completion; it is the dimension that blocks the fulfillment of our subjectivity. The objectal dimension at one and the same time opens the threat of castration and comes to fill the gap of castration. The uncanny emerges as a reality, but one which has its only substance in a positivization of negativity, a negative existence, castration. The positive presence of the objectal dimension is the "positive expression" of what Lacan, in one of his most famous dictums, has called the absence of sexual relation *("Il n'y a pas de rapport sexuel")*.
>
> *(Dolar 1991, 10)*

This passage translates the crucial element of the *negative existence* and the intricate aspects behind the quadrupled Lacanian logic upon the Freudian–Rankian double perspective. Basically, what Dolar introduces as "quadrupled" comes from Lacan's "Scheme L," which debates narcissism(s) under the Symbolic and Imaginary (with the Real as background) in a quaternary logic between two levels, (re)transmitting a fundamental logic of the subject (of the unconscious) and the consequences of its encounters with the Other. And Freud (2003b [1919], 330) explains this movement of narcissism not in a quaternary sense but under a *double* logic (an argument Freud makes on the *split-ego*, in a "mirror-like" split and a subsequent struggle between these remaining parts).

Back to Freud, the analyst further explains how the uncanny relates to all of the elements of the double, specifically from an inversion: "[t]he double has become an object of terror, just as the gods become demons after the collapse of their cult" (332–333). The double concerns a significant aspect of narcissism which is of benign significance, but when a situation triggers something which was deemed as surmounted returns, which is profoundly uncanny (2003b [1919], 332). When Dolar (re)introduces the Freudian double at Lacan's mirror-phase in order to explain how in order to affirm oneself as "I" a double is required. The mirror image of oneself is what sustains that an ego can be formed: to affirm that "this is me" thus "I am not that" means that my "ego-identity" comes from my double (2003b [1919], 12). But since this process occurs within language there are symbolic and imaginary elements traversing this very own construction. As Lacan clarifies in his "Remarks on Daniel Lagache's Presentation" [1960] (2006):

> For the Other where discourse is situated, which is always latent in the triangulation that consecrates this distance, is not latent as long as it extends all the way to the purest moment of the specular relation: to the gesture by which the child at the mirror turns toward the person who is carrying him and appeals with a look to this witness; the latter decants the child's recognition of the image, by verifying it, from the jubilant assumption in which *it* [elle] certainly *already was*.
>
> *(2006, 568)*

In a way, this brief gesture means a lot, it translates the insertion of the symbolic through the Other who bear witness to the mirror-stage of the child, settling this moment of the mirror-phase that simultaneously provides verification for the child's recognition of this (self)image only to *traverse* it through the insertion of a gap. This is why Dolar (1991) defends that the double is always already *cracked*:

> To put it simply: when I recognize myself in the mirror it is already too late. There is a split: I cannot recognize myself and at the same time be one with myself. With the recognition I have already lost what one could call

> "self-being," the immediate coincidence with myself in my being and *jouissance*. The rejoicing in the mirror image, the pleasure and the selfindulgence, has already been paid for. The mirror double immediately introduces the dimension of castration-the doubling itself already, even in its minimal form, implies castration
>
> (*Dolar 1991, 12*)

It becomes clear how castration is already at stake alongside the mirror double. Dolar makes this point, arguing how psychoanalysis sustains the impossibility of a "whole" to the subject, preventing the confection of a totalizing One which is missing (Dolar 1991, 13). Dolar's presentation of the doubling through castration, translates to a certain "loss of uniqueness," but further than that, it implies a (de)centralization inherent to our (in)humanity. This is the price paid for traversing the symbolic, a certain loss is always at stake.

More than a simplistic approach to this self-being, lies a different knowledge of an orientation vis-a-vis one's symptom. The symptom is unique to the singularity of the subject, not egoic self-being (which inevitably fails and is false anyway).[21] Dolar presents how a presence lacks, mobilizing the "opening" of reality under a certain *negative condition*, which introduces a radical inadequacy to finding a relation of the "human" as an animal, or the "human *as* human," or the human as a human-animal (which are ALL insufficient terms, these are pedagogical dyadic that simply misses the intricate complexity of negativity which Dolar notices), the introduction of the logic of the unconscious operating through this lack, (de)centralizes all these narratives for introducing an irreconcilable *lack* at the core of our being, disrupting it from being *qua* being.

Lacan's formalization of object a or as Zupančič argues, Lacan's "object-disoriented ontology" (2017, 24) concerns the "trouble with the double" which is at stake for psychoanalytic theory (and praxis) or as Dolar (1991) states

> the double is that mirror image in which the object *a* is included. The imaginary starts to coincide with the real, provoking a shattering anxiety. The double is the same as me plus the object *a*, that invisible part of being added to my image.
>
> (*Dolar 1991, 13*)

Zupančič is no stranger to this discussion on the uncanny (2005), using a joke from Ernst Lubitsch's *Ninotchka* (2005, 173) she explains objectal spectrality, the ghostly materiality of *nothing* in our everyday life. For her, comedy master the production of this kind of spectral object, the "materiality of the spectral" (2005, 174). Comedy and the uncanny are different attitudes towards nothing, towards the real, they both share commonalities and distinctions over the "materiality of the spectral" and "the production of the "impossible" (detachable and re-attachable) objects (2005, 175). She also defends how certain phantasmagoric "objects" could go to either the uncanny or to comedy.

Using Schelling's famous passage which beats at the heart of the Freudian uncanny, that is, "everything is *unheimlich* that ought to have remained secret and hidden but has come to light" (2005, 175). Zupančič notices how this can be profoundly comic as well. Her refreshing render comes from the curious trait of this paradoxical opposition: "The proximity between the comical and the uncanny seems itself both comical and uncanny. We are dealing with two phenomena that are *at the same* time extremely close to one another and extremely far away" (2005, 175). One of the best approximations of this argument (not defended by the thinker, but which makes perfect sense to be approached) lies in Edgar Wright's film *Shaun of the Dead* (2004), which is an open homage to George Romero's *Dawn of the Dead* (1978) with a comedic twist. The synopsis of the film goes as follows: "A man's uneventful life is disrupted by the zombie apocalypse." The film revolves around Shaun, a salesman of an Electronics store in Crouch End, London, who lives a comfortably resigned low to middle-class life. He shares an apartment with a friend, has little respect from his work colleagues, and although he is not in contempt, he is genuinely numb by reality and with the way things are. He is moving on with his uneventful life, and things start to collapse when his girlfriend Liz, who wanted to take a further step with their relationship but is constantly frustrated by Shaun's immobilism and numbness, she can't help but feeling neglected by him, and finally, decides to end their relation. Little did they know that the very next day from their breakup was going to coincide with the beginning of the zombie apocalypse which would reinvent their reality (the motif of the zombies is crucial to think about social (re)configurations and impasses for a multiplicity of reasons, but we won't venture towards that direction right now).

The main reason to engage with *Shaun of the Dead* is because there is a fundamental scene which encapsulates Zupančič (2005) argument between *comedy* and *unheimliche* like no other. Shaun, after the breakup, spends a night of drinking with his inseparable friend Ed at their favourite local pub. In the morning *everything* had already changed and yet, nothing immediately changed for Shaun. At this scene, after Shaun wakes up with a terrible hangover, he gets back to his daily routine as if nothing had changed[22] – clearly translating Zupančič's point that *comedy* and *unheimliche*, as two distinct universes which seem to be separated by an incredibly *thin line* (2005, 175), – but once Shaun leaves his home and walks towards the shop to get his breakfast (as he usually does), he is completely oblivious to his surroundings, he ignores the fact that the reality has been radically shattered. Here lies the comedic *avec* unheimliche, which fits Zupančič's argument: Shaun leaves completely oblivious over the escalating horrors of a dissolving reality, nonetheless, he moves on, he repeats his ritualistic daily routine, visiting the usual shop, completely blinded of the signs of destruction around him, he walks right past the zombies on the street, the broken windshields of the cars, the havoc on the street of his background scenario, *every single detail* is emblematically ignored, which is as uncanny as comedic.

This scene is profoundly ambiguous, you simply do not know what will actually take place: could Shaun have a glimpse of the destroyed reality and all of the sudden, his awareness will turn it all into a horror scene? Could his numbness prevail, and he would sustain the comedic relief of surviving his first "non" encounter with the zombie apocalypse? The ambiguity of this scene is marvelous for the way it covers many elements of this very *thin line* between comedy and unheimliche. In this scene, Shaun buys an ice cream and soda (here is another comedy sketch occurs), Shaun is so caught up and embedded into his routine – perhaps, to repress and obliterate his love loss-, he simply ignores that the clerk had already turned into a zombie and is at the back of the shop slowly moving towards him. Shaun does not even blink, he places some money at the counter to pay for his products and leaves. On his way home, Shaun ignores the dead bodies on the floor all around him, all the chaos, until the moment he is almost safe back home. He is crossing the street to get to his place and finally, he stumbles upon a zombie… but here again, the crude ambiguity of the numbness of Shaun, who mistakes the zombie with a beggar. He continues his way back home after explaining he does not have any money left, saying he was already short of money to pay for his breakfast at the grocery store. It becomes obvious that Shaun is here holding onto his position at the previous Symbolic configuration of reality and responding to an imaginary guarantee of the Other, completely unaware that the Other (*which is also barred*) was already invaded by the Real and that the previous Symbolic efficiency which was holding the (phallic) identifications will not operate for much longer, and yet, he still tries to sustain it which is *as scary as funny*. The ambiguity in this scene perfectly makes the case for Zupančič's argument.

Zupančič furthers her uncanny discussion engaging with Robert Pfaller's *The Familiar Unknown, the Uncanny, the Comic* (2005), she takes from Pfaller not only this bridge between the comic and the uncanny, but also the four main commonalities introduced by him:

> the advent of symbolic causality (something that starts as a play or a pretense takes the upper hand and starts functioning in the real), the success (not only that everything succeeds, it even succeeds too much, "more than intended"), the repetition, and the figure of the double.
>
> *(2005, 176)*

And Zupančič accompanies Pfaller's interest in Octave Mannoni's analysis of the "theatrical illusion" and "mental experiences" and she singles out how Pfaller's defends the structural difference between comedy and the uncanny is that "*the comic is what is uncanny for others*" (2005, 176). This derives from the example (or the case) of the *sneezing corpse*, first introduced by Mannoni (and further investigated by Pfaller and Zupančič). The example concerns an actor playing a dead man on the stage is laying on the floor which is a bit dusty and that all the sudden *sneezes* (2005, 176). As Zupančič breaks it down, to take the scene of the dead man sneezing as comical, a certain logic must take place: (a) to understand that the actor isn't *actually* dead (the actor is interpreting he is dead); (b) to think that somebody actually *believes* the actor is really dead (i.e., being fully tricked by the theatrical illusion), turning the sneeze into a horror scene. Zupančič suggests that the result of the experiment would be that someone not knowing they are watching a play would believe they see a dead person resurrecting in front of their eyes, which is a terrifying scene (2005, 176).

The Slovenian thinker is blunt: it is not a matter of mockery, nor a matter of making oneself "superior" or smarter over someone's ignorance. As she puts it, "[t]he point is rather that we need this other in order to be able to *relate* to the uncanny object, instead of being overwhelmed by it" (2005, 176). Although Zupančič provides a further Lacanian rendering towards the relationship between the uncanny and comedy, it is already fruitful to notice this kind of mediation at stake, to *relate* to the uncanny sustained by her. Zupančič disputes Mannoni's "theatrical illusion" as a scheme of "fetishist disavowal" or delegated belief, that is, not believing something at face value but sustaining its belief by placing it or delegating it to the Other, presupposing this belief on others. Zupančič borrows from Lacan's distinction between real and reality to examine Mannoni's point. As Zupančič explains following Lacan: the real differs from reality. The real is not a deceiving realm hiding behind an imaginary or fantasmatic coverage called reality, but something to be constructed or reached through different efforts, through certain conditions. And the artistic "fiction" can produce something of the real (2005, 177).

Zupančič remarks the constructive aspect of the real, which is different than representation or imitation and emphasizes how artistic fiction can produce a real, in a way, there is something about the artistic procedure which cannot be ignored and this is an affirmation of the unheimliche and of comedy for that matter, nonetheless Zupančič notices an important disparity peculiar to the uncanny in terms of the distinction between reality and the real:

> It is true, however, that without this something of the real being framed (delimited from reality) by a more or less explicit form of fiction, there is the risk, not of confusing reality with fiction, as one often hears, but of confusing reality with the real, which is usually to say the risk of reality "running crazy". (This is also one of the possible definitions of the uncanny: reality coincides with the real, they become indistinguishable.) So, in order to

> sustain this frame or demarcation, it is indeed necessary to rely upon the instance of the Other.
>
> *(2005, 127–128)*

Zupančič defends that reality "running crazy" is one of the definitions of the uncanny, which goes as a point of convergence between her, Žižek and Dolar's analysis on the term. But Zupančič's examination digs further, she investigates how a few additional operations must take place for these encounters with the real as "effects of the arts" can be experienced instead of becoming terrifying traumatic moments. So, some "effects of the real" within the arts can be approached for operating without being completely mixed with reality and not becoming a terrifying experience. Following Zupančič, the importance of the "guarantee" of the Other in order to indulge an experience of *belief*, this operation of the Other permits an encounter with the "effects" of the play, since it sustains that there is a reality to return to and simultaneously permits to embark into believing. From this, the author sustains the logic and the crucial point that: "as long as the big Other knows that this is only a play and not reality, I can enjoy its dimension of the real" (2005, 178). Thus, you can take something away from this experience which may become part of reality without becoming one with it, while the experiences of overdetermination of reality by the real are far from funny and can be deeply uncanny. Zupančič goes back to the "sneezing corpse" example, in order to illustrate how it can be funny (even comical), while hypothetically, in the occasion of the actor playing the part of the dead man, and after the play ends, doesn't stand to receive the applause for the performance with the other actors and remained down at the floor – that would be remarkably uncanny (2005, 178). In this hypothetical case, the Other does not hold this knowledge, does not sustain guarantees for the subject any longer (2005, 178). So, what we know (that this is "only a play") loses its support in the Other, the thin line between uncanny and comic would start to dissolve. Or as Zupančič affirms about the uncanny: the nightmarish feeling the subject gets when she suspects something is wrong, when the Other is not fulfilling its role in supporting either knowledge or experience, thus preventing any transmission to others (2005, 178). Zupančič defines the uncanny in the "emergence of the impossible-real object in the field of the Other always involves this radical severance of the subject from the Other" (2005, 178).

Zupančič uses the example of the "sneezing corpse" in order to investigate the comical and delineate its distinction with the funny, for instance, the relief experienced when, after a certain suspension of the Other (causing doubt and anguish) is felt, a reassurance of the Other's still at work "…the reality outside the fiction, thus supporting the constitutive division between reality and the real…" (2005, 179), as the Slovenian thinker defends, can make us laugh, but such relief is not yet comical. The example of "an actor playing a corpse that suddenly sneezes can be (only) funny or (also) comical" (2005, 179). Following the thinker, the example can be funny if it "*displays a lack* in the edifice of representation" (2005, 179). If the Other is holding the conditions of possibility of representation, enabling the distinction between the actor and the character he is interpreting, what happens is that the actor fails to keep on "covering all the representative space opened to him by the Other guaranteeing the difference between himself and his character. He lets his 'reality-self' disturb the character" (2005, 179). Thus, this is an operation at the level of empirical reality where the intended performance (i.e., of the representation) simply fails, becoming a funny incident. The comical, as the thinker explains, is not to the side of the actor's failure, but actually as the "knowledge of the Other," that plays a role sustaining the fictional frame all the sudden appears within this very frame: the sneezing as an object appears on the stage. This sets the difference between the two, as she describes: the uncanny concerns the emergence of an object which implies a withdrawal of the (symbolic) Other, this withdrawal implicates in the dissolution of the frame which was holding the "fictional" space. When the uncanny object is introduced, it is not funny anymore. But for the comic configuration, the frame appearing within its own scope (as an object), as Zupančič explains, it does not disappear as a frame (2005, 179).

This distinction is important, since it further appreciates the quality of the uncanny, as a withdrawal of the (symbolic) Other and the subsequent dissolution of the very own frame delimiting the space of "fiction," is distinct from the comical, which is the abrupt appearance of the very own frame (Other) which sustains the "fiction" surfaces on stage. And Zupančič defends, under Lacanian terms, that the appearance of the Other and the object *a* "on the same level is a comic scene par excellence" (2005, 179). So, the very knowledge which supports and guarantees the experience of watching a play as "just fictional" provided by the Other, if it mixes with the play itself, if the structure infiltrates the play and denounces the activity affirming to the viewers that they are watching a play while watching a play, this redoubling moment encapsulated by an object is profoundly comical. While to the side of the uncanny, which also engages with the Other and the object *a*, what takes place is an unevenness or a disparity of their level, provoking an asymmetry within reality (an infiltration of uncanny objects) or an overdetermination of the real onto reality (a shattering invasion). More than the object itself, which is almost indistinguishable between comedy and the uncanny, comedy requires a contextual operation to take place, it basically requires a

> ...space or zone that simultaneously separates and links the sneezing and its body, or the voice and its source, the smile and its face, the pleasure and its cause... It is this interval itself that becomes objectified by comic techniques.
>
> *(2005, 180)*

Another essential commonality between the uncanny and comedy is their relationship with *nothing*. Although there is a fundamental negativity which operates within our reality, there are also, different experiences of negativity are at stake between the uncanny and comedy. As Zupančič clarifies, there is a crucial "negativity which exists and functions as the condition of differentiality within our (symbolic and imaginary) world, i.e. of its readability" (2005, 181). Following her Lacanian understanding, in order to reality to constitute itself, it presupposes an element "falling out" of it, an element which supports reality itself through its very lack and because of that, it provides consistency for a given reality (2005, 181). As Zupančič explains, there exists a foundational lack that differs fundamentally from any lack we find in our reality. Unlike this constitutive lack, the lacks we encounter in reality are always reflective, constructed, and mediated by the symbolic, making them manageable within that framework. "This means they can refer to nothing as if it were something" (2005, 181). A symbol can fill this gap, mark its position, indicate an absence, and bring forth what is not present. Therefore, it's crucial to differentiate between two types of negativity: the fundamental negativity which derive from constitutive lack (which is never directly visible but allows everything else to be perceived) and an asserted or "posited" negativity, lack or absence (2005, 181).

Following Zupančič, this element refines the "spectral materiality" disputed by the uncanny objects and comedy, since both deal with the "illogical" appearance of these objects which "collapse the fundamental-constitutive negativity itself" (2005, 181). Zupančič rescues Lacan's analysis of the uncanny bounded to anxiety (anguish), and summarizes that, for Lacan, it is about the formula: "*le manque vient à manquer*, "the lack comes to lack" (2005, 181). Such constitutive lack, this lacking foundation, supports our differentiations and our symbolic edifices, because it lacks. This lack evokes an "impossible" in its place, a "surplus object that has no place in given reality and blatantly contradicts its laws" (2005, 181). Zupančič describes how this specific point sets a proximity between the comic and the uncanny for both her and Pfaller: the point of surplus-success where "things have a funny way of not only succeeding, but of succeeding too much, 'more than intended'" (2005, 181).

In a way, the notion of "the lack comes to lack" (one of the translations of the "impossible") surface from the surplus object something which should not appear in reality, but if it does, it is certainly not without consequences. As Zupančič argues: "Lacan further claims that this 'lack of the lack' is what is involved in his concept of the object *a* (as real). Which is why anxiety 'is not without object'" (2005, 181). So, Zupančič translates how Lacan's articulation of the uncanny in the operations of anxiety as "lack of the lack" means that "is not without object," it concerns the object *a* (as real). Thus, the uncanny is not lack, but a "lack that comes to lack." Zupančič explores the example of the image of someone having their "eyes being plucked out (and appearing autonomously)" (2005, 182) to argue this point often taken as uncanny. The author sustains that more than assuming how "empty" eye sockets imply lack, thus sparkling the uncanny, she captures how the real ghastly operation of the uncanny is at its *opposite* side:

> Namely, that instead of the eyes, which – on the imaginary level – always suggest an *in(de)finite depth*, an opening into a possibly inscrutable, bottomless dimension of subjectivity (eyes being considered as "openings into a person's soul"), the holes instead of the eyes are *all too shallow*, all too finite, their bottom all too visible and close. So that, once again, what is horrifying is not simply the appearance (or disclosure) of a lack, but rather that the "lack comes to lack", that this lack itself is removed, that it loses its support. One could say: the moment when the lack loses its symbolic or/and imaginary support, it becomes "a mere hole", which is to say – an object. It is a nothing that, literally, remains (there) to be seen.
>
> *(2005, 182)*

Zupančič's analysis of the uncanny under Lacanian terms concerns the moment when lack loses its support (symbolic or/and imaginary) and the horrifying which arises comes not from the lack, but from the "lack comes to lack," when the support itself is stripped away, the (uncanny) object surfaces as "a nothing that, literally, remains (there) to be seen" (2005, 182). And Zupančič analysis the other side of this image, the eyes appearing autonomously, after being removed from their sockets, these big black holes conceived as "openings" to someone's soul, it becomes the very own opposite of an opening, transforms into a surplus "abject," as defends Zupančič (2005, 182). The removed eyes turn into a surplus (an *en trop*) that cannot be "re-inscribed in the symbolic economy of plus and minus, of lack and its complement" (2005, 182)

The *en trop*, the excesses are what turns the object into an "abject," reconfiguring its own operation within reality into a horrifying capability. In this sense, this surplus "abject" simply "runs wild" in reality (infiltrating it), and missing any possibility of symbolic economic re-inscription. And Zupančič furthers Lacan's anxiety as "the lack comes to lack," noticing how once the subject "loses the very support that her desire and, broadly, her symbolic universe had in a (constitutive) lack. This is exactly why he insists that the castration complex…" (2005, 182). Thus, the uncanny is central to understand how anxiety is not stuck at the level of castration complex. As Zupančič argues: "There is, claims Lacan, a more fundamental, 'original lack', a lack in the real, a 'structural flaw [*vice de structure*] inscribed in the being-in-the-world of the subject that we are dealing with'" (2005, 182). But perhaps even more important than this argument itself, lies in her clarification, Lacan *does not* dismiss the key role of the "castration complex" for the subject, he is actually aiming at explaining it, states Zupančič. In a similar path than Freud, Lacan defends that the castration complex fulfils a central function to our experience in life, it is the procedure which allows the symbolic (and imaginary) to operate and be operated by us, it provides the stepway for symbolic support, which is why in this case, as Zupančič defends, we are dealing with "lack in the real" a key function of the symbolic (2005, 183).

Here, Zupančič summarizes how Lacan "turns the table" on Freud to explain the castration complex. For Lacan the root of anxiety, of angst, lies *not* a fear or menace of castration, not a fear or menace of reviving it. As she explains, for Lacan, what is at stake is a fear of *losing the castration itself*, which basically means losing the "symbolic support of the lack – the symbolic support provided by the castration complex" (2005, 183). The pivotal aspect of Lacan's formula of anxiety ("the lack that comes to lack") is not the fear of castration, but the fear of losing the support the subject upholds towards desire through the symbolic structure which derives from castration (2005, 183). In this sense, Zupančič explains that it is

> the loss of this support that results in the apparition of those ghastly objects through which the lack in the real is present in the symbolic as an absolute "too-muchness"; ghastly objects which dislodge the object of desire and make appear, in its place, the cause of desire.
>
> *(2005, 183)*

This illustrates the negative intricacies of the internal logical operation of the uncanny at the core of the anxiety. Zupančič delineates the expansion of the uncanny, derived from Lacan, and translates the disparity within "spectral materiality" in such ghastly objects (2005, 183). From this comprehension, Zupančič sustains a crucial distinction between: "the realism of desire *versus* the realism of the drive" (2005, 183). Remembering her commitment to differentiate the uncanny from comedy, she summarizes the uncanny:

> The uncanny relies entirely on the structure of desire, based on the antinomy of the object of desire and its (transcendent) cause. The cause of desire is the originally lost object, the loss of which opens up the scene on which all possible objects of desire appear. The object-cause of desire is constitutively excluded from the field of desire (and its objects), that is to say, from the Other. This absolute disjunction of the real-object and reality (constituted through the Other) is fundamental for the possibility of the uncanny: If the object-cause emerges on the level of the Other (instead of being "present as absent"), it produces the uncanny… If, as Lacan maintains, one can only have access to reality, to the word one can recognize oneself in, on the condition of the loss, the "falling out" of the object *a*…
>
> *(2005, 183)*

For Zupančič, there is no way around this argument:

> the uncanny is based upon, and "exploits" the realism of desire: the emergence of that what "ought to have remained secret and hidden" – to use the Schellingian definition – induces a collapse of reality (as, fundamentally, the reality of desire).
>
> *(2005, 184)*

And she adds how uncanny literature deals with the ambivalence of desire mobilized by the inherent threat of collapse (2005, 184), the operation of desire within the uncanny described by Zupančič, goes as follows:

> …a desire cannot desire the real that makes it desire; yet it is also tempted to fantasize about embracing this Cause in a self-destructive (over)realisation, that is to say, precisely the "over-realisation" that we encounter in the uncanny. It is an "over-realisation" with which we pass over to the other side – which is not the case with surplus-realisation in the comical.
>
> *(2005, 184)*

This crucial difference between the uncanny and comedy lies in the distinction between the "overrealization" and ambiguous excess which moves in self-destructive terms of dealing with the fantasy of embracing this Cause (of a desire for the real that makes it desire, but which cannot be desired). And Zupančič places the uncanny as the grammar of the "realism of desire", basically, "…the constitutive lack cannot come to be lacking without the reality constructed around this lack falling apart…" (2005, 184), which is essentially Lacan's understanding of the uncanny. And Zupančič sets her interest into the "unrealistic stance" of comedy to deal with the "realism of desire" (2005, 184) derived from the operation of the uncanny (not against it), almost like a certain operation of facing this logic behind "the lack comes to lack, the ghastly object appears where it shouldn't, the Other and the object appear on the same level…" (2005, 184), but where a different attitude takes place, a certain "*so what?*" can be questioned as a defiance of the logic behind the "realism of desire" (2005, 184). And this is how Zupančič differentiates the uncanny and the comedy: while the prior operates within the intricacies of desire, the last one deals with the intricacies of drives. But, to what extent can we *really* separate these as separated *realisms*? Zupančič understands the realism of the drives, as a comprehension of the "unrealistic" stance of the "ghastly objects" as derived from *death drive* (in its repetitive persistence), which not pushing towards self-destruction it aims at an "excess of life itself" (2005, 185),[23] as she states:

> …the vitalism of the internal contradiction of (human) life itself. Far from referring to something in us that "wants to die", or that aims at death and

> destruction, the Lacanian notion of the death drive refers to an excess of life itself. This is not to say, on the other hand, that as an excess of life the death drive saves us from our finitude, or that this "immortal, irrepressible life" (Lacan) will indeed go on living *after* we die, that something of us will survive in it.
>
> *(2005, 185)*

Zupančič takes on Žižek's distinction of object a as object-cause of desire and as object of the drive and at this moment of her philosophical development she did not necessarily settle her arguments on death drive or this dispute over realism(s) (of the drives and of desire), but certainly, the main arguments posed by her here, kept hunting the thinker all the way until *What is sex*? (2017), where she proposes (some) further articulations on these matters. Nonetheless, at this moment Zupančič stresses that: "[t]he 'real' life is precisely not beyond our life in reality (it does not lie with the Thing lost from reality); it is attached to it in a constitutively dislocated way" (2017, 186). A point which is certainly valid for comedy, but is not even a little less valid to the uncanny. And although Zupančič ends her analysis defending that:

> It is this logic of *constitutive dislocation* (as immanent nothing) that links the comedy to the dynamics of the drives, and distinguishes it from the uncanny, which is bound to the dynamic of desire with its logics of *constitutive lack* (as transcendent nothing).
>
> *(2017, 186)*

This discussion is philosophically complex and important, since it deals with the *monstrous* (Thing) and "immortality" (in-between two deaths, as Žižek discusses) (2000, 162), derived from Lacan. And at this highly theoretically speculative point, Zupančič separates the "spectral materiality" between the uncanny and comedy, as distinct operations over *nothing*: the *transcendental nothing* to the side of the uncanny (where troubles between desire and *constitutive* lack take place) and *immanent nothing* to the side of comedy (where troubles between the drives and *constitutive* displacement take place). In a way, this seems to place a distinction between *transcendence* and *immanence* at the discussion of the "spectral materiality," and yet, such points are not further explored by the thinker here – this only can only make sense under dialectical materialism. The delegation of enjoyment and interpassivity operate from the domain of the uncanny through subjective operations of belief. Although Zupančič does not further these terms, such developments seem silently present (perhaps as some "ghostly [theoretical] hauntings"), certainly resonating with more recent discussions of the author on *realism in psychoanalysis* (2017, 73) for example.

1.7 The uncanny under *creepy, eerie* and *weird* clothes

Recently many discussions concerning the uncanny appeared. Dylan Trigg's *The Memory of Place: A Phenomenology of the Uncanny* (2013), who enacts a retroactive appropriation of Freud's *unheimliche* unwittingly sustains Jentsch's line of argumentation. Basically, Trigg also reduces everything related to psychoanalysis and makes the experience between body and cognition as a response to the environment, a phenomenological orientation of the uncanny *place*, where uncanniness arises from the "lived spatiality" and "being-in-the-world" (2013, 4). Trigg reads the Freudian uncanny, mixing it with Jentsch's line of argumentation. He defends how it (only) concerns the disconnected experience between body and mental understanding at certain places (2013, 25, 27). He goes through Husserl, Heidegger, Merleau-Ponty, Bachelard as well as others, to sustains a rather risky spectrality (to which he deliberates in his final sections) as a (re)encantation of the world within the given conditions of bodies and languages (perhaps a thesis on "wordlessness"). The more troubling aspect of this line of argumentation lies in its (ideological) mystification of spectrality, almost essentializing neuroscience and calling it "good materialism," missing negativity and the dialectical point of this discussion.

In *Creepiness* by Adam Kotso (2015), the uncanny proves itself meaningful to appreciate the contradictions within the symbolic fabric of reality (e.g., the naive presupposition and uptake of normality). Kotsko's Freudian inspired (and somewhat Lacanian oriented) analysis of such traits of the uncanny, seeks to "supplant" the uncanny with "creepiness" (basically arguing that nowadays, the understanding of *creepiness* can substitute Freud's uncanny).

The main trouble about this perspective is that it only tells half of the story. Certainly, "creepiness" portrays an *aspect* of the uncanny, but does "creepiness" *encompass* all there is to it? Substituting the uncanny for creepiness risks a psychologization of the uncanny; it misses the "spectral materiality" discussion and the dialectical critique of subjectivization–objectivization about it. While Kotsko's investigation is valid, it reinforces creepiness *as* the uncanny and it would be more plausible to regard how creepiness is *a* valid grammatic of the uncanny, a mode of its appearance instead of the uncanny itself. Despite his efforts, creepiness simply does not capture the entirety of the uncanny and Kotsko reduces the uncanny to one of its possibilities, missing its openness to negativity. As a matter of fact, he *moralizes it*. And Žižek's (2009, 242) render of Kotsko creepiness is far too generous. So, the question is: is Kotsko simply giving the uncanny a new name? Probably, yes (and a rather problematic one, in this case). Nonetheless, the uncanny placed as "creepy" may concern desire or more accurately, the impenetrability of it for us and its reversal once placed onto the Other (a logic delineated previously by Žižek and previously addressed here), but this does not tell the whole story about the uncanny.

It would be unfair to argue that Kotsko "cherry picks" examples to emphasize his theorization of creepiness, especially since his engagement with "cultural" productions pedagogically exposes how different strategies of defence of the subject (of the unconscious) resonate with different encounters with the uncanny. But the key point is that what is deemed uncanny to some, could not be experienced in the same way by others. There are different qualities of uncanniness (in Lacanease, for someone whose symbolic castration is working, the idea of a hand autonomously moving away from the body could spark uncanniness, but to someone else who *denies* the symbolic castration after it took place could have a completely different reaction about chopping someone's hands). Žižek[24] locates and resumes a valid argument about Kotko's creepiness, which is: "the impenetrability of the Other desire is creepy" (2016, 189). Nonetheless, Žižek's own discussion on uncanny introduces what is missing from Kotsko's understanding of the uncanny which is the dialectical negativity between Subject and Substance. How the abject and the uncanny highlights the realm of negativity at stake concerning ontological spectrality.

Another crucial discussion about the uncanny comes from Mark Fisher. Fisher dealt with the uncanny in two works, in his PhD thesis *Flatline Constructs: Gothic Materialism and Cybernetic Theory-fiction* (1999) and on his last book *The Weird and the Eerie* (2016). Certainly, Fisher is no stranger to the uncanny, in his thesis (1999), he investigates the monstrous Golem and "a plane where it is no longer possible to differentiate the animate from the inanimate and where to have agency is not necessarily to be alive" (1999, 7). Referring to Donna Haraway's cyborg-theory as the cyber-theoretical ground to understand how "the machines are disturbingly lively, while we ourselves are frighteningly inert" (1999, 7), he portrays how such dimension challenges the theoretical failings between free will and determinism or between vitalism and mechanism. He noticed how the pairing of opposites has only reproduced their own oppositions and limitations. Fisher calls this impasse the "Gothic flatline," which is "a zone of radical immanence" (1999, 7) and he aims towards "Gothic Materialism" (1999, 7) as response.

Inspired by Wilhelm Worringer via Deleuze and Guattari, Fisher places this spectral dimension between the Gothic and Materialism, arguing it challenges the way how the Gothic was thought of (1999, 8). For Fisher "Gothic Materialism [is] concerned with a plane that cuts across the distinction between living and nonliving, animate and inanimate. It is this *anorganic continuum*, it will be maintained, that is the province of the Gothic" (1999, 8). Fisher establishes a short-circuit between Materialism and the Gothic, to rethink "materialism in terms closer to Horror fiction than to theories of social relations" (1999, 8). Further, he argues that the Gothic was on Deleuze and Guattari's side, defending the Horror with their ghostly, vampiric, lycanthropic and monstrous impasses to criticize psychoanalysis' principle of reality, stating that psychoanalysis was to the side of the renormalization of narratives (1999, 8), (a recurrent critique from Deleuze and Guattari to psychoanalysis). Fisher establishes that there are *strange* agencies which do not obey the conventional mechanistic science (1999, 8) and such *hauntings* were always in the background of Deleuze–Guattari. Fisher challenges the common boundaries between the animate–innanimate in his materialist theory, he aims at a certain *fiction* (1999, 9) coined as the cyberpunk implosion of "science fiction and body horror" (1999, 9) or a fascination with "the concepts of agency-without-a subject and bodies-without-organs" (1999, 9) giving rise to the ambivalent form of terminators, blade runners and AI's nightmarish hauntings. Fisher defends the negativity of the "un" in uncanny in all its strangeness to mobilize a more gothic materialism, something which we can only agree with.

The Gothic Materialism that Fisher engages with "is interested in the ways in which what would appear ultramodern – the gleaming products of a technically sophisticated capitalism – end up being described in the ostensibly archaic terms familiar from Horror fiction: zombies, demons" (1999, 9). He nods towards how "the nonorganic line as occupied by Gothic Materialism is to be distinguished both from 'the supernatural' (the supposed province of Horror fiction) and 'speculative technology' (the home of Science Fiction)" (1999, 9). Fisher invites *The Uncanny* (1999, 9) (through Turkle) to this discussion because psychoanalysis's engagement with "animistic traces" is detrimental to Fisher's Gothic Materialism. Nonetheless, he argues that Freud only "flirts" with "the problem of the inanimate becoming-active" because Freud is an anti-Gothic according to Fisher (1999, 10), therefore, he can only "flirt" with this dimension.[25] And Fisher defends that Freud had "dismissively" addressed the uncanny (1999, 10), since "[f]eelings of the uncanny, Freud insists, are not to be attributed to the confusion of the animate with inanimate, but to a fear of castration" (1999, 10). A position not completely fair to Freud who was concerned with *animism*, even if he did not take it as far as contemporary authors manage to do so. For Fisher, Freud didn't realize how the uncanny as a "theme has its own kind of living death, stalking him posthumously with the implacability of any zombie" (1999, 10) and Gothic Materialism benefits from the...

> ...strange, nondialectical, functioning of the "un" prefix. Thinking, no doubt, of his own remarks on the absence of negation in the unconscious, Freud establishes that the "un" of "unheimliche" does not straightforwardly reverse the meaning of the word "heimlich". In a – fittingly – disturbing way, "unheimliche" includes heimlich.
>
> *(1999, 10)*

Fisher's Gothic Materialism benefits from Freud's *uncanny* in its powerful critical deflections and circumlocutions (1999, 10). However, Fisher disputes Freud's argument of *The Uncanny* concerning castration. As Fisher explains:

> [c]astration may be terrifying, but it is not as disturbing as what Freud seems so keen to bury – precisely because it is a matter of terror, or fear. Terror or fear have an object – what is feared – and a subject – he who fears – whereas the "ominous foreboding" [Gustav] Meyrinck's character experiences arises from the inability to differentiate subject from object. There is a dispersal of subjectivity onto an indifferent plane that is simultaneously too distant and too intimate to be apprehended as anything objective.
>
> *(1999, 10–11)*

Indeed, Freud does not literally address the "terror" but the conditions of the uncanny (certainly, but not because he did not know this; but rather, because terror is a *given* for the subject – after all, they had to emerge in the world in the most terrifying way…), which are curiously closer to the insight which Fisher attributes to Gustav Meyrinck"s *The Golem*, than what he actually gives Freud credit for. The aspect of (dis)orientation within the uncanny is a far more Freudian insight than what we usually given credit for, specifically because castration cannot be the same after the uncanny, there is a certain additional openness to spectrality which was not previously possible to consider. What is certainly missing from Fisher"s analysis, is Lacan"s developments on the *unhimliche* (on anguish). Nonetheless, Fisher keeps defending how Freud's *The Uncanny* sustains an anti-Gothic basis, because "Freud keeps Gothic terror at bay by attributing the feelings of 'dread and anxiety' to a fear of castration" (1999, 26). Certainly, Freud attributes "dread and anxiety" to a fear of castration, but this operation doesn't necessarily keep the terror away as Fisher defends. Freud was attentive to the animistic perspective and the uncanny is still a concept which concerns animism, the clash between animate–innanimate according to Freud sustains this perspective.

Fisher investigates Freud's *The Uncanny* (1999, 179–80) attributing to Freud (and *not* to Deleuze–Guattari/Worringer) the more radical point at stake here. Certainly, Fisher finds in it a certain *continuum* (the life and death/ organic and non-organic/ animated-innanimate) a position which derives from his Deleuzian–Guattarian influence, when he says that:

> Freud's own concept of the death drive and Deleuze-Guattari/Worringer's concept of nonorganic life both fall short of the radically Freud's description of this continuum implies… Gothic fiction offers a ready-made term for this slate of anorganic animation: undeath. In line with Freud's analysis of the "un" prefix in his essay on 'The Uncanny", undeath, of course, does not designate the opposite state of death (life); rather it is synonymous with the concept of un life. Following Freud again, who famously maintains that there is no negation in the unconscious, we can think of unlife and undeath not as opposed to life – or death – but as designating a continuum which includes, but moves beyond, the so-called living.
>
> *(1999, 56)*

So, Fisher is right about what is at stake in Freud's text, there is indeed a nod towards a *third direction*, a different perspective which goes beyond the apparent opposition at stake. However, the intricacy of this direction concerns how *negativity* is being approached and, in a way, the clash over the "uncanny" is a re-edition of the dispute on the level of the politics of negativity, as Žižek (2011) remarks. And yet, there are productive perspectives deriving from this *site of encounter* for thinking. Although Fisher attributes the radicality of this discussion to Freud, he defends how Freud falls short concerning the animistic beliefs in everyday life. But Freud did regarded animism as a fundamental aspect of ourselves, as an ontogenetic equivalent of the phylogenetic stage of the "primitive" (Žižek 2011, 180). Certainly, Fisher noticed how Freud's *The Uncanny* is an open invitation to further *what a horror grammar deriving from uncanny* could be like, and it took him almost two decades (and a lot of theoretical transformations) to finally engage with this.

Fisher's *Capitalist Realism* (2009) is already a work which takes a lateral step from the accelerationist pressure that haunted the thinker for a while. The excitement for doing something "fresh" is finally put at bay and his (late) awakening from his political slumber (thanks to Badiou and Žižek) kicked in. Fisher's *The Weird and the Eerie* (2016) sets the score with something he felt missing about his first interaction with the uncanny. Now, Fisher starts by setting the tone: "the weird and the eerie (beyond the unheimliche)" (2016, 8), is a more "calculated" theoretical dimensioning, consistent with the idea of not missing the radical efforts which lies in Freud's uncanny. Fisher long delayed reckoning with the uncanny and its further appreciation as weird and eerie comes

> ...partly because the major cultural examples of the weird and the eerie are to be found at the edges of genres such as horror and science fiction, and these genre associations have obscured what is specific to the weird and the eerie.
>
> *(2016, 8)*

Although Fisher aims at setting the differences between the weird and the eerie, what they have in common "is a preoccupation with the strange" (2016, 8). As Fisher defends:

> The strange – not the horrific. The allure that the weird and the eerie possess is not captured by the idea that we "enjoy what scares us". It has, rather, to do with a fascination for the outside, for that which lies beyond standard perception, cognition and experience. This fascination usually involves a certain apprehension, perhaps even dread – but it would be wrong to say that the weird and the eerie are necessarily terrifying. I am not here claiming that the outside is always beneficent. There are more than enough terrors to be found there; but such terrors are not all there is to the outside.
>
> *(2016, 9)*

Fisher's delayed visit to such notions have something to do with Freud's concept of the *unheimlich*. Curiously enough, now instead of celebrating the English translation of the term and the finding of the "un," finally noticing the double negation inherent from the German term *unheimliche* (Dunker 2019) and furthering this point:

> As is well known, the *unheimlich* has been inadequately translated into English as the uncanny; the word which better captures Freud's sense of the term is the "unhomely". The unheimlich is often equated with the weird and the eerie – Freud's own essay treats the terms as interchangeable. But the influence of Freud's great essay has meant that the unheimlich has crowded out the other two modes.
>
> *(2019, 10)*

Here Fisher, refines the impacts of the uncanny in the study of horror and science fiction and "…more because of Freud's hesitations, conjectures and rejected theses than for the actual definition he provides" (2019, 10) (a more elegant resolution to Freud's investigation). Nonetheless, Fisher holds his critique of Freud for highlighting castration anxiety as the operation behind the "enigma of the unheimlich":

> The examples of the *unheimlich* which Freud furnishes – doubles, mechanical entities that appear human, prostheses – call up a certain kind of disquiet. But Freud's ultimate settling of the enigma of the *unheimlich* – his claim that it can be reduced to castration anxiety – is as disappointing as any mediocre genre detective's rote solution to a mystery. What enduringly fascinates is the cluster of concepts that circulate in Freud's essay, and the way in which they often recursively instantiate the very processes to which they refer. *Repetition* and *doubling* – themselves an uncanny pair which double and repeat each other – seem to be at the heart of every "uncanny" phenomena which Freud identifies.
>
> *(2019, 10–11)*

Fisher defends how repetition and doubling are uncanny, but he disambiguates these affects as different modalities of strangeness (2019, 11), a delicate procedure that does not hold easily if we are not aware of the tensions concerning negativity from the discussion between Lacan and Deleuze concerning *death drive* (as delineated by Zupančič 2017). Fisher aims at another grammar concerning uncanny *affects*, here are the differences between the weird and the eerie:

> Perhaps the most important difference between the *unheimlich* on the one hand and the weird and the eerie on the other is their treatment of the strange. Freud's *unheimlich* is about the strange within the familiar, the

> strangely familiar, the familiar as strange – about the way in which the domestic world does not coincide with itself. All of the ambivalences of Freud's psychoanalysis are caught up in this concept. Is it about making the familiar – and the familial – strange? Or is it about returning the strange to the familiar, the familial? Here we can appreciate the double move inherent to Freudian psychoanalysis: first of all, there is estrangement of many of the common notions about the family; but this is accompanied by a compensatory move, whereby the outside becomes legible in terms of a modernist family drama.
>
> *(Zupančič 2017, 11–12)*

Fisher raises a valid critique to psychoanalytic proceedings (much along the lines of how psychoanalysis has a certain iatrogenic procedure of raising the troubles which it enables to dissolve…), but what seems to be missing here is the realization that the "strange" is an integral part of the (dis)orientation of the subject (of the unconscious) (Zupančič 2017), and in a way, the weirdness and the eeriness are affects which suitably explore this integral uncanniness. Fisher places Freud in "the role of the Jamesian unreliable narrator…" (Zupančič 2017, 12), much along the lines of many others who eagerly wants to "murder the father" (in a way, very close to arguments made by Nicholas Royle), placing Freud as an unreachable Master instead of *a* thinker. Fisher states that: "Psychoanalysis itself is an *unheimlich* genre; it is haunted by an outside which it circles around but can never fully acknowledge or affirm" (Zupančič 2017, 12), pushing a provocative understanding of psychoanalysis. As if one could more radically benefit of the uncanny by divorcing from the methods which allow it to be formulated in the first place. And this is where Fisher's position on the weird and the eerie become more transparent but not less difficult to be grasped:

> The folding of the weird and the eerie into the *unheimlich* is symptomatic of a secular retreat from the outside. The wider predilection for the *unheimlich* is commensurate with a compulsion towards a certain kind of critique, which operates by always processing the outside through the gaps and impasses of the inside. The weird and the eerie make the opposite move: they allow us to see the inside from the perspective of the outside. As we shall see, the weird is that which does not belong. The weird brings to the familiar something which ordinarily lies beyond it, and which cannot be reconciled with the "homely" (even as its negation).
>
> *(Zupančič 2017, 13)*

Fisher remains fixated into the inside-outside pairing which the psychoanalytic uncanny constantly eludes. He seems to address the topological torsions where the limits of the subject (of the unconscious) and the impasses with the Real takes place, but without fully engaging with them (perhaps because of Fisher's Deleuzian approach which prevents a further dialectical consideration). The peculiarity of Fisher's (Gothic) materialism understands the crux of the spectral dimension concerning materialism, but at the same time, evades the troubling dialectical impasses which negativity is all about. When Fisher says that "[a] sense of the eerie seldom clings to enclosed and inhabited domestic spaces; we find the eerie more readily in landscapes partially emptied of the human… the eerie is fundamentally tied up with questions of agency" (Zupančič 2017, 14), he furthers the very dimension he aims to organize through the "eerie," since it…

> …can be posed in a psychoanalytic register – if we are not who we think we are, what are we? – but they also apply to the forces governing capitalist society. Capital is at every level an eerie entity: conjured out of nothing, capital nevertheless exerts more influence than any allegedly substantial entity.
>
> *(Zupančič 2017, 14–15)*

Fisher affirms the abstraction at the core of capitalism which abstracts itself, but he does not deal with the peculiar uncanniness this "invisibility" provokes. How capitalism manages to be nowhere and everywhere simultaneously (Wright 2020) (McNally 2011), the eeriness which Fisher advocates misses the *monstrous dimension* of capitalism itself. Curiously, Fisher argues towards this *external* dimension (the eerie affect as a direct part of the uncanny) operating *inwards*, but he does not engage with the dialectical requirements that this uncanny provokes. In a way, all efforts to further translate the grammar of the uncanny are necessary to further accommodate the troubling narratives of contemporary reality, but the weird, the eerie and Kotko's creepiness, do not supplant the uncanny, they rather further problematize and add to the uncanny dimension.

Fisher sets his *capitalist realism* under the "metaphysical scandal of capital" or as he states:

> …metaphysical scandal of capital [which] brings us to the broader question of the agency of the immaterial and the inanimate: the agency of minerals and landscape for authors like Nigel Kneale and Alan Garner, and the way that "we" "ourselves" are caught up in the rhythms, pulsions and patternings of non-human forces. There is no inside except as a folding of the outside; the mirror cracks, I am an other, and I always was. The shudder here is the shudder of the eerie, not of the unheimlich.
>
> *(McNally 2011, 15)*

Fisher's obliteration of the inside for the folding of the outside is an oversimplification of the redoubling translation which shows the Lacanian "strangeness" of extimacy and the intricacies of negativity to the subject (of the unconscious) dealing with the Other. Fisher categories of the weird and the eerie are beyond the uncanny, since it does not only concern what is distressing or terrifying (McNally 2011, 16). So, weird concerns the sense of displacement in experimental work, the encounter with something that does not belong, even if it concerns the presence of something new. But the weird also encapsulates frameworks and conceptions which are deemed obsolete.[26] Fisher argues that the encounter with the weird lies at the encounter with the strangeness of Lacanian *jouissance* (McNally 2011, 17) (nonetheless, a *strangeness* which is yet familiar, contoured by particularity and profoundly unfamiliar at first). And the eerie instead of shocking invites a certain *calm*, "[t]he perspective of the eerie can give us access to the forces which govern mundane reality but which are at the same time ordinarily obscured, just as it can give us access to spaces beyond mundane reality altogether" (McNally 2011, 18). Fisher's uptake further the intricacies of the uncanny, separating some of its most mixed aspects in Freud's designation. But with Lacan's object a and its internal unheimlich textures which dialectically operate over negativity, even these separations turn unsafe. The weird, the eerie (and Kotko's creepiness) are a valuable grammar if mobilized by negativity (if understood under Lacan *extimate* conditions). Without this operation, Fisher's categories are still operating under the symbolic-imaginary surface without responding to the differences between Deleuze and Lacan concerning the real. Although Fisher does not bypass this tension, his spectral (Gothic) materiality laks a step towards dialectical materialism which would prevent a certain essentialization of the uncanny or an intensification of ideological illusions.

After this (re)articulation of the uncanny under (Lacanian) psychoanalytic terms, we can ask, what does it mean under the framework of the "politics of negativity"? It is a formidable operator and not a forsaken element inside the psychoanalytic repertoire. It indicates where contradictions are preventing the utmost ethical stance of radical alterity to surface. This question signals to the (im)possible in its most emancipatory conditions of possibility, as a fantasmatic point of materiality to be disputed, and further, even if there is not a *grammar* yet ready to articulate such hauntings, the uncanny is *the* very own point which demands it. In a way, Žižek's *realism of the jouissance*, derives from Lacan's articulation of the object a (*with* its uncanny reversals in its core) and it furthers the discussions on how to deal with the *void* in terms of multiplicity of multiplicities, it organizes a *positioning* concerning the Real. Žižek's argument prevents a domestication of negativity and sustains a radicality to the uncanny:

> Herein consists, also, the fundamental lesson of Lacan: while it is true that any object can occupy the empty place of the Thing, it can do so only by means of the illusion that it was always already there, i.e., that it was not placed there by us *but found there as an "answer of the real."* Although any

> object can function as the object-cause of desire – insofar as the power of fascination it exerts is not its immediate property but results from the place it occupies in the structure – we must, by structural necessity, fall prey to the illusion that the power of fascination belongs to the object as such.
>
> *(1992, 32)*

For Žižek, the circuit of the object-cause of desire operate under uncanny terms, as an emissary which holds the illusion appearance to an "answer of the real" – not because we are placing such objects there – but because these are *found*.[27] But if these objects fall from this place, and reveal the empty place of the Thing, there is only uncanniness to be found. Such encounters with these "answers," touched upon the invisible power apparently "traversing the objects" and how the crucial illusion of power of fascination *seems* to emerge from the object itself. However, this has nothing to do with a naïve (re)enchantment of reality: it concerns a dialectical materialism of the contradictions which surface onto reality and the logics of desire and (death)drive. When discussing the difference between psychoanalytic unconscious and brain sciences' unconscious, Žižek (2006) notices that emotions are the core distinction. For Lacan the unconscious is not emotional (Žižek 2006, 229), and

> [w]hen Lacan deploys Freud's thesis that anxiety is the affect which does not lie (which is why anxiety indicates the proximity of the Real), the implication is that anxiety is the exception: all other emotions *do* lie, they lie in principle.
>
> *(Žižek 2006, 229)*

Therefore, *angst* has an exceptionality concerning any other emotion.

Discussing how music can deceive emotions, Žižek articulate Romanticism and the uncanny as an antidote (Žižek 2006, 229). He claims that the "true heart of the subject, which is what Hegel called the 'Night of the World,' the abyss of radical negativity" (Žižek 2006, 229) and that music carries out its message beyond the words of the Rational Logos, from Enlightenment to another metaphor concerning the Romantic subject of the "Night of the World," that is, the metaphorical change from Day to Night. Žižek attributes to the uncanny the unique feature of advancing a tipping point of precipitation, translating a moment of transformation with the arising of Romanticism and this shifting of metaphors,[28] where

> the Uncanny [is] no longer the external transcendence but, following Kant's transcendental turn, the excess of the Night at the very heart of the subject (the dimension of the Undead), what Tomlinson called the "internal otherworldliness that marks the Kantian subject."
>
> *(Žižek 2006, 229)*

This is where monstrosity as an invitation towards a *new* grammar (the arrival of *new* signifiers) and the discussion about the uncanny seems to meet. Žižek summarizes "the underlying 'noumenal' flux of *jouissance* beyond linguistic meaningfulness. This noumenal dimension is radically different from the pre-Kantian transcendent divine Truth: it is the inaccessible excess which forms the very core of the subject" (Žižek 2006, 230).

Notes

1 Mladen Dolar understands "masses" as a *site* of political intervention but not *political agents* (2008, 28).

2 Nicholas Royle (2003) further defends how such the uncanny could earn a field for itself, throughout his herculean effort of placing it beyond a certain Derridean perspective and beyond a Freudian psychoanalytic comprehension.

3 In Mladen Dolar (1991): *"I Shall Be with You on Your Wedding-Night": Lacan and the Uncanny*, the philosopher summarizes Freud's discussion and articulates the uncanny with what Lacan's the *object a*.

4 Freud's metapsychology (which for psychoanalysts do not mean theory *per se*, but impasses derived from the clinic…) concerns the *unbegriff* [that which lacks], an openness to knowledge in the formulation of concepts and clinical developments. There are no specific books or texts that will *define* Freud's metapsychology, what we have are *movements* which are *metapsychological* in terms of attempts at translating, thinking and transmitting solutions to psychoanalytic impasses.

5 As Royle explains:

> For it is possible to recognize the dominance in the unconscious mind of a 'compulsion to repeat' proceeding from the instinctual impulses and probably inherent in the very nature of the instincts…All these considerations prepare us for the discovery that whatever reminds us of this inner 'compulsion to repeat' is perceived as uncanny (U, 360–361).
>
> (Royle 2003, 89)

and "All of these aspect are 'difficult to judge': they give rise to intellectual uncertainty or insecurity (*der intellektuellen Unsicherheit*)" (Royle 2003, 90).

6 E.T.A. Hoffmann's "The Sandman" is a short story revolving around Nathanael, who as a child is exposed to an uncanny tale by his nanny about a creature "The Sandman" and out the curiosity, Nathaneal who sneaks into the night trying to meet this creature, who is with his father in the form of the lawyer Coppelius. Nathanael gets discovered and in order to prevent the devilish Sandman from plucking his eyes out, his father intervenes asking to spare his son and after that, an explosion takes place and Nathanael's father perishes at the event, causing Nathanael to fall ill. Years later, now as a young adult, Nathanael who has no memory of the events, has a girlfriend and is starting his life, when he is reintroduced to the devilish makings of "The Sandman"… The figure of The Sandman, "disguised" as the optician Coppola, sells to Nathanael a small telescope. And through these lenses, Nathanael gets a hold of Olympia (the living doll) who lives with Professor Spelanzani right across his own place. Nathanael (who was in a relationship with Clara) falls deeply in love with the living doll Olympia and once he is invited to finally meet Spelanzani's daughter at a party, he was about to propose to Olympia, when he is interrupted by a discussion between Spelanzani and Coppola (about who was responsible for building Olympia's eyes and clockwork). Coppola is revealed as Coppelius, who wins the fight and takes Olympia's who is now missing her eyes and

the sight of Olympia's eyes on the floor drives Nathanael to break down and attack Spelanzani, which results in Nathanael being committed to an asylum. Later on, Nathanael recovers and decides to marry Clara, at an estate nearby his hometown. On a visit to this place, Clara points out something and Nathanael takes his telescope to gaze upon it, when he looks through Coppola's lenses again, he goes mad and leaps to his death.

7 Freud's interpretation of the uncanny is intimately related to Otto Rank's "The Double" [*Der Doppelganger*] (2011). The two main aspects of the psychoanalytic investigation of the *double* by Rank are precisely: (1) the impossibility to love by those implicated with the double and (2) its intimate intercorrences with death. Freud makes reference to Rank's work in his "Uncanny" (2003b, 327), in order to sustain the intercurances of oneself and otherness (but otherness within oneself), a duplicity later on explored by Lacan at his developments on the ego Ideal and Ideal Ego from Freud's first and second narcissisms (his first five seminaries are mostly dedicated to this).

8 Freud refers to Henry Thode, Michelangelo, Kritische Untersuchungen über seine Werke, I. Bd., 1908. [5] Thode, l. c., 197. [6] Vom Grabdenkmal des Papstes nämlich.

9 Originally from 1922, this text was posthumously published in 1940 in *Internationale Zeitschrift für Psychoanalyse* (a journal Freud helped to create) and Chaves (2013) points out how this was probably supposed to have become a larger study that was never concluded by Freud. See the original at: https://www.pep-web.org/document.php?id=gw.017.0047a.

10 Concerning the Medusa, perhaps one could speculate how she possesses the phallus and thinks nothing of doing so and how this is the most horrific point of Medusa – she is the figure of the uncanny at its most sublime: feminine jouissance who thinks nothing about the phallus she possesses. Complete indifference in the face of ambivalence. I owe this point to Cindy Zeiher.

11 As Lacan states: "unknown occupant that appears in an unexpected way is absolutely related to what's encountered in the Unheimliche…" (2004, 75).

12 Or as Lacan explains the *aphanisis*:

> The subject's relation to the signifier necessitates the structuring of desire in the fantasy and the functioning of desire implies a syncope of the function of the *a* which can be defined temporally and which necessarily fades and vanishes at such and such a phase of the fantasmatic functioning. This *aphanisis*; of the a, the vanishing of the object inasmuch as it structures a certain level of the fantasy, is what we have a reflection of in the function of the cause.
>
> (2004, 217–218)

13 As Krutzen (2009, 240) facilitates Lacan addresses this neologism in only four different occasions: Seminar 7, Seminar 9 and twice at Seminar 16.

14 This traces back to Lacan's paradox of the One (1962 [2004], 67) and Lacan reversal of the position around the One from Kant's *Einheit* ["unity"] towards *Einzigkeit* ["uniqueness"], to translate Freud's *Einverleibung* ["incorporation"] as "consumption of the enemy", the rivalry with father (1962 [2004], 212) as primary identification and not second identification (the function of the unary trait).

15 Žižek discusses "abject" from Julia Kristeva's usage:

> What happens when we stumble upon a decaying human corpse or, a more ordinary case, upon an open wound, shit, vomit, brutally torn-out nails or eyes, even the skin that forms on the surface of warm milk? What we experience in such situations is not just a disgusting object but something much more radical: the disintegration of the very ontological coordinates which enable me to locate an object into external reality 'out there'. The phenomenological description of such experiences is Julia Kristeva's starting point in her elaboration of the notion

> of abject: the reaction of horror, disgust, withdrawal, ambiguous fascination, and so on, triggered by objects or occurrences which undermine the clear distinction between subject and object, between 'myself' and reality 'out there'.
>
> (2016, 261)

One could say Kristeve "hit and miss," the dimension of the abject has further implications and should not be assumed as such, against the background of the uncanny itself.

16 One could argue that this is also where the uncanny is actually located – where the familiar yet new feeling which can't be altogether articulated because it seems to emerge from beyond the symbolic of speech and complete knowability and at the same time, it hystericizes the subject into "going there"... Confronting the ambiguity. Another point I owe to Cindy Zeiher.

17 But Lacan was also very specific about this, philosophy ought to be employed in psychoanalysis. Philosophy is simply useful to psychoanalysis sometimes, as is art, as is politics, as is the uncanny which mediates the relationship between psychoanalysis and philosophy nicely (as one could try to establish).

18 As Dolar elucidates this rather complex Lacanian operator: "The L-scheme was introduced in order to situate the imaginary ego produced by the mirror phase in relation to the symbolic, to the Other of the symbolic order, and to a subject that is not an ego" (1991, 8). Remembering that the real was not formulated by Lacan yet, but it could be implicitly speculated, as Dolar defends.

19 Cixous' investigation of the uncanny as "Disquieting Strangeness," defends that

> [t]here is something 'savage' in the *Unheimliche*, a breath or a provocative air which at times catches the novelist himself off guard, overtaking him and restraining him. Freud and the object of his desire (i.e., the truth about the *Unheimliche*) are fired by reciprocal inspiration.
>
> (1974, 13)

Cixous understands the function of psychoanalysis vis-a-vis the uncanny, its emergence from psychoanalysis and dependence of it for its own instance (*but only until a certain point...*). Cixous assumes Freud as a *writer*; for instance, Cixous says Freud's main argument against Jentsch (concerning the dispute about Hoffman's text and the uncanny) is that the psychiatrist was not enough of a "writer" to capture the uncanny (1974, 17), in a way, reducing the psychoanalytic discourse as a *mastery* subjugated to the Literary phantasy of fiction, or as Cixous says: "Literature is the objective of psychoanalytic inquiry" (1974,17) which (although profoundly creative) is certainly not correct – analytic inquiry does not aim at Literature, but to analytic cure – nonetheless, Cixous perhaps signals how the arts could procedurally mediate a certain encounter with the Real, but to say that this is the objective of psychoanalytic inquiry is to reduce its discursivity instead of opening it up.

20 Another film that translate this point is Craig Gillespie's "Lars and the Real Girl" (2007), which tells the story of Lars who establishes a romantic bond with anatomically correct sex doll named Bianca. Lars lost his mother at his birth, making his father to be distant from both him and his older brother Gus. When their father dies, Lars inherits the garage where he lives and Gus, now married to Karin, the proper house. All attempts to socialize Lars are unsuccessful, until one day, he warns his family that he is expecting the visit from a missionary he met on the internet, named Bianca. Here, his delusion was actually beneficial towards his possibility of socialization and not the way around, more in the Lacanian *sinthome* (2016) sense of the term, than the symptomatic sense, which we notice from Nathaniel.

21 Certainly, this is a complex point and for it to work some critique is required. For instance, from a Lacanian perspective, the *object a* is an imaginary object and thus, already has a fantasmatic knowledge attached to it. The object a is not an object *per*

se. It is very clearly a fantasmatic object of knowledge singular to the subject on the couch. At the same time, Dolar is not incorrect, but how he makes this point is not entirely clear. For the Lacanian, the object of knowledge is unconscious knowledge and never the object (*object a* or *not*), which is elevated in the Symbolic order.

22 Certainly, this could be interpreted as the experience of love loss, which certainly transforms one's reality, but there is also the combined unawareness over the fact that the Symbolic coordinates of reality itself had been radically disintegrated....

23 Zupančič rescues the distinction between *objet-petit a* as object-cause of desire and as the object of drive from Žižek, *The Ticklish Subject*, Verso, London & New York 2000, 163–167 and gave a more recent re-appreciation and further exploration to this point in *What is sex?* (2017) 110, in a way answering the intricacies of the conclusions derived from her own argumentation here.

24 As Žižek puts it:

> How does the abject relate to subjectivity? Is a subject – which is excessive in its very notion – simply abjective, an outgrowth disturbing the harmony of the world, opening up a gap in its very heart? One has to draw a clear distinction here: 'abjective' is ultimately the inside of a living object (like the depth of Irma's throat from Freud's dream about Irma's injection), while the inside of a subject is 'creepy' – as Adam Kotsko has shown in his Creepiness, 'creepy' is today's name for the Freudian 'uncanny', for the uncanny core of a neighbour: every neighbour is ultimately creepy, which is why the title of the book's last subchapter is quite appropriately 'The creepiness of all flesh'. What makes a neighbour creepy is not his weird acts but the impenetrability of the desire that sustains these acts. For example, creepy is not primarily the content of the Marquis de Sade's writings (their content is rather dull and repetitive) but 'why is he doing it?' – everything in Sade is a 'sadist' perversion, everything except his writing, the act of doing it, which cannot be accounted for as a perversion. So the question is: what does a creepy neighbour want? What does he get out of it? An experience, an encounter, gets creepy when we all of a sudden suspect that he is not doing it for the obvious reason one does what he is doing....
>
> (Žižek 2016, 189)

25 This is a far more complex topic: could Freud be assumed as a Gothic or an anti-Gothic or a thinker of Enlightenment or an anti-Enlightenment thinker? The Brazilian psychoanalyst Inês Loureiro (2002) after tracing a cartography of influences behind Freud's developments, coined Freud as a dark-Enlightenment thinker (2002, 344). This nuanced tone is much more suitable one than the anti-Gothic argument placed by the young Fisher. Nonetheless, Hegel's aesthetic is not a romantic endeavour and this is why Lacan's picking up the uncanny is crucial for our debate.

26 For Fisher:

> ...the weird is a particular kind of perturbation. It involves a sensation of wrongness: a weird entity or object is so strange that it makes us feel that it should not exist, or at least it should not exist here. Yet if the entity or object is here, then the categories which we have up until now used to make sense of the world cannot be valid. The weird thing is not wrong, after all: it is our conceptions that must be inadequate...In many ways, a natural phenomenon such as a black hole is more weird than a vampire. Certainly, when it comes to fiction, the very generic recognizability of creatures such as vampires and werewolves disqualifies them from provoking any sensation of weirdness. There is a pre-existing lore, a set of protocols for interpreting and placing the vampire and the werewolf. In any case, these creatures are merely empirically monstrous; their appearance recombines elements from the natural world as we already understand it.
>
> (Fisher 2016, 20–21)

27 A certain supplement is required to be undertaken here concerning this potential democracy of uncanny objects: what Žižek fails to point out is that although there is a potential to, not any object can function as the object a. The placeholder is very specific to the fantasy and how the subject envisages themselves as circulating the object a. It has to necessarily produce the uncanny eeriness, as Fisher defends for it to be a proper *object a*, in order for metonymy to take place. Perhaps, Žižek is referring to metaphor here but the uncanny rests upon metonymy which is also the failing of Royle's thesis. (I'd like to thank Cindy Zeiher for this comment.)

28 And one could add, it concerns the non-Romantic Romanticism of Freud, which does not fall so far from his own dark Enlightenment perspectives, as previously discussed. More importantly, one must not encapsulate nor diminish Freud's attempts at the psychoanalytic method from the Romantic dimension of his own time. By inviting a more Hegelian perspective to negativity, one must invite *movement* which fights against a certain static Kantian rendering from Freud's developments (Žižek 2012).

References

Badiou, Alain. *Being and Event. 1998*. London: Continuum, 2005.

Badiou, Alain. *Conditions*. London: Continuum, 2008.

Badiou, Alain. 2009. [1982] *Theory of the Subject*. London: Continuum.

Chaves, Ernani. Tradução: "A cabeça de Medusa" (Sigmund Freud, 1940/1922) [Translation: Medusas'Head] In: *Clínica & Cultura*, Vol. II, No. II, 91–93, 2013.

Chaves, Ernani. O Paradigma Estético de Freud [Freud's aesthetic paradigm]. In *Sigmund Freud: Arte, Literatura e os artistas* [*Sigmund Freud: Art, Literature and the Artists*]. Minas Gerais, Brasil: Editora Autêntica, 2015.

Cixous, Hélène. La fiction et ses fantômes: Une lecture de l'Unheimliche de Freud. In *Prénoms de Personne* (Col. Poétique). Éditions du Seuil, 1974.

Dolar, Mladen. "I Shall Be with You on Your Wedding-Night": Lacan and the Uncanny. *Rendering the Real*, Vol. 58, 5–23, 1991.

Dolar, Mladen. Freud and the Political. *Unbound (Harvard Journal of the Legal Left)*, Vol. 4, No. 15, 15–29, 2008.

Dunker, Christian Ingo Lenz. Animismo e Indeterminação em "Das Unheimliche". In *Obras Incompletas de Sigmund Freud: O Infamiliar*. Belo Horizonte: Editora Autêntica, 2019, 199–218.

Ellison, David. *Ethics and Aesthetics in European Modernist Literature. From the Sublime to the Uncanny*. Cambridge: Cambridge University Press, 2001.

Fisher, Mark. Flatline Constructs: Gothic Materialism and Cybernetic Theory-fiction. PhD Thesis defended in Warwick, 1999. http://wrap.warwick.ac.uk/110900/1/WRAP_Theses_Fisher_1999.pdf

Fisher, Mark. *Capitalist Realism*. London: Zerobooks, 2009

Fisher, Mark. *Weird and Eerie*. London: Repeater, 2016.

Freud, Sigmund. Negation. *Standard Ed*, Vol. 19, 235–239. 1925. See link: http://faculty.smu.edu/dfoster/English%203304/Negation.htm

Freud, Sigmund. Totem and Taboo and Other Works, trans. James Strachey. In *The Standard Edition of the Complete Works of Sigmund Freud*, Vol. 13. London: The Hogarth Press and the Institute of Psychoanalysis, 1955.

Freud, Sigmund. Dostoievsky and Parricide. In *The Standard Edition of Complete Psychological Works of Sigmund Freud Vol. XVIII (1917–1919)*, translated by James Strachey. 1928. Great Britain: The Hogarth Press, 1961a.

Freud, Sigmund. The Moses of Michelangelo. In *The Standard Edition of the Complete Psychological Works of Sigmund Freud, Volume XIII (1913–1914): Totem and Taboo*, 1961b.
Freud, Sigmund. *Beyond the Pleasure Principle and Other Writings. 1920*. London: Penguin Books, 2003a.
Freud, Sigmund. *The Uncanny. 1914*. London: Penguin Books, 2003b.
Kotso, Adam. *Creepiness*. Winchester: Zero Books, 2015.
Krutzen, Henry. *Jacques Lacan Séminaire 1952–1980 Index référentiel*. 3a édition. Paris: Ed. Economica, 2009.
Lacan, Jacques. [1959–60] *The Ethics of Psychoanalysis: The Seminar of Jacques Lacan, Book VII*. New York: W. W. Norton & Company, 1992.
Lacan, Jacques. *Le Séminaire livre X. L'angoisse. 1962–1963*. Paris: Seuil, 2004.
Lacan, Jacques. *Écrits*. New York: W.W Norton & Company, 2006.
Lacan, Jacques. *Anxiety: The Seminar of Jacques Lacan, Book X. 1962–3*. London: Polity, 2014
Lacan, Jacques. *Transference: The Seminar of Jacques Lacan, Book VIII. 1961*. London: Polity, 2015.
Lacan, Jacques. *The Sinthome: The Seminar of Jacques Lacan, Book XXIII: 23. 1975–6*. London: Polity, 2016.
Le Rider, Jacques. *Modernité viennoise et crises de l'identité*. Paris: Presses Universitaires de France - PUF, 1992.
Loureiro, Inês. *O Carvalho e o Pinheiro: Freud e o estilo romântico*. [*The Oaktree and the Pine tree: Freud and the romantic style*]. São Paulo: Ed. Escuta, 2002.
Masschelein, Anneleen. *The Unconcept: The Freudian Uncanny in Late-Twentieth-Century Theory*. New York: State University of New York Press, 2011.
McNally, David. *Monsters of the Market. Zombies, Vampires, and Global Capitalism*. Leiden: Koninklijke Brill, 2011.
Rank, Otto. *The Double - A Psychoanalytic Study*. North Carolina: The University of North Carolina Press, 2011.
Royle, Nicholas. *The Uncanny*. Manchester: Manchester University Press, 2003.
Ruda, Frank & Hamza, Agon. Interview with Alenka Zupančič: Philosophy or Psychoanalysis? Yes, Please! *Crisis and Critique*, 02 April 2019. https://terada.ca/discourse/wp-content/uploads/2020/09/Crisis-andCritique-Zupancic-Interview.pdf
Safatle, Vladimir. Lacan, revolução e liquidação da transferência: a destituição subjetiva como protocolo de emancipação política. *Estudos Avançados*, Vol. 31, No.91, 2017. https://doi.org/10.1590/s0103-40142017.3191016
Trigg, Dylan. *The Memory of Place: A Phenomenology of the Uncanny (Series in Continental Thought)*. Ohio: Ohio University Press; Reprint Edition, 2013.
Wright, Ian. *What Is Abstract Labour and Who Does the Abstracting?* 2020. https://ianwrightsite.wordpress.com/2020/06/13/what-is-abstract-labour-and-who-does-the-abstracting/
Žižek, Slavoj. *Looking Awry - An Introduction to Jacques Lacan through Popular Culture*. London: MIT Press, 1992
Žižek, Slavoj. *Organs without Bodies*. London: Routledge, 2004.
Žižek, Slavoj. *Parallax View*. Harvard, MA: MIT Press, 2006.
Žižek, Slavoj. *For they Know Not What they Do: Enjoyment as a Political Factor*. 1991. London: Verso Books, 2008.
Žižek, Slavoj. *The Plague of Fantasies*. London: Verso Books, 2009.

Žižek, Slavoj. 2011. *The Politics of Negativity in Frank Ruda Hegel's Rabble: An Investigation into Hegel's Philosophy of Right*. London: Bloomsbury.
Žižek, Slavoj. *Less than Nothing: Hegel and the Shadow of Dialectical Materialism*. London: Verso Books, 2012.
Žižek, Slavoj. *Disparities*. London: Bloomsbury, 2016.
Zupančič, Alenka. *Ethics of the Real*. London: VersoBooks, 2000.
Zupančič, Alenka. Reversals of Nothing: The Case of the Sneezing Corpse. *Filozofski vestnik Volume/Letnik XXVI*; Number/Številka, Vol. 2, 173–186, 2005.
Zupančič, Alenka. *What Is Sex?* Cambrige, MA: Mit Press, 2017.

2

MONSTROSITY IN DISPUTE

Monsters in history and its implications to thinking

2.1 A brief discussion of monstrosity in philosophy: disturbances and tensions in history

The investigation about monstrosity is far from being a *new* one. But up until now, this text has defended a certain topological position which deserves further discussion. The main objective of this section does not lie in a detailed "historical" appreciation of monstrosity, but on philosophical discussion about it (e.g., philosophies focused on languages and bodies, as Badiou would describe). We can say that there is a certain ongoing thrust behind thinking about monsters, which poses important questions. The chapter is organized as follows: (1) a brief engagement with monstrosity in general history of the field; (2) monstrosity picked up from the 20th-century thinkers of the "adventure of French Philosophy" (Badiou 2012) and (some of) its implications; (3) historicism surpassing time in the French adventures of thinking; and finally, (4) an offering of speculative explorations of monstrosity after the 20th-century French philosophy. The overall idea is not to introduce a parallel discussion but to highlight the impasses of monstrosity. It would be rather naïve to pretend that this section is a profound or a detailed approach to the general history of monstrosity. This is why the present section is nothing but a *brief* interaction with the general history of how monstrosity has emerged *philosophically* and how it has been (re)articulated by Lacanian psychoanalysis (and its debate with *l'univers morbide*).

There is an important study in the history of monstrosity called *Marvels of the East* from Rudolf Wittkower (1942) which sets the scene for our discussion. The German historian argues how the "survival and transmission of this Greek conception of ethnographical monsters" (Wittkower 1942, 159) come to

DOI: 10.4324/9781003437543-3

be "[a]nd their power of survival was such that they did not die altogether with the geographical discoveries and a better knowledge of the East, but lived on in pseudo-scientific dress right into the 17th and 18th centuries" (Wittkower 1942, 159). One of the first arguments presented illustrates how the Greeks managed to forge and disseminate their perspective about India (Wittkower 1942, 160), from early writings tracing back from Herodotus,[1] passing along to Ktesias from Knidos (around 4th century B.C.) who added outlandish tales to the one's already circulating about the East since Homer's time. Following Wittkower findings, it was after Alexander the Great's invasion (around 326 B.C.) that western ideas about India seemed to change. His expeditions were known to have been documented but most of these registers have been lost (Wittkower 1942, 161). Yet, one of the most important books registering such endeavours came to be only after the end of the campaigns through the hands of Megasthenes (around 303 B.C.) whose treatise survives in Diodorus Siculus, Strabo, Pliny, Arrian, Aelian and others (Wittkower 1942, 162). Megasthenes adds more stories[2] of Indian marvels, with tales on fabulous races and animals, and a fascinating point remarked by Wittkower is how such (rather marvelous) additions were undisputed for almost 1500 years (Wittkower 1942, 162). A long period of political struggles, disputes and confusions emerging in the East originated from the direct contact by land between the West and India which was made difficult for a long period of time (up until monsoon navigation was discovered, which led to merchandise exchanges) (Wittkower 1942, 163). As Wittkower tells us, the Greek and Roman authors (of the last centuries B.C.) reproduced the classical accounts of India because of their lack of direct geographical and ethnological contact (Wittkower 1942, 163).

According to the historian, there are many incurrences which sustain how the bestiary mixes the Ancient Greeks and Indian incursions.[3] However, there are also cases, where even without much basis, Greek writers concocted creatures such as satyrs and sirens and there are also occasions where observations could have "transfigure" the bottom of some creatures, for example, "unicorns" could perhaps have only been Indian rhinos (Wittkower 1942, 164). Nonetheless, Wittkower maintains how most

> of the fabulous stories were of literary origin; they were borrowed from the Indian epics. Megasthenes himself said that he owed his knowledge of some of the marvels to the Brahmans, and he had, of course, no reason to distrust the reports of the highly esteemed cast of philosophers.
>
> *(Wittkower 1942, 164)*

Moreover, even an "accurate observer," such as Megasthenes (as the Historian defends), would not be strange to have believed such fabulous stories, since these were a part of the Greek inheritance and had the Indian verbal and literary tradition to rely on (Wittkower 1942, 165). Wittkower addresses that there were those who were critical of such marvels, wonders and fabulous stories, such as Strabo (responsible for *Geography*, wrote at the year one of our era) (Wittkower 1942, 165). Although he criticized old superstitions, he also had to rely in the material on India from Megasthenes and other writers of Alexander's time to do so (Wittkower 1942, 165).

Taking a step forward to mediaeval times, Wittkower argues that one key source for the mediaeval lore of monsters was Pliny's *Historia Naturalis* (finished 77 A.D.). Where most of the miraculous stories are well accepted (unlike Strabo, as the Historian tells us), yet it was Solinus (who in the 3rd century A.D. wrote *Collectanea Rerum Memorabilium*), the chosen author by the Christians over Middle Ages, nonetheless his work was influenced by Pliny's work. As Wittkower tells us, Medieval writers needed such books to sustain their geographical material, that instead of relying on judgement and knowledge had chosen imagination, oddities and marvels (Wittkower 1942, 167). However, Christianity could not "swallow" pagan antiquity, thus it had to pay its dues to the authority of the Bible (Wittkower 1942, 167). For instance, in "St. Augustine, Chapter 8 of the 16th book of the *CivitasDei* is entitled: 'Whether certain monstrous races of men are derived from the stock of Adam or Noah's sons?'" (Wittkower 1942, 167). And St. Augustine's answer has a certain "cunning ingenuity" (Wittkower 1942, 167), since if fabulous races *do* exist and these are actually humans, they *must* have descended from Adam. Augustine realizes there are monstrous births in individual races, leading to the hypothesis that monstrous races must exist from their shared origin. The theological argument is that man should not judge these races because these are part of God's creation. So, Augustine argues that God could have created fabulous races for us not assume the monstrous births as a failure of His wisdom (Wittkower 1942, 168)

As Wittkower notices, Augustine's proposals were deeply embraced by Middle Age' writers. For instance, the encyclopedic work of Isidore in "the *Etymologiae* (written probably between 622 and 633), simply states that monstrosities are part of the creation and not 'contra naturam'" (Wittkower 1942, 168) but more interesting than that, as Wittkower notes, this explains how the notion of monstrosity reconnects with the idea of portend and foretelling the future which derived from Babylonia and travelled to Greece and Rome, finding its reintroduction through Christian lenses (Wittkower 1942, 168). Instead of a monstrous race, Solinus (who influenced Isidore), deals with "individual monsters," yet he never defines what monstrosity means. The comprehension of the monster as a magical prodigy traces back to Rome and Greece and Babylonia (Wittkower 1942, 168). As Wittkower explain, the ancient knowledge from the period is separated by two branches: geographical and magical. What this means is that, for authors like Isidore, monstrosity and monsters are a designation concerning geographical distance. The Isidorean approach depicts a hierarchy from the Holy Trinity, to Church, to mankind and he places the fantastic races as inhabitants of far parts of the world and finally, the animals (Wittkower 1942, 169).

A long list of fabulous races and marvels follow this period (7th century onwards), where, as Wittkower defends, fabulous descriptions of geographical mythology gained popularity with the cartography from Isidore and Solinus. The relevance of such marvels can be attested by the great encyclopedias from the 12th and 13th centuries, which gave notoriety to such occurrences.[4] Besides the literary transmission

> from Ktesias and Megasthenes through Pliny and Solinus to Isidore and down to Vincent of Beauvais and the encyclopedists of the later Middle Ages was not the only way in which the western world came into contact with the Marvels of the East.
>
> *(Wittkower 1942, 171)*

Wittkower's investigation at this juncture continues: there are also pictures of these fabulous races in antiquity, from "St. Augustine's mentions of a mosaic in the harbour esplanade with elaborate representations of monstrous peoples…"(Wittkower 1942, 171) to many copies of Solinus's from the 9th century on with illustrations and miniatures (Wittkower 1942, 171). These treatises survived bringing forward these representations of the *Marvels of the East* (Wittkower 1942, 172), gaining different translations which popularized these "classical" creatures which were described as "Eastern" non-classical monster (Wittkower 1942, 173). For example, the ancient centaur depicted as a partial men combined with a wild bottom and birdlike legs (Wittkower 1942, 173) hints to the composition of antique models that solidify inaccuracies to textual depictions.

Wittkower traces back how Panofsky and Saxl, through Hrabanus, have copied from Isidore spreading the "monstruaries" through the 11th century all the way towards the 15th century (Wittkower 1942, 173). However, Wittkower talks about the works where marvels can be found in prototypical maps of the world as a constant feature (Wittkower 1942, 173). For example, the Hereford map, where fabulous races and animals distributed all around the world (around the 13th century).[5] Yet, there is another group of influences of images which came from the "[m]anuscripts of Kazwini's cosmography, the Arabic Pliny of the 13th century" (Wittkower 1942, 174), shows a representation of fabulous races (a cynocephali group) remarkably similar to the western types. In short, such a large stock of classical marvel illustrations have reached the Middle Ages through many different channels, as Wittkower explains:

> the maps of the world, the monster treatises, the illustrated Solinus and probably the illustrated Isidore. It is this visual material which, together

> with the literary transmission, impressed itself on the minds of the people and proved so influential in many branches of mediaeval thought.
>
> *(Wittkower 1942, 176)*

Following Wittkower, it becomes clear how the infiltration of such marvels into the field of religious art becomes clear from the 12th century onwards, which assumed fabulous races as products of God's will who "is righteous in all his ways and holy in all his works" (Wittkower 1942, 176). A similar line of argumentation is presented around 1486 by Heinrich Kramer and James Sprenger, who debate the implications of witchcraft in their *Malleus Maleficarum* (The Hammer of Witches), where demons influence still must be conceived within God's creation and plan (otherwise, it would be outside of God's omnipotence).[6,7,8] While this is skipping ahead, it is important to note that what Wittkower addresses how the iconographical program introduced through many different moments in that period, was slowly *moralized* through Christian's lenses and a key creation at this point were the *bestiaries*. Originally produced by mediaeval craftsman, the bestiaries compile interpretations of a series of monsters present in ecclesiastical art. And after the 13th century, the marvels were incorporated into a group of Bestiaries, which re-united the encyclopaedic and the mystical branches of Bestiaries, argues Wittkower. This attribution present in the Westminster Bestiary provided the marvels with new allegorical meanings, for example,

> the pygmies stand for humility and the giant for pride, the cynocephali typify quarrelsome persons and the people who cover themselves with the lower lip are the mischievous, according to the word of the psalm: "Let the mischief of their own lips cover them" (P1. 44c).
>
> *(Wittkower 1942, 177)*

As Wittkower goes on to explain, with allegorical perspectives and interpretations of the world such as the one from M. Capella, into an enclosed comprehensive system, the idea of looking at the monsters as "moral prodigies" started to be conceived in the later Middle Ages embracing the moralization of the Bible. Another example Wittkower uses to illustrate this point, are "people with long lower lip [are] symbols of justice" (Wittkower 1942,178) or those with "long ears listen to the word of God" (Wittkower 1942, 178) from the 175th tale *"De mirabilibus mundi"* (in *Gesta Romanorum*) which contains a full account of other examples like "the cynocephali are the preachers who ought to be coarsely clad just like the dog-headed people, and the headless monsters are the symbol of humility, and so on" (Wittkower 1942, 178). Although the influence appears obvious in the illustrations and literature of the 13th, 14th and 15th centuries, Wittkower notices how complex it is to define how (re) interpretations took place, but a valid example comes from the monsters compiled in the Westminster Bestiary with "modernized" versions of the old lores or the 15th century work of Thomas of Cantimpre's *Liber de monstruosis hominibus* (Wittkower 1942, 178).

Another popular imagery which was translated from the original in Greek and vastly spread in the early Middle Ages was the *Romance of Alexander* which contains under the guise of the great king's adventurous campaigns many of the Indian fables (Wittkower 1942, 179). Wittkower notices how the tales of Alexander's incursions at Asia, counted with the illustration of the fantastic creatures encountered at the journey, but such illustration got many different artistic interpretations (Wittkower 1942, 180). In a way, the marvels were actively participating in making history, since they were a significant part of the mystification which excited the people over the 12th and 13th centuries in Europe and such perspectives echoed until the 17th century, as Wittkower defends (Wittkower 1942, 181). For instance, there is the story of the great Christian kingdom of Prester John in the remote East, containing countless marvels, which is the common medieval geographic location to portray "Paradise in the extreme East" (Wittkower 1942, 181). This is a central example how the 'mixing marvels' influences the theme of monstrosity in this moment of history. Nonetheless, there is also the point of moralization related with a "heated" discussion during the Middle Ages: the *existence of the Antipodes*. Basically, men who walk with their feet opposite ours that live in the other side of the world. Such belief was deemed heretical after the 8th century, but the heated argument concerned if Noah's descendants could have reached that far and how could Christ bring salvation to all mankind, if this portion was inaccessible (Wittkower 1942, 182)?

These polemic undertakings of monstrosity alongside the circumspection of Christianism have gone hand in hand for a while, but things took a slow turn towards a change of perspective concerning the *occult*. The moral panic of the occult is usually rooted in the accumulation of theological impasses of the "Christianization" over reality across world's history. In the 14th century, Nicolas Oresme and Henry of Hesse started to oppose occult science and the belief in monsters, but it took time for this perspective to become hegemonic. Even through the Enlightenment of the 15th century and the geographical expansion that spread the known borders didn't immediately break with tradition, as Wittkower explains (Wittkower 1942, 182). Thus, modern authors from that period, instead of pursuing different perspectives preferred to adhere to old superstitions and to rediscover "old Isidorian patterns of the ages of the world…" (Wittkower 1942, 182). This conservative spirit explains the Isidorian influence which can be found in innumerable illustrations, for example, Sebastian Franck's Chronicle of 1531 and this spirit persisted throughout the second half of the 16th century (Wittkower 1942, 183).

Wittkower argues about the difficulties that previous writers had in order to dispute authority and their legacies on such matters, counting here with the clashing opinions of two cosmographers from the 16th century, Andre Thévet and Sebastian Münster (Wittkower 1942, 183), who either bluntly denied stories of marvels or were sceptical about the construction of previous marvels (Wittkower 1942, 183). While Thévet took on the pictorial tradition to dispute and doubt, Münster still accepted fabulous tales and creatures like griffins, but remained "hesitant about the monsters' races" (Wittkower 1942, 184). For Wittkower, works like Münster and Schedel's are above all link to tradition concerning monsters (Wittkower 1942, 185). It was Conrad Wolffhart (under the pseudonym Lycosthenes), who took a step away from cosmologies and encyclopaedias and back into the world of magic. Basically, Lycosthenes is an exponent of ideas resulting from the non-surmounted notions revived from "the circle of German emperor Maximilian." (Wittkower 1942, 186), and "their effect was immediate and widespread, and they brought to the surface popular beliefs which had had no place in the official mediaeval conception of the world." (Wittkower 1942, 186)

A famous interpreter of the awe of monsters is A. Warburg (in *Gesammelte Schriften*, II, 522 ff), who resulted in the collection of "prodigies by Joseph Gruinpeck for Maximilian's secretary Blasio Holtzl (1502) and by Jakob Mennel for the emperor himself (1503)" (Wittkower 1942, 186). Many superstitions were maintained here, such as the power of the stars, omens and portents. Wittkower notices how Luther and Protestant circles were certainly not immune to any of this sustaining trend (Wittkower 1942, 186) and in the beginning of the 16th century, many treatises based on monsters surfaced in European countries (Wittkower 1942, 186). Wittkower comes up with a list of authors (Aldus Manutius, Pierre Boaistuau, Marcus Frytschius, Jacob Rueff, Ambroise Paré and Cornelius Gemma) who correlated monstrous births with political events (Wittkower 1942, 187). Although these births didn't derive directly from monstrous races, writes ponder upon a genetic linkage between the individual monsters and the monstrous races (Wittkower 1942, 187). The central argument revolves around the destruction of tower of Babel in the Bible, explains Wittkower, where the earth shared one language and speech, but later, God scattered people all over the earth. And Lycosthenes argues how monster races and the individual monsters come to live after God's dispersion of mankind (Wittkower 1942, 187).

Wittkower's argumentation delineates how such horror stories propel an imaginary background which was integrated through pictorial and literary transmissions which always found a way to resurface and re-invent the idea of monstrosity dressed in different clothes. This is a clear influence within such 'marvels from the East' on Ancient Greece and Rome, which migrated and were transformed at the Middle Ages further reshaping its approach to monstrosity under the orthodox understandings of the Bible. Nonetheless, the effort of sustaining such tradition for some authors did not just stop at repeating previous claims but rather, it created new trajectories of monstrosity by mixing entrenched traditions with new interests which were being developed at that period (e.g., physiology and natural studies). Following the *Historian*, it was precisely this orientation that lead up to the studies of *teratology*:

> The works by Jacob Rueff, Cornelius Gemma, Ambroise Pare and others are not histories or annals like those of Schedel, Mennel, Lycosthenes and Wolf – they are concerned with a systematic study of monstrosities, that branch of natural science for which the term teratology has been generally accepted.
>
> *(Wittkower 1942, 188)*

From 16th century onwards, Europe was flooded with studies deriving from such orientation. Basically, the product of a compilation of all known classical and post-classical sources, methodologically organized and interpret along with the new biological and anatomy research. But the scientific perspective was "overshadowed" by the overwhelming "cases" at hand: mythological creatures and fantastic monsters which were held under the same scrutiny of direct observations to represent an investigation of different monsters (Wittkower 1942, 188).

For Wittkower, the scientific research influenced the debate on monsters as much as it was a central topic of the science from that period. The investigations of individual "monstrosities" and its connections with questions around pathologies where popular at that time. Yet, this certainly, does not mean that scientific discursivity *took over* old mythological traditions. Wittkower presents (Wittkower 1942, 189) how behind the encyclopaedic spirit of grouping monstrosity according to irregularities at the level of the body, classical sources such as Lycosthenes influenced overshadowing scientific observation. Wittkower offers that before those discussions focused on deformities located at parts of the body, the link to such deformities via the fabulous races can be found in many different sources (Wittkower 1942, 189).

But prior to this orientation, there was a more progressive group of scholars inspired by Aristotle's logical understanding of nature against pure randomness, attempted to classify the biological causes that produced monstrosities (Wittkower 1942, 190). Basically, this different approach relates to causality in nature and the pursue of its functions (Wittkower 1942, 190). The pioneers of this branch, as Wittkower offers, were J. Rueff and A. Paré (Wittkower 1942, 190) who "paradoxically enough, did not even escape from the belief in the monster as a portent, and they regarded God's will or rather His wrath as the primary reason for monstrous births" (Wittkower 1942, 190). He emphasizes how teratology and the attempts to systematize studies on monstrosity, were still very much embedded with previous renders from *bestiaries* and how such "modern" step certainly does not represent an obliteration of old tendencies, but it's opposite. Another example is the anatomist and botanist Caspar

Bauhin (1560–1624) whose work on monsters provided a table with reasons for monstrous births and in his ranking, the influence of the stars, the winds and the wrath of God appeared above biological causes. For Wittkower, the Aristotelian review of monsters is due to Fortunio Liceti and a new systematizing effort along the Aristotelian lines came from other fields, that is, *zoology*7$_{F}$ As Wittkower carefully demonstrates this growing interest from the 17th century took the stage regarding the dispute between "classical authority and exact observation" (Wittkower 1942, 191). Here, the Historian demonstrates that this clash has a curious genesis which descends from when "Ktesias compared a tailed race in India with satyrs" (Wittkower 1942, 191) and the surface of "anthropological and ethnological knowledge" (Wittkower 1942, 192) from the 16th and 17th centuries, pushed new perspectives on old fabulous races. This certainly changed the former balance between old and new perspectives somewhat established in medicine, zoology and anthropology, prior to the 17th century. As Wittkower defends, scepticism about the existence of fabulous races was always present, but it took a more incisive shift in the 17th century with the incisive text from John Spencer's (1663) "discouraging of a superstitious study of the singularities in nature" (whose fame is derived as being the founder of comparative religion), a text which had "this authoritative body, which finally banished all marvels and fabulous stories and based research solely on experiment and exact observation." (Wittkower 1942, 193)

Wittkower's rendering of the 'marvels of the East' provides crucial refinements to the studies of monstrosity. The fabulous races and marvels which were classically projected on India until the 15th and 16th century also kept its hold over Europe. But over time (with the help of travellers' reports), India stopped being the "birthplace" location of monstrosity. Wittkower notices how this geographical connection got lost, while it *simultaneously* de-territorialized monstrosity as such, "spreading out" geographically throughout and within the globe. This revitalized perspective gained thrust in "prognostications, teratological treatises and popular imagery," (Wittkower 1942, 194) and although the geographical "India" was lost, the monsters "from the East" persisted everywhere. For Wittkower, the contributions from observers did not further "natural sciences, ethnology or geography" (Wittkower 1942, 194), because solid observations and fabulous traditions (Wittkower 1942, 195) where too mixed in knowledge production of their period. He goes on to hypothesize that perhaps, "their imagination was fed from childhood with stories of marvels and miracles which they found because they believed in them." (Wittkower 1942, 194) and such influence is rather profound. He concludes this by saying that:

> Monsters-composite beings, half-human, half-animal-play a part in the thought and imagery of all peoples at all times. Everywhere the monster has been credited with the powers of a god or the diabolical forces of evil.

> Monsters have had their share in mythologies and fairy-tales, superstitions and prognostications. In the Marvels of the East this old demonic inheritance was at the same time preserved and made pseudo-rational. But their ethnological shadow existence sank back into the sphere of magic whenever the innate awe of the monster came to the fore. The Greeks gave to some of these primeval conceptions visual forms which were generally accepted for 1500 years. They shaped not only the day-dreams of beauty and harmony of western man but created at the same time symbols which expressed the horrors of his real dreams.
>
> *(Wittkower 1942, 197)*

Wittkower makes it clear how disputing such marvels, despite the observations made and the claims repudiating them, still took a significant amount of effort to be transformed and even so, these creations seem to linger, populating under different symbolic-imaginary aspects of our reality. Our attentiveness to contingency and singularity is at stake within monstrosity and this brief historical appreciation already permits a closer look at the power influence of the theme and its dwelling through many moments of existence.

Patrick Tort's (1980) *L'order et les monstres*, picks up the question of *teratology* (congenital abnormalities) and presents an in-depth investigation of the "origins of monsters as a relevant problem to medical and anatomy science" (Wittkower 1942, 6). Tort pursues how teratology burst into Europe and that monstrosity is its heritage, it charged the field with moral connotations and designations to investigate monstrosity. Tort pursues the trends of teratology which Wittkower (1942, 190) previously introduced. Moreover, Tort corroborates with Wittkower's stance on the difficulty of overcoming some elements of monstrosity (e.g., the moralization of the relationship between the order and exceptions) and how its prior designations seem to be carried along. For Tort, teratology leads to the questions of "abnormalities" and dysmorphology and monstrosity investigated under teratological terms deals with a certain organization of physical anatomy and its impasses. A good example is the investigation of the polydactyls (who were those that could *reproduce* their 'monstrosity') addressed by Tort.

Tort discusses how "abnormalities" at the level of the body occupied a differentiated position when modern science tried establishing a certain encyclopaedic organization of categories. The *polydactyls* are a valid example to illustrate anti-metaphysical attempts to organize accidentalism and to move beyond preformationism. And this normative organization built into discourse changes reality as such, it is a formalization of monstrosity against religious and metaphysical instances. The polydactyls interest teratologists because they possess an inherited "form of monstrosity" (Wittkower 1942, 226) and "[s]uch an observation, which corresponds to a genetic fact since proven, could then have several consequences on the general representation of monsters" (Wittkower 1942, 227).

The implications highlighted by Tort are (1) the implications of hereditary trait and (2) the existence of a "double observation established the existence of a heredity in the paternal line (Godeheu), a heredity in the maternal line (Maupertuis), which added to the already perceived insufficiency of the two versions – ovist and animalculist – preformationism"(Wittkower 1942, 227) and finally, (3) how "this observation did indeed constitute 'proof', as regards the cases of polydactyly, that the hypothesis of a generation by accidental confusion of germs was gratuitous and without foundation" (Wittkower 1942, 228).

For Tort, these three implications are the key impasse of teratogenesis. Even if at the level of observation, one can correctly see hereditary traits, "the ethology of the monstrosities was once again excluded from the most fruitful avenue of research which would have been opened during the preceding decades" (Wittkower 1942, 228). As Tort explains, teratogenesis are in constant tension with metaphysical possibilities and preformationism. An example of this is how

> [t]he last word of the preformed monster thesis had been, on the metaphysical level, that of the almighty wisdom of God extending beyond the capacity of human intellect, and, on the scientific level, that of the statistical impossibility of the convergence into a single body of an "almost unpronounceable number of mechanical hazards producing organization."
>
> *(Wittkower 1942, 219)*

A point that corroborates this Aristotelian perspective on random accidentalism and which were highly influential during the time, juxtaposes Christian lenses by turning monstrous births as signs of the wrath of God (Wittkower 1942, 234). Nonetheless, there is also a second approach, which tends to provide a more secularized discourse of "nature," admitting "…deviations, errors, irregularities, disappointment of apparent ends, capacity for abortion or failure. The theologian demand for perfection seems to have practically died out, for it was to this that the demand for regularity was due" (Wittkower 1942, 235). For Tort, the status of the monsters pose a problem concerning the reflection of "laws of Nature" and the history of scientific reflection (portrayed by the teratological efforts clearly attest to this point), delts "in the polemical context which is that of the quarrel of the monsters, that is to say, in a debate whose the object is precisely identifiable *a priori* as the exception to the laws of nature" (Wittkower 1942, 235). Basically, Tort is attesting to the delicate debate on how *exceptions* can rule[9] in discourse. Yet, Tort is dealing with what where the embedded questions at that moment for teratology, explaining how the influence of Christian orthodoxy played a significant part of this debate on the laws of nature:

> In a Christian universe, in a very general way, the laws of nature, guaranteeing the regularity of phenomena, are fixed, immutable, and willed such by God. Once the world is harmoniously completed, God gains a kind of

> exteriority which means that the laws governing the functioning of his creation are sufficient to maintain the order which has been imposed on him, without the Creator having to intervene in it at any time. corrective or rebalancing purposes – this being a consequence of the sovereign perfection of its own nature, by virtue of which "nothing imperfect can come out of its hands". From this point of view, the Cartesian theory of continued creation is itself only another figure, another mode of representation of the lasting stability of the laws of nature.
>
> *(Wittkower 1942, 235)*

In a way, this attests to the many attempts at finding a balance to accommodate different (perhaps competing) narratives. However, the issues concerning monsters change more drastically when a shift towards "the preformationist theory of generation and the systematic anatomical observation of monstrous organisms" (Wittkower 1942, 236) appears. This shift tries to organize monstrosities as part of the Christian creation by considering every origin of species coming from God. Therefore, God as responsible for "deviations" and how it "proves" God's almighty freedom (Wittkower 1942, 237).

Tort's investigation on the (re)birth of monstrosity under the scope of teratology, indicates how in its efforts to step away from preformationism and towards "a generalization of the antimetaphysical hypothesis of accidental formations should have freed science from the obsession with absolute beginnings, and cuts" (Wittkower 1942, 242). This should have been a sparkle from accidentalist teratogenesis to stand up against the emphatic religious perspective on monstrosity (monstrous *race* or *individual* monsters). Or as Tort defends:

> In the vertical movement of parallels and analogies, it plays the role of the *clinamen*. Because natural history and anatomy could have produced endless parallels and analogies without departing for a moment from the providentialist metaphysics of physical theology. Accidentalist teratogenesis rejects the idea of a divine plan for the deviant organization in general by maintaining the essential idea of a heterotaxic repair of the functions of life, where life itself begins to be grasped in the intuition of life as a property common to organized beings. It helps to secularize the general thought of living things, insofar as it grasps its general analogies at the very heart of the deviations which exclude its transcendent command. To find, in naturalistic and no longer metaphysical terms, the science of the order of the living world, it was necessary to go through that of deviance and disorder.
>
> *(Wittkower 1942, 242)*

The radical implications of monstrosity aren't elevated here but forcefully reduced to a certain "naturalization of empiricist discursivity" and to its constraints, minimalizing "the gap between the organic and the subject via finding the organic causes of the subject" (Zupančič 2017, 75). Obviously, Tort's critique of teratological efforts is central to our discussion, but he was not attentive to this point. The realm of monstrosity as a philosophical operator introduces a dialectical materialist perspective to impasses beyond the level of *bodies and languages*, it reaches the implications of discourse over societal symbolic-imaginary edifices. It is an operator of strangeness that shifts the perspective of classic oppositions.

This section has briefly summarized the theme of monstrosity under a broader scope, investigating how it spread out through culture through religiosity and then, migrated towards scientific discourse, disputing metaphysical and anti-metaphysical arguments. Nonetheless, a *nuanced* discussion about *domination* and ideological stances of the wonders and marvels may push this discussion towards a more crucial aspect to studying monstrosity. The present incursion into monstrosity here is an introduction to how "monsters" seem to have gained different symbolic meaning through different cultures over time. However, monstrosity has shaped and (re)shaped our imagination through history. And in more recent times, monstrosity seems to have shifted from a forceful imaginary stance (in a more mythic and metaphysical stance) to occupy a symbolic position of transformative change in discourse, evidencing how monstrosity was a turning point in history representing the embodiment of a contradiction to a norm, as the embodiment of a torsion in discourse, demanding a transformation. In vulgar terms monstrosity is used to designate something or someone to be appalled but under philosophical terms, monstrosity can be the position of radical alterity against oppression. An invitation to think about difference and strangeness under different terms.

Throughout this section, the philosophical dimension of monstrosity was portrayed as a point of negativity in discourse; yet, what have become more evident is how monstrosity concerns a certain radical *topos* for thinking. In a way, this section illustrates how "monsters" have populated the imaginary through oral tradition determining roots of prejudice on alterity and difference through different periods of time. But with the further advancements of rationalist illuminism and with the scientific discourse, the realm of monstrosity which was once a certain point of preontological undecidability started to change its position. This was not a cut and clean moment of symbolic transformation of reality (far from it), a lot of time was required to subsume the metaphysical attributes posited over monstrosity, but this does not mean that there aren't animistic reminders of the fear of radical difference, these fears are still very much present in the societal fabric of our relations.

2.2 Monstrosity and the 20th-century "adventure of French Philosophy": a discussion

It is indisputable that French theorists left a mark in contemporary philosophy. This section borrows from Badiou's *The Adventure of French Philosophy* (2012) and *Pocket Pantheon* (2009) that add to our discussion. For instance, Badiou comments on Georges Canguilhem, who investigates monstrous and monstrosity in *Knowledge of Life* (2008), a crucial text that introduces monstrosity to contemporary philosophical terms.

This section has no intention of summarizing Canguilhem's life work or to consolidate a systematic approach to his philosophical developments. Our only concern here lies in the thinker's contribution devoted to monstrosity. In *Knowledge of Life* (2008), Canguilhem investigates the relation between knowledge and life, avoiding the assumption of a conflict between them (Canguilhem 2008, xvii). For him, the conflict lies not between thought and life, but "between man and the world in the human consciousness of life" (Canguilhem 2008, xvii). Thus, thought and knowledge are present in life sustaining a regulatory role, not as blind and mechanic force contrasting with thought (Canguilhem 2008, xviii). Canguilhem's supports a "reasonable rationalism" (Canguilhem 2008, xx) to understand the origins of life in a rational manner, or as he states: "The thought of the living must take from the living the idea of the living" (Canguilhem 2008, xx). His appraisal on life and death, health and sickness through the medical developments of his time, lead him to his first definition of monstrosity between normal constitution and monstrous form in certain organisms. For him, monstrosity can be interpreted as "an arrest in development or a fixation" (Canguilhem 2008, 15), leading to the expression of unusual properties in the expected morphology in human development.

Canguilhem's first approach to monstrosity is very biologistic. But it addresses that lack of engagement between modern medicine and philosophy for questions about life and death, normal and pathological, critical normativity and so on. This is the direction chosen by Canguilhem's philosophical investigation, the ideological impasses of the scientific method, the medical discursivity, its practice and experimental methods. As the philosopher defends, the experimental methods did not cover an essential issue: "to what extent do experimental (i.e., artificial) techniques thus instituted permit us to conclude that natural phenomena are adequately represented by the phenomena thus rendered perceptible?" (Canguilhem 2008, 18). For him, biologists construct knowledge of what is and happens without accounting for the participation of their active observation disturbing the phenomenon they observe. So, how to adequately conclude between the normal from the experimental itself, ponders Canguilhem. Relying on Etienne Wolff's argument, the mechanism of production of living beings (normal and monstrous) generates elucidations for both teratology and embryology (Canguilhem 2008, 18).

Going through the history of species in Biology, Canguilhem defines *monstrosity* as a significant stumbling block, as a proper impasse which requires a shift in perspective. One we could call a fundamental point of "knowledge of the Real" (Žižek 2000, 77) or an impasse of the (non)relation between science and philosophy (Zupančič 2017). Canguilhem (2008) investigates the difficult definition of "normalcy" and "pathology," while introducing a general notion of what *human life* is. For him, "[h]uman life can have a biological meaning, a social meaning, and an existential meaning" (Canguilhem 2008, 121–122). Basically, a diseased human being can maintain such meanings. In short, Canguilhem does not introduce any axiomatic position or definition to substantiate his claim, he only defends that life relates to *meaning*.

Canguilhem finds in the ambiguity of *normality* his justification for philosophically appraising knowledge in life. For him, it's all a matter of meaning, the individualization of the norm and how it obliterates the boundaries between the normal and the pathological, if there is meaning to support it (Canguilhem 2008, 130). Following Canguilhem, what is pathological for some can be normal in some cases, but this is not enough to abolish a boundary between normality and pathology (Canguilhem 2008, 130). Thus, he formulates that when an individual gets sick, the affirmation of his sickness (Canguilhem 2008, 130) is a traversal into another universe: this individual "become a different man" (Canguilhem 2008, 130). This is how Canguilhem manages to integrate two different perspectives: Claude Bernard's thought,[10] who assumes a homogeneity between the pathological and the normal, differing only as a matter of quantitative variation (Canguilhem 2008, 131) and the positivist thesis rooted in François Broussais and Auguste Comte, which branched in the 18th century to the physician discussions about the theory of irritability (Canguilhem 2008, 131). The "atomist pathology" derives from *quantitative variations* of a predetermined understanding between normal and pathological, for example, fever (Canguilhem 2008, 131), high blood pressure and so on. But the consolidation of "atomist pathology" can be problematic since, for Canguilhem, the a "diseased" organism turns into "other" in its entirety (Canguilhem 2008, 131).

Only from this point on, Canguilhem starts to clarify his concept of the "pathological." For him "pathological" is *not* the contrary "normal," as he clarifies, "for life in the pathological state is not the absence of norms but the presence of other norms. Rigorously speaking, "pathological" is the vital opposite of "healthy" and not the logical contradiction of "normal" (Canguilhem 2008, 131). The pathological is seen as a certain "distortion." Yet, Canguilhem cannot depart from Goldstein's[11] claim that:

> ...the norms of pathological life are those that oblige the organism to henceforth live in a "shrunken" milieu, which differs qualitatively, structurally, from its former milieu of life; the organism is obliged by its incapacity to confront the demands of new milieus (in the form of reactions or undertakings dictated by new situations) to live exclusively in this shrunken milieu.
>
> *(Canguilhem 2008, 132)*

Basically, Canguilhem argues that overcoming organic crises and establishing new physiological order is the luxury of the healthy being and by contrast, the diseased one has a decreased potential for transformation (Canguilhem 2008, 132). Under Canguilhem's biological perspective, the typical straightforward materiality of the "matter" does not strictly apply to his discussion. Nonetheless, he is still entrapped under the self-relating production of discursivity (of bio-medical discourse) without quite fully realizing or addressing a way out of it: he is entrapped by scientific discourse at the level of body and language. He attempts to escape by jumping towards psychology and psychiatry, arguing that someone mentally ill "is" a different person, is a "other" person; he argues that mental illness is not a prolongation or exacerbation of the normal psyche. For him, "the abnormal is truly in possession of other norms" (Canguilhem 2008, 132). From this insight, Canguilhem emphasizes how biology and medicine are branches of "anthropology," but since their "anthropology" is embedded in morality (Canguilhem 2008, 133) only a philosophical appraisal of "normal" could rid biology from its normative moralism.

It is precisely at this point that Canguilhem introduces his discussion on *Monstrosity and the Monstrous* (Canguilhem 2008, 134), since the existence of monsters can teach us something of life itself (Canguilhem 2008, 134). For him, "monster" is a fundamentally organic designation (there are no mechanical or mineral monsters) which has something to do with a "breach of confidence" in the face of divergency in a morphological level. How difference at the level of appearance, how an equivocal aspect in comparison to its species is usually receive as a cause for *radical fear* (Canguilhem 2008, 134). And so, monsters evoke "fear" (Canguilhem 2008, 134)

> [b]ecause we are living beings, real effects of the laws of life, and ourselves possible sources of life in our turn. A failure of life is of double concern to us, for such a failure could touch us or could come from us. It is only because we humans are living beings that a morphological failure is, to our living eyes, a monster. If we were beings of pure reason, pure intellectual machines of observation, calculation, and explanation, and thus inert and indifferent to the occasions of our thinking, then the monster would be merely what is other than the same, an order other than the most probable order.
>
> *(Canguilhem 2008, 134)*

Canguilhem says monstrosity must be conceived under certain criteria, which is why he determines that "[s]omething with no rule of internal cohesion, something whose form and dimensions cannot be seen as divergences from a module that can be expressed in terms of a measure, mold, or model, cannot be called monstrous" (Canguilhem 2008, 135). This means that rocks can be "enormous" but never "monstrous," only if raised under a mythical treatment (like in fantastic tales) (Canguilhem 2008, 135). As one could expect, the philosopher brings forward a distinction between "enormous and monstrous" from Kant's argument on monstrosity in *The Critique of Judgement*' [1790] (which will be explored on the next chapter). However, his approach concerns how both are "outside the norm" (Canguilhem 2008, 135). Basically, the enormous finds a way to evade from the metric norm and enormity portrays an expansion towards monstrosity, when quantity provokes questions over quality, as he claims (Canguilhem 2008, 135). Thus, the "ambiguity of gigantism" (from Kant's profound debate on monstrosity, this is what Canguilhem highlights), he ponders, could the giant be an enormous or a monster? Since its size obliterates the "end that constitute its concept" (Canguilhem 2008, 135). Forcing Canguilhem to conclude that "[t]he monster is a living being with negative value… the monster is not only a living being of reduced value, it is a living being whose value is to be a counterpoint" (Canguilhem 2008, 135). Although this "theory of values" is not fully explored, he highlights how a certain value is attached to the relation between a mode of being and a given milieu consistent as a species (Canguilhem 2008, 135). Thus, his definition of the monster, concerns the counterpoint that nods the precarity of stability in life. For Canguilhem the countervalue of life is monstrosity and not death, because monstrosity introduces contingency against the supposed stability of habits which is turned into law to understand life, the repetition of species, morphological comprehensions and so on (Canguilhem 2008, 135).

Canguilhem explains monstrosity at the level of the body *and* language. He defines how "[m]onstrosity is the accidental and conditional threat of incompleteness or distortion in the formation of the form; it is the limitation from within, the negation of the living by the nonviable" (Canguilhem 2008, 136). Explaining the reason why monstrosity causes confusion, concerns the ambivalence in human understanding towards the monster, which attributes awe instead of an appreciation of the values of life (Canguilhem 2008, 136). For him, "fear" and "fascination" are at the level of the body, "[t]he monstrous is the marvelous inverted, but it is marvelous nonetheless" (Canguilhem 2008, 136). Therefore, monstrosity is an embodiment of negative magnitudes. Indeed, Canguilhem notices a very important element to be introduced at the level to uncanny discussion: the point of torsion where symbolic and imaginary takes place to deal with the real of the body concern negative magnitudes, but he risks the essentialization of the bodies in a rather positivist and troubling sense.

And yet, Canguilhem surprises us with an insightful point, that is, how life's does not only produce exception but also "spontaneous transgressions of its own habits" (Canguilhem 2008, 136), introducing a certain dialectical stance to negativity which suggests subjective transformation. Canguilhem ponders upon how monstrosity is the sparkle for such movement. He claims "Life is poor in monsters. The fantastic is world" (Canguilhem 2008, 136). He is addressing this negativity.

His examination on the history of monstrosity, lies in finding the "relation" between monstrosity and monstrous. As he argues that both concepts share the same etymology and serve two modes of normative judgement: the medical and juridical which were embedded in religiosity and were then secularized (Canguilhem 2008, 137). While Canguilhem summarizes the impasse of normativity, he pursues how the monstrous earned its social "reputation," its ideological stance in modernity. For him:

> [t]he passage from hybridization to monstrosity is easy. The Middle Ages retains the identification of the monstrous with the criminal but also enriches it with a reference to the diabolical. The monster is at once the effect of an infraction of the rule of the sexual segregation of species and the sign of a will to perversion in the table of creatures.
>
> *(Canguilhem 2008, 137)*

The idea which Canguilhem will argue concerns how monstrosity relates more to the "licentiousness of the living" than to a consequence of the contingency of life (Canguilhem 2008, 137).

Canguilhem defends that the monster, when it refers to man, becomes a more emphatic case: "the question of the illicit eclipses that of the irregular; responsibility eclipses causality. If the Orient deifies monsters, Greece and Rome sacrifice them" (Canguilhem 2008, 137). After his research of monstrosity in Ancient Greece and Rome he debates monstrosity in the Middle Ages through the work of Ernest Martin ("History of Monsters"). It is a work which connects "…teratology to demonology [which] appears to have been the result of a persistent dualism in Christian theology" (Canguilhem 2008, 138). Canguilhem argues that his interest lies in how the monstrous, which is initially a juridical concept was gradually turned into an imaginary category that allowed for a displacement of responsibility (Canguilhem 2008, 138). Thus, explaining how the development of a human embryo somehow altered, was quickly to be assumed as having something to do with a demonic apparition, perhaps an incubus or a succubus, which is to blame by some authority (judge, theologians or philosophers). Here, he introduces more additional layers to his brief historical investigation, debating how humans became so familiarized with the idea of having lived amongst monsters and places an argument like Rudolf Wittkower (1942, 170): the legends of monsters were blended with history in such way that reality and fiction were undissociated. Thus, with a fertile ground to believe in the actual existence of monsters because these were imagined, this fictionalized mold starts to shape reality and authenticates fiction itself, he defends (Canguilhem 2008, 139).

Investigating the "monstrous-monstrosity" dialectic, Canguilhem denotes how teratology during the Middle Ages and the Renaissance is more than a cartography of monstrosities, it is actually a "celebration of the monstrous" (Canguilhem 2008, 139). He defends this point inspired by Julius Obsequens (4th century) and Conrad Lycosthenes (1557) whose iconographical approaches juxtapose monstrosity and the monstrous (Canguilhem 2008, 140). Moving through centuries, Canguilhem sums up his incursion denoting that the Middle Ages were a period in history were the mad lived in society with sane individuals and monsters lived amongst the "normal," while in the 19th century, the madman was expelled from society, locked away and institutionalized in asylums for the sake of reason and the monsters turned into an example of medicine to teach the norm (Canguilhem 2008, 140).

The exceptional century of monsters, as Canguilhem defends, was the 18th century. It was a century which "espoused the paradox of looking to aberrant organisms for entryways to an understanding of regular phenomena of organization" (Canguilhem 2008, 141). Monsters "reappear" under a resurface of the Renaissance, as a certain insurrection against the legislation of Nature by mechanistic physics and philosophy, as a nostalgic embrace of the non-distinction of norms. For him, the monsters legitimate a perspective of life where fecundity dissolves order (Canguilhem 2008, 141). But it is at the 19th century that monstrosity finds the correlative reduction of the monstrous, or to put it better, when the monstrosity was more emphatically "contained" under the realism of scientific discourse. As Canguilhem explains that teratology results from the combination of comparative anatomy, embryology and the theory of epigenesis. A certain teratological consensus of the time about monstrosity is that it concerns a development fixation of the organ at a certain stage which was surpassed by the others (Canguilhem 2008, 142).

Canguilhem exposes that in the 19th century, under further efforts on natural sciences, for example, Isidore Geoffroy Saint-Hilaire "*Histoire des anomalies de l'organisation*" (1837), which illustrates a "domestication of monstrosities," after the classification and organization of anomalies through a methodological pairing with nomenclature, a naturalization of the composite monster was established. From that point on, an understanding of fully development or incompleteness was solidified around monstrosities (Canguilhem 2008, 142). This localizes how anomaly and variety would become at the end of the century a key point for theories of evolution (Canguilhem 2008, 142). It is after this Historical period (close to the birth of biology as a scientific field that transformed natural history in experimental science), that definitions, categorizations and descriptions methodologically arranged turned teratology into a natural science (Canguilhem 2008, 142–143). As Canguilhem summarizes, monsters were contingencies of nature and contemporary science turn them into "games of scientists" (Canguilhem 2008, 144). Although Canguilhem argues for a more open scientific discourse, that does not mean Canguilhem questions the symbolic fabric derived from the science discourse itself in its interactions with the Real.

After this discussion, Canguilhem finally explains his point: "that life is poor in monsters, while the fantastic is a world" (Canguilhem 2008, 145). What Canguilhem means by this lack in monsters concerns how structural oddities at the level of organism only takes place only for a brief moment in early development (Canguilhem 2008, 145). While this "fantastic that is a world," he means that the fantastic, the unfathomable power of imagination can populate an entire world (Canguilhem 2008, 145). Canguilhem assumes a Bachelarian understanding of imagination, that is, "a function without an organ. It is not one of those functions that cease functioning to recuperate their functional power. It feeds only on its own activity" (Canguilhem 2008, 145). And this is how the French thinker finally explains how the "monstrous proliferation insofar as it is imaginary. Poverty on the one hand, prodigality on the other-this is the first reason for maintaining the duality of monstrosity and the monstrous" (Canguilhem 2008, 146). (An interesting point never fully explained by the thinker.) Thus, Canguilhem sustains how *the monstrous works as an imaginary operator and monstrosity persists in actualizing it*. And he rests his case on monstrosity, explaining how life does not transgress its laws not its structural framework, which means that there is "nothing monstrous about monstrosities" (Canguilhem 2008, 146). He seems to ponder upon negativity in terms closer to the Hegelian *Night* (a certain pre-ontological realm of negativity for the subject) in life, where the fundamental conditions of monstrosity concerning ontological inconsistencies are instituted, but he does not go towards that direction. Canguilhem criticizes a strict positivist formulation which restrains the world of imagination (Canguilhem 2008, 146). Following Canguilhem, he critiques an anticosmos created through an imaginative fabrication of a reign of exceptions without laws, which can haunt those who have created it, one that insists in an exceptionality departed from material conditions, which is a different understanding of contingencies. The world of the monstrous is the imaginary antiworld or the reign of well-constructed imaginary fantasies, which forgets that exceptions only come from laws (Canguilhem 2008, 146).

This seems to be Canguilhem's "fear" of monstrosity realizing its negativity in *full*. Certainly, Canguilhem satisfy his perspective under the restraint of scientific discourse and the idea of a lawless world of monstrous pre-ontological condition limited to the Imaginary, but this does not tell the whole story. Considering Badiou's discussion on Canguilhem, we can understand how he was a "discreet master" (Badiou 2012, 5) for a generation. Badiou praises Canguilhem's academic efforts on the genealogy of concepts and epistemology, saying how "Canguilhem is … to the life sciences what Koyré and Bachelard are to physics" (Badiou 2012, 7). His philosophical procedure aims at "seeking coherence," (Badiou 2012, 10) or to better put it, "[t]he order of thought means nothing without the irrepressible demand that finds its subjective consistency," explains Badiou (2012, 12).

But at the same time, Badiou (2012, 39) criticizes Canguilhem's lack of interest in a theory of subject, which weakens his philosophical endeavour. For Badiou, Canguilhem discusses the subject without giving it a proper (theory) of subject (Badiou 2012, 40). This is a strategic attempt on Canguilhem's part, which Badiou denounces as "the fault lines or discontinuities between the tectonic plates of

Canguilhem's thought and what it controls in its actualization"(Badiou 2012, 40). Badiou points out three discontinuities in Canguilhem:

> A quasi-ontological discontinuity which within the natural presentation separates the living from the non-living.
>
> An operational discontinuity which distinguishes technique from science.
>
> A primarily ethical discontinuity which, in medicine, links together the dimension of knowledge and what might be called the dimension of closeness.
>
> *(Badiou 2012, 40)*

For Badiou, Canguilhem understands living as "a pre-subjective disposition on the basis of which any possible subject arises, it is because the living can be understood only in connection with the three essential notions of centre (or centring), norm and meaning" (Badiou 2012, 40). Here, Badiou debates how there is a "formal schema or virtuality of the subject," to think between norm and meaning (related to the previous discontinuities stated by Badiou). Badiou states how "Canguilhem absolutizes reality in the unified form that, at least ideally, physical science attributes to it" (Badiou 2012, 40), a point easily spotted in our discussion. Badiou reminds us that the concept of the subject is a modern one, which picks out the conflict of absolute, and he continues:

> ...the absolute character of the objective universal milieu is coupled with the absolute character of subjective need, the latter giving its energy to the triplet of centring, norm and meaning. This conflict of absolutes implies that what is truly real, what determines differences within reality, varies from one whole to the other depending on the place from which one is speaking. With regard to the absolute universe, or universal milieu, living milieus have no meaning that would enable them to be classified or compared.
>
> *(Badiou 2012, 42)*

But Canguilhem would not simply oppose the "absolute character of the universal milieu to the pre-subjective absolute character of the centring by the living being" (Badiou 2012, 43), explains Badiou. For Canguilhem, "the human subject in any case is entailed in both terms of the conflict" (Badiou 2012, 43) and the fundamental point, neatly summarized by Badiou is that "the notion of a 'subject' somehow designates not just *one* of the terms of the clash of absolutes, but rather the enigma of this discordance itself" (Badiou 2012, 43). Canguilhem's efforts of debating a knowledgeable subject in the life sciences, provides a crucial step towards monstrosity (in its negative counterpoint and potency) and ontological inconsistencies. Although Badiou praises Canguilhem for his contributions, he is also aware of his shortcomings. In a way, the realm of negativity presented by monstrosity in Canguilhem, is a central dimension but one not explored by him. It becomes clear that there is a fragile impasse in Canguilhem's philosophy, concerning his trust in the subject of knowledge embedded in the scientific discursivity, not necessarily facing the troubles of normativity which is also produced by such discursivity. Although respectful of Canguilhem's philosophical project, one can easy to assume that Badiou (2009, 10) would place him under the category of thinkers limited by bodies and languages (a thinker rooted into "biopolitics").

In a way, we can identify Canguilhem as the precursor of what would later become the realm of *biopolitics*. Zupančič (2016) develops a good critique of biopolitics while investigating one of Canguilhem's disciples: Michel Foucault. She presents how Foucault engages in sexuality in his three volumes of *The History of Sexuality* (1976), but all too quickly dropped the category of sexuality to investigate the concept of biopolitics instead (Zupančič 2016, 50). Zupančič aims at investigating sexuality and psychoanalysis on Foucault whilst criticizing biopolitics' shortcomings (Zupančič 2016, 50). Pursuing question: "What is the version of psychoanalysis that Foucault *needs* in order to develop, with its 'help', his concept of biopolitics, and why?" (Zupančič 2016, 50). Zupančič's strategy is two-fold:

> on the one hand, [she] will insist on what is quite dramatically missed (and missing) in Foucault's account of psychoanalysis; on the other hand, [she] will try to show how this leaves a significant symptomatic trace in his theory of modern power as biopolitics.
>
> *(Zupančič 2016, 51)*

The thinker determines the central missing element in Foucault's discussion: the unconscious. Zupančič makes it clear how Foucault attributes an importance to Freud's approach to sexuality but simultaneously dislocates it completely from the unconscious, not even quoting a single time through his entire book. As Zupančič explains, sexuality is "constitutively unconscious" and Foucault tries to separate sexuality from the unconscious… Following Zupančič, "in so far as something about sexuality is constitutively unconscious – [it is] constitutively problematic, lacking, irreducible to any kind of truth about itself" (Zupančič 2016, 51). Thus, the proper way to translate the 'unconscious'

> …does not mean the opposite of consciousness, it refers to an active and ongoing *process*, *work* of censorship, substitution, condensation and so on, and this work is itself intrinsic to sexuality (desire) and its deadlocks, rather than simply performed in relation to it.
>
> *(Zupančič 2016, 51)*

And Foucault simply obliterated both notions of the unconscious and repression (*Verdrängung*) from his work (Zupančič 2016, 51).

Zupančič follows Foucault's argument about how "in modern societies, sexuality has been *anything but* repressed; we have been witnessing – in respect to sexuality – a gigantic 'incitement to discourse'…" (Zupančič 2016, 52) and she explains,

> [p]art of this '*invention*' of sexuality, of its discursive implantation, has also been to institute it as the ultimate secret that *has to* be talked about and revealed; it has been made the locus of truth and the ultimate object of knowledge, sustained by its very secrecy…[12]
>
> *(Zupančič 2016, 52)*

and this is not an unintended aspect on Foucault's part but a deliberate strategic manoeuvre (which concerns Foucault's substitution of the term 'unconscious' for the 'secret') (Zupančič 2016, 52). This strategy of advocating for "secrecy" as an attempt to cover up the subject (of the unconscious) and the unconscious itself, while simultaneously trying to keep sexuality (in all its radical stance) at bay, certainly provides a profound uncanniness throughout his work. One could say that the strategy of turning the 'unconscious' into a 'secret', is analogous to the uncanny in its most Schellingian sense: something which was supposed to be kept a secret, but which comes to light…

Following Zupančič's investigation on Foucault, it becomes clear how he decided not to rigorously engage with psychoanalysis (Zupančič 2016, 52). Nonetheless, Zupančič explains this is a far more complicated point, since both Freud and Lacan "…were trying to account for it [perceptions produced], as well as counteract it" (Zupančič 2016, 52). This is why Zupančič defends that "the perception according to which psychoanalysis holds sexuality to be the secret and ultimate answer to everything is a defence against the main discovery of psychoanalysis, and needs to be analysed as such" (Zupančič 2016, 52). Here, Zupančič sides with Lacan and Freud, and states her main critique to Foucault:

> That sex is not *verdrängt* because it is considered (excitingly) dirty; rather, it is considered '(excitingly) dirty' and in need of regulation (by prohibition or incitement – no big difference here) because something about it is constitutively unconscious, that is because something about it is involved in the gap (ontological inconsistency) of the discursive being as such.
>
> *(Zupančič 2016, 52–53)*

This is a fundamental element to be integrated into our discussion about monstrous implications and its dialectics. Zupančič also points out how Foucault turns psychoanalysis into a *biopolitical instrument*, a technology of power where

> we think that what resists works against the deployment of power, but actually this resistance is its inherent condition, as well as a pacifying trap which makes us prey to the illusion of how subversive we are if we speak of sex, or give voice to this resistance.
>
> *(Zupančič 2016, 53)*

For Foucault, psychoanalysis is two-fold: one side would be resisting secret and the other side "(almost) endlessly revealing it and seeing its manifestations everywhere" (Zupančič 2016, 53). Zupančič argues that Foucault's claims are fragile, since: "Psychoanalysis comes as that which will save sexuality from its confinement that it has itself declared as such ('invented'). Psychoanalysis is like the proverbial lawyer who helps us deal with problems that we would not have without him" (Zupančič 2016, 53). For her, the Foucauldian understanding of the unconscious makes no room for the Freudian thesis of the unconscious, where sexuality and unconscious simply cannot be separated. A key reason why Zupančič wages on Freud's theory of the subject as intrinsically libidinal rather than Foucault's historical approach.

Focusing on Foucault's harsh criticism on how psychoanalysis becomes the pervasive technology for locating biopolitics, she counters it with the Lacanian argument that psychoanalysis was aware of the "pathological structures it produced," Zupančič defends:

> Far from producing liberation, the retreat of symbolic authority paves the way for a morbid, infinite scrutiny that Freud associated with the logic of the superego – it is this logic that generalizes guilt, infusing it on the 'microphysical' level. And it is important to note that this shift and the pathological structures it produced is the very ground analysed by psychoanalysis. In other words, the 'generalization of illness' (what Freud called, for example, the psychopathology of everyday life) is the way in which psychoanalysis has detected and conceptualized the new modus operandi of power (and a new kind of law). In this sense, the birth of psychoanalysis could be seen as intrinsically linked to discerning and theorizing the effects of what Foucault will call 'biopower', its 'symptoms' – whereas Foucault cast psychoanalysis as contributing to the generalization of illness as a means of implanting and exercising 'biopolitics'. If everyday life is psychopathological, it is – this is Freud's thesis – because 'power' finds a way of inhabiting it from within, because 'power' is already operative in the (seemingly) most neutral aspects of life. The theory of the superego is not a psychologization of the social power structure, but a reminder that the social power structure can already be fully operative at the level of the 'individual psyche'.
>
> *(Zupančič 2016, 54)*

For Foucault, the *confessional* structure of psychoanalysis links sexuality to a "no way out" logic of complete scrutiny. But something is always missing in language, something will always be missing from complete scrutiny. The only structure of complete scrutiny is the Freudian superego ("as different from the structure of an external authority: 'nothing could be hidden from the superego, not even thoughts'") (Zupančič 2016, 55). And as Zupančič notices, Foucault's usage of Bentham's Panopticon[13] translates the superego logic far better than Freud's examples, since "[t]he point of the latter is not simply its being designed in such a way as to assure absolute visibility, at all times, of its subject" (Zupančič 2016, 55) but most importantly, how it is all about the internalization of authority:

> This internalization of authority, however, is only one aspect of the Freudian concept of the superego – we could call it the disciplinary aspect. The other is its 'economic' aspect – that of a properly perverse economy, described by Freud as follows: the more virtuous the man is, the more severely and distrustfully the superego behaves, 'so that ultimately it is precisely those people who have carried saintliness furthest who reproach themselves with the worst sinfulness' (*CD*, 318).
>
> *(Zupančič 2016, 55)*

Foucault's passage from "disciplinary to security" seems to follow Freud's double aspect of the superego structure logic between the disciplinary to the "economic," as Zupančič explains. Foucault's shift also resonates with Lacan's claim on the superego structure (made prior to the publication of the first volume of *The History of Sexuality*): "that 'nothing forces anyone to enjoy (*jouir*) except the superego. The superego is the imperative of jouissance – Enjoy! Here, we see the turning point investigated by analytic discourse" (Zupančič 2016, 56) and which concerns this 'obscene figure' of the law:

> The superego is described as an 'obscene figure' of the law (Lacan 2006, 434), which, far from prohibiting enjoyment, binds 'pleasure with compulsion', makes pleasure imperative, and makes it an object of infinite scrutiny; it traps us in a vicious circle where we can never fully live up to its demand. Consent combines with inquisition. It is a 'perverse' law that does not work from 'above', but from beneath and from within.
>
> *(Zupančič 2016, 56)*

The psychoanalytic logic of the superego as "the only thing that forces anyone to enjoy" (Zupančič 2016, 56) concerns the "socially dominating" trait which is "perceived by Lacan in terms of a historical occurrence" and is a pacific point of agreement between Foucault and Lacan. Yet, Zupančič also points to another convergence between Lacan and Foucault: their critical position against FreudoMarxism and their defence of the 'repressive hypothesis', following the events of May 1968 in France (Zupančič 2016, 57). On this point, Zupančič explains Foucault's position as a *reversal* concerning the 'repressive hypothesis':

> And a *reversal* it is indeed: sex is not repressed, the opposite is the case; sex was 'put into discourse', the notion of 'sexuality' has been invented and became part of just about everything. Similarly with family, society and capitalism: the very concept of the family was invented not to hinder and pose an obstacle to sexuality, but on the contrary to implement it and make it our constant obsession. Society and capitalism did not repress sexuality; on the contrary, they gave it a discursive support and opened up an infinite number of spaces where it could proliferate, prosper and – in doing so – be both profitable and a perfect means or paragon of micro-politics and bio-power (control).
>
> *(Zupančič 2016, 57)*

Indeed, Lacan agrees with the rejection of the 'repressive hypothesis'. But Zupančič highlights a central divergence between them:

> The difference (perhaps barely perceptible at the outset) comes from the fact that, thinking in a Freudian lineage, the question of sexuality and its repression makes no sense for Lacan without a third term or element, that of *Verdrängung*. *Verdrängung* is not one with repression (*répression*); neither is repression the cause of *Verdrängung*.
>
> *(Zupančič 2016, 57)*

Only through the introduction of this third term (*Verdrängung*), that Lacan manages to disassociate any confusion or misconception concerning his own position,[14] and from this remark, Zupančič notices how *Verdrängung*

> makes sex the *delayed and displaced* cause of its own repression, and it is also why this particular repression can very well take the form of what Foucault describes as incitement, even encouragement, or simply that of the deployment of sexuality.
>
> *(Zupančič 2016, 58)*

Lacan's position and answer to this debate, fully assumes the concept of the unconscious and of *Verdrängung* in order to "understanding how (and why) power works" (Zupančič 2016, 58). Zupančič explains that for Lacan:

> It is not simply part of the workings of power, nor is it simply its effect; rather, it is its foundation, its 'other side', its underpinning. As discursive,

> power is structured around or above its own point of lapse or contradiction. The 'primary' character of *Verdrängung* implies that *Verdrängung* is one with the (institution of the) discursive. There is a structural gap that pertains to discursivity as such, and this gap is what gives to the unconscious its structure, and it is involved – by default – in all relations of power
>
> *(Zupančič 2016, 58)*

When Lacan (re)introduces the Freudian theme of *Urverdrängung* (primal repression, which is the *condition* to any other repression), his "[t]he point is to acknowledge that, whatever the object of power, the latter never operates simply in relation to this object, but also in relation to its own structural gap" (Zupančič 2016, 58). The crucial question lies in Lacan's theory of the discourses *as* 'social bonds', that is, "[t]he crucial question is always the question of the relationship between the 'object' of power and the latter's own structural hindrance or flaw" (Zupančič 2016, 58). This is why the (Freudian) unconscious (under these Lacanian lenses) implies a *redoubling*, as Zupančič explains:

> The Freudian concept of the unconscious is fundamentally about this redoubling, or double dimension: it is never simply about what is repressed, but also about where it gets discharged, and why there. As formations of the unconscious, symptoms are of various kinds and take different paths: these differences are by no means irrelevant, but can tell us something about the very core of the problem. In other words, the question is always (also): what is the discursive ('systemic') repression (*Verdrängung*) that is being sustained (covered and/or exploited) with and through different particular repressions and their different modalities?
>
> *(Zupančič 2016, 59)*

Zupančič explains that the gap which 'neurosis ties up with a real' (as Lacan states) is a constitutive impasse (impossibility) *of* "discursive reality" (Zupančič 2016, 59). This is not a matter of "psychological" disposition, but a consequence of "*a flaw of the discursive reality itself*, because the gap of the unconscious is out there, 'built into' speech and discourse as structuring our reality" (Zupančič 2016, 59). Thus, Zupančič translates how power as a social phenomenon enacts a response to the impossibility (gap) of the discursive structure (Zupančič 2016, 59). A certain *realism of the signifiers* derives from the belief posited by individuals to the Other through language, but language itself is inconsistent. Or as Zupančič puts it:

> For psychoanalysis the concept of the unconscious is precisely the concept of the limit of my language, whereby 'limit' is to be taken here in the sense of its inconsistency or 'leak': the limits of my language have themselves a limit.
>
> *(Zupančič 2016, 59)*

This is why language is the "locus of contingency" as Zupančič explains, language is a limit with a gap (Zupančič 2016, 60) opening and closing while creating and subtracting signifiers, gluing and dissolving meaning. Following Zupančič, "[c]ontingency is always double: it does not simply refer to the fact that something unpredictable happened, but also and perhaps above all to the fact that it happened" (Zupančič 2016, 60). The Freudo–Lacanian unconscious makes room for contingency because it's open to its own negativity, the political understanding which derives from this is different than the affirmative micro-politics defended by Foucault. For Lacan politics is a divide, as Zupančič explains:

> [t]he alternative between an (always) singular division (resonant with politics proper) and a multiplicity of power struggles, divides, disputes, subjectivations (resonant with biopower) is a wrong alternative, because the two are not situated on the same level: there is a divide – or: there are divides – between multiple instances and layers of the social being, but there is also a divide that structures this multiplicity – that structures, 'distributes' it in a certain way.
>
> *(Zupančič 2016, 61)*

And Zupančič *refines* this 'political' division sustained by a Lacan, affirming the importance to not confuse the different levels of these *divisions*, since these are not on the same level. This frames Žižek's render of the Marxist concept of *antagonism* quoted by Zupančič (Zupančič 2016, 61) which is

> ...not simply antagonism *between* different classes or social groups; it is above all that which structures the very field where these classes or groups appear (and hence dictates how they appear) as suggested earlier, the micro-relations of power are always also a response to an impediment (gap) implied in the very structure that sustains them. This is the *Verdrängung* that creations such as family and society are built from. Politics, in the strong sense of the term, always involves the reactivation of this gap, whatever the structure (and functioning) of power in the given context.
>
> *(Zupančič 2016, 61)*

Zupančič defends how antagonism structures the very own field where classes and groups appear, and the power relations are established as a "response" to the gap within that very own structure that sustain them (and this is why the debate on *Verdrängung* is crucial here, as the philosopher defends). Against this precise background, Zupančič introduces how Foucault's deliberate "'omission' of the concept of the unconscious" (Zupančič 2016, 61) could be what makes sexuality become such a "suitable" notion to biopolitics, mostly because Foucault's concept of power operates similarly to Freud's sexuality.[15] However, as Zupančič emphasizes, the discrepancy is the missing element of the unconscious (Zupančič 2016, 61). The paradoxical redoubling which the unconscious and sexuality (under psychoanalytic terms) invites, as Zupančič defends, a closer appreciation of the structural gap, which is missing from any biopolitics or biopower, as the thinker concludes:

> For psychoanalysis, the described functioning of sexuality is itself a symptom – it is related to a signifying negativity as its inherent divide and propelling force. The truth is not that everything is sexual, but that there is something that can make anything sexual. Anything – including the act of copulation ('sexual intercourse') itself. And it is here, in this paradoxical redoubling, that we can perceive the structural gap which is conceptualized by psychoanalysis as that of the unconscious. What is lacking from the notion of biopolitics or biopower is precisely the conceptualization of this redoubling, which is at the same time essential for its functioning. True, power can be everywhere, but it is crucial to think that which can turn anything into a power structure, activating it as power. Without taking into account this redoubling, this point through which power effectively becomes power, 'biopolitics' risks appearing itself as something of a biopolitical concept: that is, as a concept actively closing, 'stitching up' the gap introduced by Freud in the field of thinking social relations.
>
> *(Zupančič 2016, 61–62)*

Zupančič's examination of Lacan *avec* Foucault introduces a sober critique to biopolitics and biopower under a concise point: it lacks the psychoanalytic unconscious. Foucault's manoeuvre of abdicating from a rigorously debate of the unconscious is not without consequences. Here, Zupančič engages with Lacan's argument, noticing a certain redoubling which the unconscious introduces (under the understanding of *Verdrängung*) and how this radical negativity seems to (re)articulate political terms to an understanding about life. Thus, biopolitics encloses and closes the gap of inconsistencies, not making room for structural multiplicity to transform. Biopolitics is entrapped between bodies and languages and any micro-political attempt reinforces the ideological system in place.

So, Canguilhem and Foucault can be placed side by side in terms of biopolitics since both make no room for negativity nor contradiction in dialectical terms. Both Canguilhem and Foucault's philosophies are restrained by languages and bodies. The missing element of the subject of the unconscious seems to restrict and limit his philosophical endeavours. Nonetheless, this section portrays how monstrosity has been of great interest for philosophy, but also, how until now monstrosity has been constrained at the level of bodies and languages (Badiou 2009), never being considered under a dialectical materialist approach. The growing scientific discourse over time, the marvels and the awe that once derived from monsters have not ceased to exist, they simply migrated towards another discourse. However, the realm of monstrosity, restrained under the dimension of the scientific narratives of the bodies and language, cannot fully appropriate its negativity, its excess. Because monstrosity concerns the multiplicity which lies at the crux of this debate, it concerns the dimension of the Real and this dimension has never gained a proper examination.

2.3 A philosophical understanding of history and monstrosity

We need to talk about monsters. This section presents passages that address the creatures which populate our shared imagination: monsters. Most of the monsters found in TV shows, films, and theatre nowadays come from literature. This is an overall discussion to better accommodate how monsters appear in our history, setting some prerogatives about monsters and monstrosity *from within* past periods of time and their resurface in culture. Because monstrosity takes place in history as a necessity to change, slavery was and still is a monstrosity. The exoticism ideologically imposed over bodies was and still is present in our reality, which is another aspect of monstrosity. The extermination camps, the genocides, the horrors of domination and oppression, the structural ruling over black, native and women bodies, these are all historical and structural elements of monstrosity. This only reinforces the philosophical prerogative that monstrosity appears where contradictions are at stake, where better politics are required to surface. Most of the violences from the "past" still occurs today, but our sensibilities have become far too numb over time. Perhaps, the popularized appearance of creatures and monsters in our culture expresses this very own ambiguity: to know things are going for the worse, that contradictions are intensifying, but having our sensibilities are too overwhelmed to transform ourselves or the reality which surrounds us. This section aims at a philosophical approach to the moments in which monstrosity gained more (or less) traction within our reality. But we must not lose sight of the main point of this section, which is *how* monstrosity informs *something* about the very *symbolic and imaginary fabric* in which they were formulated. Also taking into consideration that the future is as much at risk as our past, and the best way to move forward is to face our contradictions head on instead of repressing them. Monstrosity is a powerful ally in this process, it teaches about our fears and makes us question the oppressions which we normalized over time.

The overall idea behind this section is to portray how creatures, monsters and monstrosity occupy a role within reality, one which changes over time. Certainly, this does not mean to retell history from the standpoint of monstrosity in a speculative sense. Our point here is *not* to conduct a "deconstructive" historicist which re-enforces relativism but to discuss the truth-value in monstrosity regarding its symbolic and imaginary representations. For Žižek (2000), this means to sustain considerations on both the *universal*, the *particular* and the *subject*, avoiding a naive "clean cut" narrative which excludes the infiltration of ideological impositions in "theoretical" thinking (i.e., true science versus pre-scientific mythology within the Eurocentric hegemonic agenda) (Žižek 2000, 101).

Žižek asserts that the main problem of a *relativist* perspective to history is that it misses any inherent *truthvalue* in the name of a compartmentalized analysis of moments in time which become "*different* discursive formations" (Žižek 2000, 101) based on "social-political status and impact" (Žižek 2000, 102). Even further, Žižek explains how *historicist relativism* relies on "ontological and epistemological presuppositions about the nature of human knowledge and reality…" (Žižek 2000, 102).

And Žižek introduces another perspective:

> First, the point is not simply that 'all concepts are metaphors', but that the very difference between a concept and a metaphor is always minimally metaphorical, relying on some metaphor. Even more important is the opposite conclusion: the very reduction of a concept to a bundle of metaphors already has to rely on some implicit *philosophical (conceptual)* determination of the difference between concept and metaphor, that is to say, on the very opposition it tries to undermine. We are thus forever caught in a vicious circle: true, it is impossible to adopt a philosophical stance delivered from the constraints of everyday naive life-world attitudes and notions; however, although *impossible*, this philosophical stance is at the same time *unavoidable*.
>
> *(Žižek 2000, 102)*

In a way, this minimal metaphorical element invites a redoubling between the *impossible* and the *unavoidable*, is what is at stake here. Our point is that monstrosity is a figure of negative crucial to consider structural material contradictions. While discussing Derrida, Žižek states that "[w]e should always bear in mind this delicate stance on account of which Derrida avoids the twin pitfalls of naive realism as well as of direct philosophical foundationalism…" (Žižek 2000, 102). Basically, Žižek denotes the Derridean nuanced impasse which makes him a "meta-transcendentalist, in search of the conditions of possibility of philosophical discourse itself" (Žižek 2000, 103), his deconstructionism finds its validity (especially, against Foucault) for facing this *impossible* and yet *necessary* "philosophical foundation" of how everything we understand and perceive what is already "overdetermined by a horizon of pre-understanding" and yet, such horizon remains ultimately impenetrable (Žižek 2000, 103).[16]

And far from settling with Derrida, Žižek criticizes his oscillating deconstructionism and presents his own point about *truthvalue* from *within* a paradoxical interconnection, as follows:

> ...what is deeply symptomatic in Derrida is his oscillation between, on the one hand, the hyper-self-reflective approach which denounces in advance the question of 'how things really are' and limits itself to third-level deconstructive comments on the inconsistencies of philosopher B's reading of philosopher A, and, on the other hand, a direct 'ontological' assertion about how differance and archi-trace designate the structure of all living and are thus already operative in animal nature. One should not miss here the paradoxical interconnection of these two levels: the very feature which forever prevents us from grasping directly our intended object (the fact that our grasping is always refracted, 'mediated', by a decentered otherness) is the feature which connects us to the basic protoontological structure of the universe.
>
> *(Žižek 2000, 103)*

Žižek's philosophical discussion here advances a significant impasse for this text, that revolves around the two prohibitions presented by "deconstruction": (1) the 'naive' empiricist approach and (2) "a global non-historical metaphysical theses about the origin and structure of the universe" (Žižek 2000, 103), which interests our main discussion about *monstrosity* in history and since it also places it at a crucial philosophical 'battle' of recent times: *the current proliferation of ontologies* (which will be addressed, through the course of the text). Going back to Žižek's argument, the thinker notices how cognitivist Cultural Studies recently have violated both prohibitions of deconstructionism for the sake of empiricist "freshness" and the rehabilitation of metaphysical problematics under recent terms. While *naive empiricism* is a false theoretical prerogative of "*freedom*" provided by cognitivists, who forcefully inform us how *empiricism can be empirically false*; Žižek reinforces the troubling pretense examination of any given object in reality without having no "background of a global theory" which can quickly presuppose a certain sense of *neutrality* that is flat out fallacious. And if this renewed *passion* for (naive) empiricism wasn't in itself troubling enough, there is also the other side of the contemporary trends in Cultural Studies *relativism*, which is the resurrection of metaphysical commitments that Žižek denounces as some troubling *zombified* Hegelian project, that returns to "life" from the dead, trying to synthesize metaphysics and science into a global theory of everything which the Slovenian thinker states is nothing but a "false ideological specter of Hegel" (Žižek 2000, 104).

Here, Žižek's blows some fresh air against the dusted catacombs of Hegelian thought and reintroduces the "Hegelian dialectic of the Notion" (Žižek 2000, 104) as indispensable to a proper critique of historicism. This is how that *paradoxical* interconnection that Žižek addressed earlier comes forwards. By introducing Hegelian *Begriff* (Notion) as it purports a "non-existing theoretical position analyzing a non-existing [something]..." (Žižek 2000, 105) or as he refines it: "...something that cannot simply be explained, accounted for, in terms of historical circumstances, conditions and reactions, but acts as a structuring principle that displays dynamics of its own..." (Žižek 2000, 106). And if a certain "notion" does not adequately fit the empirical multitude it attempts to *articulate*, as the Hegelian motto goes and Žižek sustains: "so much worse for reality!" (Žižek 2000, 106). Obviously, Hegelian *Begriff* has much more complex implications and as Žižek pursues it later:

> ...Hegel uses the term *Begriff* (notion) in two main opposed meanings: 'notion' as the very core, the essence, of the thing, and 'notion' as 'mere notion' in contrast to 'the thing itself'; and one should bear in mind that the same goes for his use of the term 'subject':" the subject as elevated above the objective, as the principle of life and mediation of objects, and the subject as designating something 'merely subjective', a subjectively distorted impression in contrast to the way things out there really are.
>
> *(2016, 79)*

Žižek presents the *crux* of his postulate about *historicism* traversed by the Hegelian dialectics of *notion* and introduces how *reflexive determination* – in the strict Hegelian sense – is at stake here, "although it seems to designate a property of its object... it effectively involves a reference to the gaze of the subject perceiving it" (Žižek 2000, 105). A common example comes from Marx invocation of this Hegelian coinage in a footnote in Chapter 1 of Capital, propagated by Žižek: "individuals think they treat a person as a king because he is a king in himself, while, effectively, he is a king only because they treat him as one" (2009, 79). So, a certain *retroaction* is what Žižek discusses here. The *misperceptions* and *impasses* of reality, which were given into the symbolic exchange or reality present within the designations and contours of a *given notion*, through *retroaction* of this very own notion, permit to shed new lights on those very own *misperceptions* that created it, providing a whole different perspective to reality[17] itself. Although this seems a bit loose, erratic or even like a long detour to address *historicism*, this is the heart of this discussion: a Hegelian understanding of the notion of history itself through a Hegelian notion of *notion*, must be conveyed in order to face its own impasses, and this is why Žižek's arguments are crucial here. Otherwise, we could easily fall into the entanglements of a pseudo-*anthropomorphizing* of past temporalities, a certain naive believe that this attempt to ponder into the past have no consequences, almost like a belief that we could just easily *address* past discursivities without having to pay any dues along the way.

Žižek's Hegelian dialectics of a notion of history, does not pay tribute to a dead teleological dream of Hegel's theory in its 'evolutionary' march of history. Going along the lines of what Hegel himself puts it in *Lectures on the philosophy of world history* (1975) [1857] that "History is the process whereby the spirit discovers itself and its own concept" (1857, 62), Žižek's fidelity goes more along these lines. And this is also how Žižek argues for a *latent reason of history* in Hegel's philosophy, but in the name of a Hegel that manages to escape the entrapments of a *teleological* linear understanding of history and also, one that aims at escaping the interpretation of Hegel as a sheer speculative philosophical exercise of reasoning (as some Hegelian scholars tend to defend or analytical philosophers). What Žižek's reading of Hegel allows us to do is to notice a *nuanced* rendering of the inherent contradictions within reality but simultaneously sustaining a *logic* that reaches beyond the *immobilism* of its restraints. Thus,

> ...teleology relies on linear evolutionary logic in which the lower stage already contains in nuce the seeds of the higher stage, so that evolution is just the unfolding of some underlying essential potential, while here, the lower (or, rather, previous) stage becomes readable only retroactively, insofar as it is itself ontologically 'incomplete', a set of traces without meaning and thus open to later reappropriations.
>
> *(2000, 107)*

Such *incompleteness* is a crucial aspect to be consider, and if we briefly stop and take a closer look at it, the approach towards "*main*" historical narratives solidified in themselves with their interpellation (and also in its *misintepellation*) (Martel 2017) can be transformed through this dialectical (re)appropriation that retroacts upon the "lower stage" and manages to provide a *truth-value* and essential potential that was latent and not yet fully manifested, transforming completely our understanding of historical events. A crucial examination of *how* this approach works can be found in Susan Buck-Morss' *Hegel, Haiti and Universal history* (2009); her Hegelian discussion about slavery sheds a better light at the historical ideological construction of Eurocentrism and the role of Haiti in this process (2009). As she elegantly insists about Hegel (1974) and history supporting "...a shift in knowledge away from traditional hierarchies of significance. It insists that facts are important not as data with fixed meanings, but as connective pathways that can continue to surprise us" (2009, 13). Žižek's development of Hegel's fits quite accurately with Buck-Morss dedicated investigation, nonetheless, the Slovenian thinker adds that:

> ... when black slaves in Haiti recognized themselves as the subjects of human rights declared by the French Revolution, they of course in some sense 'missed the point' – the fact that, although universal in their form

> ('all men'), human rights effectively privileged white men of property; however, this very 'misreading' had explosive emancipatory consequences. This is what Hegel's Cunning of Reason is about: human rights were 'really meant' to be accepted only by white men of property, but their universal form was their truth. It was thus the first interpellation which was wrong, but the true interpellation could only actualize itself through the false one, as its secondary misreading.
>
> *(2016, 103–104)*

So, Hegel's Cunning of Reason (1975), which is an implicit nod towards the *truthvalue* of universal form (1977) and if we also know that Hegel makes the case that "[t]o comprehend what is, this is the task of philosophy, because what is, is reason" (1967 [1821], 11), than certainly seems necessary to grasp what a *notion* is made of, especially if it concerns that which allows us to be surprised beyond the fixed meanings of facts (paraphrasing Buck-Morss). And as Žižek (2016) cunningly explains what a Hegelian notion of a notion is all about:

> ...[t]he act of abstraction, of tearing apart, can also be understood as the act of self-imposed blindness, of refusing to 'see it all'. What Hegel calls 'negativity' can also be put in the terms of insight and blindness, as the 'positive' power of 'blindness', of ignoring parts of reality. How does a notion emerge out of the confused network of impressions we have of an object? Through the power of 'abstraction', of blinding oneself to most of the features of the object, reducing the object to its constitutive key features. The greatest power of our mind is not to see more, but to see less in a correct way, to reduce reality to its notional determinations – only such 'blindness' generates the insight into what things effectively are.
>
> *(2016, 78–79)*

This "ignoring" of certain elements of (symbolic-Real and imaginary-Real) reality, this self-imposed blindness involved in abstraction as a tearing apart, certainly provides this "building of a plane in mid-flight" aspect to the *act of abstraction*, which is what ontological incompleteness ultimately revolves around. The very own philosophical attempt at developing a *notion*, is always a somewhat failed enterprise, but its validity lies within its own process, but especially if we somehow manage to be *surprised* beyond given fixed narratives along the way. And here is where a certain surprising element of this *gaze*, this *viewing*, needs to be addressed, since if there is a certain "seeing less," a certain "squint" concerning the notion (as defended from Žižek's last passage), there is also *another side*, which the side of "seeing more" ("...deprivation opens up a space to be filled in by phantasmatic projections...") (2000, 110) or "seeing too much"... and this is where Žižek's *parallax view* (2014) is crucial. Through such *shifting* perspective there is a possibility *of seeing*: "the ultimate dialectical paradox of truth and falsity: sometimes, the aberrant view which misreads a situation from its limited perspective, can, on account of this very limitation, perceive the 'repressed' potentials of the observed constellation" (2000, 110). So, Žižek's "seeing less" and "seeing more" through a *parallax view*, sustains the theoretical notional *act of abstraction* that does not only *suspend* apparent "truths" in reality, but it also sees towards "*libidinal truth*" (which is what Lacan has in mind in the famous passage from his forth Seminar[18] "that truth has the structure of a fiction: the very suspension of literal truth opens the way for the articulation of the libidinal truth" (2000, 108). And this point can be made clearer by using our historical example of the Haitian revolution (Buck-Morss 2009; Žižek 2016, 103): they "saw less" *because they've seen further*. The Haitian (mis)interpellation of the French guiding *myth* of its own revolution, perfectly exemplifies Hegel's *Cunning of Reason* because it sets the record straight with its *truthvalue* behind it, the Haitian revolution was the proper *realization* of the French revolutionary terms (noticeably, only *retroactively* we could understand this, nonetheless, this changes everything that we could perceive as once *fixed*, either in terms of subjectivization and established narratives). Even the imaginary guiding myths of the French prerogative, after the (mis)interpellation of the Haitian Revolution and their *materialization* of the mythical triad *seen through* and *from within* their eyes, through the eyes of the slaved and dominated, did not only re-shaped completely the French narrative in its Eurocentrism, it did also placed true to the side of the oppressed as a more truer possibility than the ones given, up until that point.

The overall idea behind this discussion is only to provide a better work frame towards the investigation of monstrosity and specifically because it has *a* monster in mind, a fundamental component into the development of the *monstrosity* which concerns us here: *global capitalism*. And the overall strategy of providing this philosophical background to *historicism*, does not only justify its implication towards not falling into the traps of Foucault's discursiveness (as argued previously) and not falling into the troubling oscillations of a Derridean perspective (as also previously presented), but it wants to philosophically engage with *how* one can approach *monstrosity* (and its symbolic accumulation). But far more, the justification behind this thesis is not to address monstrosity (*only*) as the *figments of our imagination* (which they are), but to further develop a certain theoretical perspective concerning their *symbolic significance* and *critical efficiency* towards impasses of reality. A justification in line with a certain Žižekean translation of Badiou's *understanding* of our current predicaments, which means that is not enough to signal the contours in order to "undermine" the symbolic hierarchical edifice and its social "groundings," but to provide alternatives towards *thinking* (2016, 12).[19] Basically, *thinking* as a philosophical radical procedure that provides alternatives beyond the nihilist dangers of a cynical grammar towards today's (neo)liberal reality and all its anxiety-induced *immobilism*.

It is true that the Žižekian notion of *disparities* (2016) not only develops as *refines* the historicism debated here. And there is no need to reinvent the wheel, so the text will ride on the intricacies of disparities. Taking that into account, a more *creative* way to understand the present efforts behind this text, we could affirm that we can only take monstrosity seriously *after* Žižek's (Hegelian) *Kraken*. Or to put in other words, this means that *monstrosity* understood *after* Žižek's foundations towards *new dialectical materialism* (2014), is an understanding of a certain theoretical engagement with a certain *monstrous grammar* in order to go *beyond* the subterranean work of the *mole* (from Hegel, Marx, Derrida and criticized by Negri and Hardt's "Empire") (2016, 13). This work aims at providing further theoretical contours towards this *monstrous grammar* drawing its consequences from the abject monster creature already presented by Žižek (and its impasses with global Capitalism), but also, consolidating grounds towards a psychoanalytic comprehension of its consequences. From understanding that *monstrosity* could set the steps of what a *(in)humanity's grammar* could look like and also, moving against the *biopolitical* democratization of (mis)understanding appearances.

Hopefully, this brief section made it clear that it had no intention of solving or even exhausting the intricacies behind the Hegelian philosophical impasses concerning history, showing how what is deemed as pacified in history is not quite as such and, that the truest dialectical materialist perspective concerns *always* focus on emancipation against domination. Every single moment in our lives is at stake, each second counts to realize emancipation to people. This critique of *historicism* comes to prevent the reinforcement of a certain classical historical attempt at "accuracy" (which can easily be deemed as *classist*) (Badiou 2005, 34; Lazarus 2015, 110), but also, to present what does it mean to conceive monstrosity, monstrous and the monster in relation to the monster of *global capitalism*. The proper dimension of dialectical materialism benefits from the contradictions which monstrosity points out.

Up until this point, the discussion of monstrosity presented has shown how it detains the philosophical depth of positing the topos of a point of excess. Throughout different moments of our 'history' this designation has changed and transformed, nonetheless, the excessive aspect of monstrosity establishes a non-relation with its monstrous self. This curious vanishing point plays its part not only under symbolic and imaginary stances, but it is also a certain attempt to defend against the pre-ontological remainders which remain non-surmounted in our "reality." The point of uncanniness which is experienced by the subject (of the unconscious), assumed as experiences of encounter with emission of the Real, can certainly be rendered comic or perhaps tragic, but only if assumed against its proper monstrous background. Without the assumption of the unconscious, the uncanny quickly became a mere cognitive mistake and its stances are limited to sciences of the body and the restraints of language. Yet, as Zupančič (2016, 60, 2017, 40) pointed out, language itself experiences its own limits, and this is what structures it. In a way, this collateral result of the symbolic operation, which (in)humanizes us, faces additional leftovers and monstrous inconsistencies. Monstrosity *as a topos* engages precisely with that.

Notes

1 As Wittkower presents in Herodotus Bk. IV, 44 and Bk. III, 97-Io6, there are condensed remarks about India. In the end of his life, Herodotus wrote his History (around the 5th century B.C.). For Wittkower, his account on India was probably based on Hekataios of Miletus "(written about 500 B.C.) who in his turn drew on Skylax's report of a journey made c.515 B.C." (Wittkower 1942, 159).

2 Wittkower (1942) emphasizes how Megasthenes talks about

> serpents with wings like bats, of winged scorpions of extraordinary size; he repeats from Herodotus the story of the gold-digging ants… The Hyperboreans, he relates, live a thousand years; there are people who have no nostrils, with the upper part of their mouth protruding far over the lower lip, and others who have dog's ears and a single eye in their forehead.
>
> *(Wittkower 1942, 162)*

3 As Wittkower (1942) explains, the cynocephali and the cyclopic races where creatures present in the Greek culture with ideas similar to those of the Indians, perhaps they might share a common mythical origin in ancient past (Wittkower 1942, 164).

4 Same examples highlighted by Wittkower are the *Imago Mundi* of Honorius Augustodunensis, Gauthier of Metz's *Image du Monde* (I246), Gervase of Tilbury's Otia imperialia, Bartholomew' encyclopaedia from around 1220s, the *Trésor* of the Florentine Brunetti Latini from the 1260s, and Vincent of Beauvais' encyclopaedia of the later Middle Ages (Wittkower 1942, 170–171).

5 As Wittkower explains, India and Ethiopia detain the most marvels according with Solinus: the sciapodes, the pygmies, the giants, the mouthless people, the martikhora, the unicorn, the horse-hoofedmen, the people with long ears, Anthropophagi, Hyperboreans, the Arimaspians who fight with the griffins, the satyrs and fauns, the people with long lips and people with their head in their shoulders and breasts, by basilisks and gold-digging ants, etc. (Wittkower 1942, 174).

6 The first part of Heinrich Kramer and James Sprenger' *Malleus Maleficarum* (1971) [1486] on witchcraft (Devil, Witch and the permission of almighty god) encapsulates this argument, where they address the twisted justification that burning women to the stake was a "preferable alternative" than feeding them to the beast for their heretic crimes (1971, 6).

7 This is an important detour, Hegel in "The Science of Logic" [1832] (2010) debates how exceptions establish a dialectical relation with the rule. While discussing the mathematical infinitesimal and its magnitude and on how it establishes the philosophical infinite, that which denies it is the very own thing which founds it:

> The dialectic just cited is also the same as the understanding deploys against the concept of *infinitesimal* magnitude given by higher analysis… These magnitudes are so determined that they *are in their vanishing* – not *before* this vanishing, for they would then be finite magnitudes; not *after* it, for then they would be nothing. Against this pure thought, it is objected and endlessly repeated that these magnitudes are *either* something *or nothing*; that there is no *intermediary state* between being and nothing ("state" is here an inappropriate, barbaric expression). – Assumed here is again the absolute separation of being and nothing.

> But we have shown against this that being and nothing are in fact the same, or to speak in the language cited, that there *is* nothing which is not an *intermediary state between being and nothing*. Mathematics owes its most brilliant successes to precisely that determination which the understanding rejects. This form of argumentation that falsely presupposes the absolute separation of being and nothing, and insists on it, should be called not *dialectic* but *sophistry*.
>
> *(79–80)*

Yet, Žižek [1989] finds a similar logic on *The Phenomenology of the Spirit* while debating Badiou's notion of undecidability ("undecidability means that there are no neutral 'objective' criteria for an Event: an Event appears as such only to those who recognize themselves in its call; or, as Badiou puts it, an Event is self-relating, it includes itself – its own nomination – among its components.") (Žižek 2009, 98) which is

> uncannily similar to the Hegelian dialectical process in which, as Hegel himself made clear already in the Introduction to his *Phenomenology*, a 'figure of consciousness' is not measured by any external standard of truth but in an absolutely immanent way, through the gap between itself and its own exemplification/staging. An Event is thus 'non-All' in the precise Lacanian sense of the term: it is never fully verified precisely because it is infinite/unlimited, that is, because there is no external limit to it. And the conclusion to be drawn here is that, for the very same reason, the Hegelian 'totality' is also 'non-All'.
>
> *(Žižek 2009, 98)*

And finally, "What this means is that the externality of Nature with regard to the Idea is not that of the Idea's constitutive exception:

> it is not that Nature is set free as the exception that guarantees the Wholeness of the Idea's self-mediation. It is not the case that, once this mediation is completed (that is, after the Idea's dialectical progress can no longer be propelled by the Idea's own incompleteness – its failure to correspond to its own notion), the completed Idea needs an external Other (Nature) to sustain complete and closed circle of itself-mediation. Nature is, rather, the mark of the non-All of the Idea's totality.
>
> *(Žižek 2009, 99)*

8 Bernard, Claude. *Cahier de notes 1850–1860*. Paris: Gallimard, 1965. *The Cahier Rouge of Claude Bernard.* Trans. Hebbel H. Hoff, Lucienne.

9 Goldstein, Kurt. The organism: A Holistic Approach to Biology Derived from Pathological Data in Man. New York: Zone Books, 1995.

10 As Zupančič explains:

> It would seem…that the concept of the unconscious is for Foucault simply the way in which psychoanalysis conceptually institutes sexuality as secret, as *the* secret — the latter being the very condition of its endless exploitation and of exercising power through it.
>
> *(Zupančič 2016, 52)*

11 As Zupančič explains, for Bentham's Panopticon

> … to work, nobody actually needs to occupy the central tower and survey the inmates. In other words, even if nobody occupies the point from which everything can be seen, the mechanism of power and control not only works perfectly, but emerges, so to speak, within each individual cell of the prison.
>
> *(Zupančič 2016, 55)*

12 From this disjunction derives an insight on analytic cure and the transformative potency to operate towards a dissolution of identificatory traits of domination. See more in (Gonsalves 2020).
13 Zupančič delineates this point between Foucault's notion of 'power' and Freud's sexuality:

> it has no central, clearly delimited place, no proper substance of its own, which is why it can be found everywhere, even in the most unlikely context; the very resistance to sexuality, its taming, hiding, prosecuting can itself have a strongly sexual character; the fundamental mode of sexuality is that of a 'polymorphous perversion', a kind of sexual micro-physics.
>
> *(Zupančič 2016, 61)*

14 In Nicholas Royle's (2003) *The Uncanny*, we can find an entire chapter dedicated to this Derridean notion which the British author coins as the *mole* (Chapter 18). Basically, Royle addresses the intricacies of Derrida's philosophical thinking which aims at *undermining* philosophical discourse *from within*, much like Žižek points out (2000, 103).
15 Žižek uses countless examples to illustrate this retroactive movement: from Hegel's famous passage of "Napoleon on a horse in the streets of Jena after the battle of 1807, Hegel remarked that it was as if he saw there the World Spirit riding a horse" (2009, 79) to the arising of *film noir* as a *notion* concerning a certain *gaze* that retroacts upon the inherent contradictions within cinema (2000, 103–110).
16 As Lacan argues while discussing the structure of myths and their role in *La relation d'objet* (1956–57): "La nécessité structurale qui est emportée par toute expression de la vérité, est justement une structure qui est la même: la vérité a une structure – si on peut dire – de fiction" (128) (see in: http://staferla.free.fr/S4/S4.htm). Pfaller (2005, 2014) also deals with the illusions in our everyday life.
17 As Žižek states it:

> The problem is that, today, simple opposition gets complicated: our global-capitalist reality, impregnated as it is by our global-capitalist reality, impregnated as it is by sciences, is itself 'prodding', challenging our innermost presuppositions in a much more shocking way than the wildest philosophical speculations, so that the task of a philosopher is no longer to undermine the hierarchical symbolic edifice that grounds social stability but – to return to Badiou – to make the young perceive the dangers of the growing nihilist order that presents itself as the domain of new freedoms.
>
> *(2016, 12)*

18 In a very simplistic sense, Žižek's *Kraken* is a Hegelian reappropriation of Deleuze's notion of 'rhizome' under different terms, the justification behind this criticism comes from Deleuze's inclination towards Jung in order to sustain such a notion. Zupančič is who clarifies this best, Jung's "revisionist" psychoanalysis which confuses libido as 'instinctual/drive force' [*Triebkraft*] sustaining a certain "monism of the substance libido" (2017, 39, 100).
19 Zupančič clearly explains this point on Lacanian psychoanalysis and language:

> To a great extent, Lacanian psychoanalysis seems compatible with this account, and it is often presented as such. The primacy of the signifier and of the field of the Other, language as constitutive of reality and of the unconscious (including the dialectics of desire), the creationist aspect of the symbolic and its dialectics (with notions such as symbolic causality, symbolic efficiency, materiality of the signifier)…all of these (undisputed) claims notwithstanding, Lacan's position is irreducibly different from the performative ontology described above. It is not simply that Lacan has to take into account and make room for

> the other, 'vital' part of the psychoanalytic notions (such as the libido, the drive, the sexualized body), which would be defined as 'real,' as opposed to belonging to the symbolic. This kind of parlance, and the perspective it implies, are very misleading. Something else is at stake: taking the signifying order as his starting point, Lacan sees it as the locus of a fundamental *split*. While the signifying order creates its own space and the beings that populate it (which roughly corresponds to the space of performativity described above), *something else gets added to it*. It could be said that this something is parasitic on performative productivity; it is not produced *by* the signifying gesture, but together *with* and 'on top of' it. It is inseparable from this gesture, but, unlike what we call discursive entities/beings, not created by it. It is neither a symbolic entity nor one constituted by the symbolic; rather, it is collateral for the symbolic.
>
> *(Zupančič 2017, 40–41)*

References

Badiou, Alain. *Being and Event*. 1998. London: Continuum, 2005.

Badiou, Alain. *Logics of Worlds: Being and Event II*. London: Continuum, 2009.

Badiou, Alain. *The Adventure of French Philosophy*. London: Verso Books, 2012.

Buck-Morss, Susan. *Hegel, Haiti, and Universal History*. Pittsburgh: University of Pittsburgh Press, 2009.

Canguilhem, Georges. *Knowledge of Life*. New York: Fordham University Press, 2008.

Gonsalves, Rodrigo. Paradoxes of Transference and the Place of the Psychoanalyst: Commentary on Session XXIII. In *Reading Lacan's Seminar VIII. The Palgrave Lacan Series*, edited by G. Basu Thakur and J. Dickstein. Cham: Palgrave Macmillan, 2020. https://doi.org/10.1007/978-3-030-32742-2_19

Hegel, Georg Wilhelm Friedrich. *The Philosophy of Right. 1821*. edited by T. M. Knox, London, New York: Oxford University Press, 1967.

Hegel, Georg Wilhelm Friedrich. *Jenaer Realphilosophie. Frühe politische Systeme*. Frankfurt: Ullstein, 1974.

Hegel, Georg Wilhelm Friedrich. *Lectures on the Philosophy of World History. 1857*. Translated by H. B. Nisbet, Cambridge: Cambridge University Press, 1975.

Hegel, Georg Wilhelm Friedrich. *Phenomenology of Spirit. 1807*. Translated by A. V. Miller, edited by J. N. Findlay, Oxford: Clarendon Press, 1977.

Hegel, Georg Wilhelm Friedrich. *The Science of Logic*. 1832. Translated by George Di Giovanni. Cambridge: Cambridge University Press, 2010.

Kramer Heinrich and Sprenger, James. (aprox. 1486.) *Malleus Maleficarum* [*The Hammer of Witches*]. New York: Dover Publications, 1971.

Lacan, Jacques. 2006. *Écrits*. New York: W. W. Norton.

Lazarus, Sylvain. *Anthropology of the Name*. 1996. London: Seagull Books, 2015.

Martel, James. *The Missinterpellated Subject*. Durham, NC: Duke University Press, 2017.

Pfaller, Robert. *On the Pleasure Principle in Culture: Illusions Without Owners*. London: Verso Books, 2014.

Pfaller, Robert. The Familiar Unknown, the Uncanny, the Comic. In *Lacan's Silent Partners*, edited by S. Žižek. London: Verso, 2005.

Royle, Nicholas. *The Uncanny*. Manchester: Manchester University Press, 2003.

Tort, Patrick. *L'Ordre et les monstres*. Paris: Editions Le Sycomore, 1980.

Wittkower, Rudolf. Marvels of the East. A Study in the History of Monsters. *Journal of the Warburg and Courtauld Institutes*, Vol. 5, 159–197, 1942. http://www.jstor.org/stable/750452

Žižek, Slavoj. History Against Historicism. *European Journal of English Studies*, Vol. 4, No. 2, 101–110, 2000.

Žižek, Slavoj. *The Monstrosity of Christ*. Cambridge, MA: Mit Press, 2009.

Žižek, Slavoj. *Absolute Recoil: Towards a New Foundation of Dialectical Materialism*. London: Verso Books, 2014.

Žižek, Slavoj. *Disparities*. London: Bloomsbury, 2016.

Zupančič, Alenka. Biopolitics, Sexuality and the Unconscious. *Italian Biopolitical Theory and Beyond: Genealogy, Psychoanalysis, and Biology*, Vol. 39, No. 1, 49–64, 2016. https://doi.org/10.3366/para.2016.0183

Zupančič, Alenka. *What Is Sex?* Cambridge, MA: Mit Press, 2017.

3

THE UNCANNINESS OF MONSTROSITY (OR IS IT THE OTHER WAY AROUND?)

The contours towards another grammar between philosophy and psychoanalysis

3.1 The Kantian triad: the monstrous remains

Kant's *The Critique of Judgement* [*Kritik der Urteilskraft*] [1790] finishes his Critical endeavours for philosophy. The two main points made in the ending chapter of his text for philosophy integrate his perspective concerning aesthetics and teleology, consolidating the previous steps from his *The Critique of pure reason* [1781] and *The Critique of practical reason* [1786]. This section does not aim at exhausting all the elements from Kant's final Critique or accommodating the many interpretations of this Classic text, but it aims at highlighting a quintessential element for our discussion: *monstrosity*. So, the brief presentation and elaboration of this section has the sole purpose of highlighting and integrating Kant's discussion about monstrosity, therefore, all the intricate details concerning the rest of his aesthetical elaboration are consciously left out of this section.

The German philosopher introduces this work by setting out where this Critique ends and fits within his overall endeavours for thinking by also defending his overall Critical endeavour. Kant clearly summarizes in his original Preface [1790] how his first Critique focused on establishing a secure possession of *understanding* as "…far as it contains constitutive a *priori* cognitive principles, has its special realm, and one, moreover, in our *faculty of knowledge*…" (2007, 3); while his second Critique, the critique of practical reason, aims at how: "*reason*, which contains constitutive *a priori* principles solely in respect of the *faculty of desire*" (2007, 3) finds its own domain. Finally, his final Critique introduces: "the *power of judgement*, which in the order of our cognitive faculties forms a middle term between understanding and reason" (2007, 4).

DOI: 10.4324/9781003437543-4

The highlight of this middle term, provided by Kant, aims at feelings of pleasure and displeasure, the in-between faculties of cognition and desire, but also, remarks what does it mean for the understanding in its aprioristic laws and for reason, to have this intermediate link (2007, 4).

Kant's justification behind his final chapter lies not in a formation of taste, but towards the investigation of the faculty of aesthetic judgements, connected to its transcendental traits (2007, 5). This extension, this "appendage to the theoretical part of [his] philosophy" (2007, 5), does not contribute to the *knowledge* of things, as Kant defends, but it concerns *feelings*, nonetheless a very particular kind of feeling since it must be detached from the crucial grounds of the faculty of desires, as previously determined on his second Critique. Thus, he investigates in this third Critique the limits in-between understanding (concerning its cognitive connections to *a priori* laws) and reason, as a faculty for the transcendental[1] subject to ponder upon nature, especially when facing the feelings of pleasures and displeasures and its logical location within his previous Critiques (2007, 5). This text has two parts: the first part focuses on the critique of aesthetic judgement, where he addresses the judgement of taste in aesthetic, his triad of delightfulness, and his famous exhaustive distinction between the beautiful and the sublime, along with his thoughts on artistic creation. Second, his "critique of teleological judgement" concerns his teleological approach to the role of ends and purposes, within natural sciences. Kant tends to muscle his third work to fit with his previous dedication towards epistemology (on his first Critique) and ethics (his second Critique).

The most common engagement we seem to find concerning this last Critique is Kant's designation of and distinction between the beautiful and the sublime. For Kant, the notion of beautiful (2007, 35) is a *subjective mediation* established through imagination with objects in reality:

> If we wish to discern whether anything is beautiful or not, we do not refer the representation of it to the object by means of the understanding with a view to cognition, but by means of the imagination (acting perhaps in conjunction with the understanding) we refer the representation to the subject and its feeling of pleasure or displeasure. The judgement of taste, therefore, is not a cognitive judgement, and so not logical, but is aesthetic—which means that it is one whose determining ground *cannot be other than subjective*… This denotes nothing in the object, but is a feeling which the subject has of itself and of the manner in which it is affected by the representation.
>
> *(2007, 35)*

So, Kant is determining how judgements of beauty can be established in the first place, separating how predicative of taste and predicative of beauty can be fruits of aesthetically grounded logical judgment, but are not aesthetic *per se* (2007, 45). Kant illustrates this point with an example of a rose:

> For instance, by a judgement of taste I describe the rose at which I am looking as beautiful. The judgement, on the other hand, resulting from the comparison of a number of singular representations: Roses in general are beautiful, is no longer pronounced as a purely aesthetic judgement, but as a logical judgement grounded on one that is aesthetic.
>
> *(2007, 46)*

Kant continues, analysing how the beautiful, apart from a concept, pleases universally (which is how he ends his second moment) (2007, 51), then he discusses *purposiveness*[2] in order to establish the grounds that judges the beautiful, allowing Kant to emphasize how "[*o*]*bjective* purposiveness can only be cognized by means of a reference of a the manifold to a determinate end, and hence only through a concept" (2007, 51). This makes it clear for Kant to argue that the beautiful is "judged on the ground of a mere formal purposiveness, i.e., a purposiveness without a purpose, is wholly independent of the representation of the good" (2007, 51). So, objective purposiveness is separated by Kant into external (or utility) and internal (or perfection) of the object (2007, 51). Although Kant goes into the intricacies of the philosophical debate that is, whether perfection surfaces to address beauty, for our discussion, this brief designation will suffice. Concerning the differentiation between beautiful and the sublime, Zupančič helps us to understand that:

> Kant associates the beautiful with the so called "purposiveness without a purpose". This is to say that beautiful things have no purpose outside themselves, yet they are structured as if they had one. The simplest definition of beauty could be that it is a *sense-full* form which draws its fascination from the fact that we know this form is entirely coincidental, contingent, unintentional. If we take, as Kant does, an example from nature, for instance the beauty of a crystal form, we can say that the beauty strikes us as a kind of proof that nature *knows* (what it is doing). On the other side, the sublime is explicitly a *senseless form*, it is more like the incarnation of chaos (the eruption of volcano, a turbulent ocean, a stormy night,...). It appears as pure excess, as the eruption of *"jouissance"*, as pure waste. In other words, if we said that the beautiful is the place where *Nature* knows, we can say that the sublime is the place where *Nature enjoys* and it is precisely this *jouissance* of the Other, the *jouissance* that doesn't serve anything, that fascinates us.
>
> *(Zupančič 1992, 59–60)*

Kant's *sublime* is separated into two notions: the mathematical sublime (Zupančič 1992, 78) and the dynamic sublime (Zupančič 1992, 90). Kant's first definition of sublime (derived from the mathematical) can be explicated as such:

> *Sublime* is the name given to what is *absolutely great*. But to be great and to be a magnitude are entirely different concepts (*magnitudo* and *quantitas*). In the same way to *assert without qualification* (*simpliciter*) that something is great, is quite a different thing from saying that it is *absolutely great* (*absolute, non comparative magnum*). The latter is *what is beyond all comparison great*.
>
> (*Kant 2007, 78*)

Kant attributes how the capability of establishing measurements must derive from *a concept of judgement* or something connected to one, which "introduce as basis of the judgement a subjective purposiveness of the representation with reference to the power of judgement" (Kant 2007, 79). And this is how Kant reaches his link with the debate on *magnitudes*:

> Given a multiplicity of the homogeneous together constituting one thing, and we may at once cognize from the thing itself that it is a *magnitude* (*quantum*). No comparison with other things is required. But to determine *how great* it is always requires something else, which itself has magnitude, for its measure.
>
> (*Kant 2007, 79*)

Kant remarks magnitude from the multiplicity of homogeneous within one thing, immediately cognizable in the thing itself. However, when we come to "how great," a certain *counting* is needed. Kant argues that in order to establish the judgement of magnitudes, not only "the multiplicity (number of units)" must be accounted but also the "magnitude of the unit (the measure)" (Kant 2007, 79), which forces the philosopher to defend the impossibility of an absolute concept of a magnitude, since the magnitude of a given unit always requires a comparison against something else to establish its own measure and standard (Kant 2007, 79). As for the other side of the notion of the sublime, the dynamic sublime, Kant connects it with *might* and the *dominion* which is imposed by it:

> If we are to judge nature as dynamically sublime, it must be represented as a source of fear (though the converse, that every object that is a source of fear is, in our aesthetic judgement, sublime, does not hold). For in forming an aesthetic judgement (no concept being present) the superiority to hindrances can only be judged according to the greatness of the resistance. Now that which we strive to resist is an evil, and, if we do not find our powers commensurate to the task, an object of fear. Hence the aesthetic

> judgement can only deem nature a might, and so dynamically sublime, in so far as it is looked upon as an object of fear.
>
> *(Kant 2007, 90–91)*

Zupančič draws our attention towards the curious move from Kant's side of establishing that the core of the Idea of sublime lies in the estimation of magnitude (1992, 61), noticing how this is a very strange pairing from Kant's side to establish his work, as she summarizes:

> First of all he counterposes mathematical and aesthetical estimation of magnitude in order to formulate afterwards the latter as the basis of the former. Briefly: mathematical estimation of magnitude operates with numerical concepts, whereas the aesthetic estimation of magnitude implies a comprehension of the magnitude solely and simply in intuition *(Anschauung)*, and is, as Kant puts it, "*nach dem Augenmasse*", "cut to the measure of the eye". We can get a determinate concept of how large something is only by estimating the magnitude mathematically, i.e., by using numbers that can progress to infinity. However, for the mathematical estimation of magnitude we need a first or basic measure, a unit that serves as the means of all measuring. And this basic measure can only be comprehended in intuition. All mathematical, scientific calculations are based, ultimately, on the aesthetic estimation of magnitude which represents the irreducible prescientific or "transcendental" moment of mathematical science.
>
> *(1992, 61–62)*

Here lies a mathematical attempt to sustain calculations in Kant's determination of magnitudes which are aesthetically mediated (Fugate 2016). The One as a fundamental One, which "proceeds any counting and that makes it possible" (Zupančič 1992, 62), makes it possible to count the "one" in the series ("1,"2,3,...), and so Zupančič translates: "...it is an absolute magnitude: we may not say that it is of some magnitude or other, it simply is magnitude, it incarnates, so to speak, the very being of magnitude itself." Thus, the "[a] esthetic comprehension of magnitude is the gesture by which we mark out the basic measure with the help of which imagination operates when presenting numerical concepts" (Zupančič 1992, 62). Zupančič sustains how Kant forces a ""speculative judgement": the absolute magnitude = I" (Zupančič 1992, 62). In order to allow such a measuring, such speculative judgement establishes itself as an unit of measure, and this "is precisely the means by which infinitude is "included" into the finite, and by means of which in the most finite and limited thing we come across the paradigm of absolute magnitude..." (Zupančič 1992, 62). Zupančič notices the necessity behind Kant's transcendental subject to operate under speculative judgment.

But Kant's 26th paragraph of the *Critique of Judgement* deserves our attention for another reason, this is where the philosopher defines the *monstrous* [*das Ungeheure*] (Kant 2007, 87). In the middle of Kant philosophical construction of "[t]he estimation of the magnitude of natural things requisite for the idea of the sublime" (Kant 2007, 81), he establishes the curious connection between the (numeric or algebraic) estimation of magnitudes and the aesthetic intuitions from what our eyes can see (Kant 2007, 81), this is where he *defines* monstrosity. Kant deals with a mathematical fascination between measured and measurement, and here he settles for *an estimate*, for an *approximation*. Clearly, not out of poor mathematics on Kant's part, but rather for how intuitively Kant seemed to ponder upon an intrinsically complex mathematical relation concerning *infinites* not yet established by the mathematics of his time. Yet, he needs to sustain his transcendental subject (Zupančič 1992, 62) through a "speculative judgement" (a point addressed further). Kant explains that for a magnitude to be accounted for, the magnitude of its measurement must be a *known quantity* (Zupančič 1992, 81) otherwise, no comparison is viable, thus no definite concept of a given magnitude can be logically found (Zupančič 1992, 82). Thus, Kant assumes that what we already grasp intuitively with the help of our imagination relates to numerical concepts and provides the estimation of the magnitude of the fundamental measure (Zupančič 1992, 82).

Kant systematizes this argument presenting how the mathematical estimation of magnitude lies to the side of infinity, therefore, it cannot have a greatest possible magnitude; while its other half, the aesthetical estimation *certainly* does. As he defends: "that where it is considered an absolute measure beyond which no greater is possible subjectively (i.e. for the judging subject)"(Zupančič 1992, 82) – this is the idea of the Kantian sublime – precisely in this formulation, that:

> ...calls forth that emotion which no mathematical estimation of magnitudes by numbers can evoke (except in so far as the fundamental aesthetic measure is vividly preserved for the imagination): because the latter presents only the relative magnitude due to comparison with others of a like kind, whereas the former presents magnitude absolutely, so far as the mind can grasp it in an intuition.
>
> *(Zupančič 1992, 82)*

Kant's awe takes him towards the two faculties derived from the sublime: apprehension (*apprehensio*) and comprehension (*comprehensio aesthetica*). While Kant sees no problem with *apprehension* (since it can be carried on *ad infinitum*) (Zupančič 1992, 82), is to the side of *comprehension* to keep up with apprehension progressing towards its maximum that things become more troubling, when the aesthetical greatest fundamental measure to sustain this estimation of magnitude falls short (Zupančič 1992, 82). As Kant defends, imagination is a boundary not to be traversed concerning the sensual intuition attempted by comprehension efforts to represent when apprehension goes towards infinity, even when the first units absorbed by comprehension are disintegrated in the process of keeping up with the further new ones, or as Kant says: "…is lost at one end as is gained at the other…" (Zupančič 1992, 82). So, in a way, Kant's sublime is in a way, a deliberate (mis)calculation on his part between apprehending and comprehending, which carefully must not move towards imagination.

After defending this argument, Kant invites Savary's observations in his account of Egypt (2007, 82), to exemplify the sublime, and Zupančič already remarks how this example is far from being neutral (1992, 64) on Kant's account. Kant's example of the sublime[3] is configured through:

> … Savary's narrative, together with some consequences that Kant points out. Already in this basic frame we encounter the air of mystery, of the uncanny, which is quite important in the sentiment of the sublime. The "Letters on Egypt", the narrative, the story-is it not all about passing on a mystery, in this case the mystery of the pyramids? The pyramids, belonging to another time and another place are also catacombs and labyrinths, they always confront us with some enigma.
>
> *(1992, 65)*

A certain uncanny that lies towards the sublime, defends the thinker. This is a crucial significant placement for *uncanniness*, since it is in this passage from Kant's discussion that the monster surfaces. Literally after engaging with this example, Kant notices a delight which he will not engage with, that of a representation which presents its own inadequacy and its subjective lack of purposiveness for our judgement in the estimation of magnitude. Interestingly he do not engage with this manoeuvre because he admits *pure* aesthetic judgement "(*unmixed with any teleological judgement* which, as such, belongs to reason)" (Zupančič 1992, 83), and the example Kant finds for those are not in works of art, not "where a human end determines the form as well as the magnitude" (Zupančič 1992, 83), but in "raw nature merely involving magnitude (and only in this so far as it does not convey any charm or any emotion arising from actual danger)" (Zupančič 1992, 83). For Kant there is nothing *monstrous* in this example of the sublime, nor "magnificent or horrible," and he continues:

> …the magnitude apprehended may be increased to any extent provided imagination is able to grasp it all in one whole. An object is *monstrous* where by its size it defeats the end that forms its concept. The *colossal* is the mere presentation of a concept which is almost too great for presentation, i.e. borders on the relatively monstrous; for the end to be attained by the

> presentation of a concept is made harder to realize by the intuition of the object being almost too great for our faculty of apprehension.—A pure judgement upon the sublime must, however, have no end belonging to the object as its determining ground, if it is to be aesthetic and not to be tainted with any judgement of understanding or reason.
>
> *(2007, 83)*

So, for Kant, the final element of his triad – the beautiful, the sublime and the monstrous (the negative of the sublime) – relates to a size defeating the end that forms its concept; but still, the monstrous is not the colossal (a concept almost too much to fully present) which borders on the relatively monstrous, as Kant says. If a "pure judgement upon the sublime must have no end belonging to the object as its determining ground" (2007, 83), and "an object is monstrous where by its size it defeats the end that forms its concept" (2007, 83), there is valid consideration on how sublimity relates to monstrosity through a certain going beyond its own end, something unattainable that lies within a certain (im)possibility. More pointedly, the monstrous for Kant is not on the side of imagination, neither on the side of beauty nor on the side of the sublime. Rather it is a negative point that keeps them all in check. In a way, the uncanny related by Zupančič's text, seems to interestingly articulate the puzzling in-between ends of the monstrous, its conceptual defiance of concepts and its curious relation to unfitting itself. Thus, there is an interesting aspect from Kant's monstrosity, to consider about our own (in)humanity and how it's fundamentally negative (a perspective that only makes sense beyond the Kantian philosophical scheme).

3.2 The Hegelian contours of monstrosity

The proper monstrous dimension makes more sense taken under Hegelian lenses. This brief section has no intention of summarizing the entirety of Hegel's philosophical endeavour, but to present his dimension of negativity and the subject in his *Phenomenology of Spirit* [1807] (1977).

The notion of subject which psychoanalysis is concerned about is not the transcendental one (or the Kantian one), but a Hegelian one. The subject of the unconscious as Lacan defends derives from Hegel. The proper negative dimension introduced by the movement of consciousness and recognition through language present Hegel's phenomenology, highlights negativity as the motor to transformation and change in everything that we do. This negativity founds our (in)humanity and sets the ground for the need for a *monstrous grammar*. Not a soothing positive, but an inherent negativity. The motor of negativity which drives the dialectical movement introduced by Hegel explains the subject as constant transformation instead of a transcendental subject like Kant wanted. Hegel's definition of subject redefined the notion of subject for philosophy.

The discussions concerning the interpretation of Hegel's *Phenomenology of Spirit* is in itself a long philosophical trouble which is difficult to find shortcuts around. Hegel's first text of philosophical maturity (Houlgate 1991, 50) provides many debates even until this day. The *Phenomenology of Spirit* indicates key elements of his philosophical system and invites a new grammar to philosophy itself through Hegel's discourse (Lebrun 2004). While arguing against the epistemological limitations of the Kantian philosophical project, Hegel introduces his approach to "experience" and to "subject" through the dialectical movement, which as Gérard Lebrun defends, dissolves dichotomies and apparent impasses by setting a transformative role to the subject circumscribed to his historical conditions. Hegel's influence is impossible to be ignored, even if it means to acknowledge it in a certain anti-Hegelianism. One point is clear, the German philosopher was key to contemporary thought in the field.[4]

Hegel's philosophy provides the foundations for thinking scientifically in philosophy, and accounting for the awareness of thinking scientifically through this operation. Hegelian dialectics sets the condition of possibility to consider transformation into philosophy in a radical form. Hegel takes the relation between subject and object through dialectics and reframes the field in terms of thinking transformation, potency and movement. He breaks out from the Aristotelian logical framework and provides an alternative for the Spinozist substantialist endeavour (Moder 2017). One could argue that it is only after Hegel's turn on its head of the philosophical field, that the condition of transformation and movement could finally sustain something *radically* new. In a more profound way, the internal logic of negation and tension inherent to conceive transformations beyond the conditions of given possibilities, is the key feature of Hegel's philosophy.

Hegel's phenomenological project could be (pedagogically) separated into six pairs of basic oppositions: (1) depth vs. surface, (2) eternal/enduring vs. passing, (3) necessary vs. accidental, (4) essence vs. appears, (5) universal vs. particular, (6) One vs. multiplicity (Dolar 2018). Thus, Hegel assumes the philosophical program of antinomies but instead of being shackled by them, he provides through his dialectical logics a movement to traverse "impossible" oppositions and actualizing them into new possibilities. It is only after Hegel dialectics that negativity gains its proper and more radical meaning, when it becomes a movement for transforming the given condition of (im)possibility towards emancipation.

This brief section does not try to encompass Hegel's philosophy, but it defends how *negativity* can be taken as a condition of possibility (a dialectical movement to actualize given impossibilities into a certain condition of possibility), being attentive to its implications for thinking and to approach transformation itself in a radical way. The discussion towards monstrosity depends on Hegel, since it connects intimately with the dialectical movement but also, for its approach to language and thinking, through his journey of conceptual formation. In a way, the monstrous is inherently connected with Hegelian dialectics, it concerns the abruptness of Hegel's dialectics, facing the *das Ungeheure* in his debate with Adam Smith's capitalist argument (Buck-Morss 2009), but at a deepest level, at the moments where impasses of lack itself surface and struggle at the face of the dialectical movement of negation. For instance, moments where the question of Hegel's openness is simultaneously its best feature, but also its more debatable one. For example, Hegel famously argues towards the subsequent higher unity after crucial contradictions tear the symbolic fabric of a given moment in time, but what about moments in recent history, such as Nazism and other states of exception (which struggle to be *fully* subsumed)? Žižek (2015) argues how Nazism is a point beyond the countless genocide in human history, but different than other genocides, it operated through the programmatic degradation of subjectivity towards its bare minimum. And yet, under Hegel's own logic, what could it mean that *such a wound* would have become "undone"? Rescuing Žižek's discussion about the healing of the wound (of the Spirit):

> ...for Hegel, wounds are healed in a much stronger sense than just as steps towards a higher unity: they literally disappear, they are "undone" – how? Recall Wagner's "*Die Wunde schließt der Speer nur der sie schlug*" from the finale of Parsifal – Hegel says the same thing, although with the accent shifted in the opposite direction: the Spirit is itself the wound it tries to heal, i.e., the wound is self-inflicted. That is to say, what is "Spirit" at its most elementary? The "wound" of nature: subject is the immense – absolute – power of negativity, of introducing a gap/cut into the given-immediate substantial unity, the power of differentiating, of "abstracting", of tearing apart and treating as self-standing what in reality is part of an organic unity. Consequently, the Spirit heals its wound not by directly healing it, but by getting rid of the very full and sane Body into which the wound was cut. It is in this precise sense that, according to Hegel, »the wounds of the Spirit heal, and leave no scars behind«: Hegel's point is not that the Spirit heals its wounds so perfectly that, in a magic gesture of retroactive sublation, even their scars disappear; the point is rather that, in the course of a dialectical process, a shift of perspective occurs which makes the wound itself appear as its opposite – the wound itself is its own healing when perceived from another standpoint.
>
> *(Žižek 2015, 810)*

Žižek emphasizes the shift of standpoint as a proper topological shift, not as a psychological abstraction (in a metaphysical sense), but as a negative ontological capability of finding means to heal such wounds. The monstrous *topos* defended here (which is inherent to Hegelian dialectics itself), concerns how

Hegel's dialectical movement (in its more open and wild fashion) provides the fundamental movement to sustain the necessity of transformation and the requirements of negativity.[5] Here is where it seems valuable to approach Alain Badiou's philosophical work, since he criticizes Heidegger (who critiques Hegel's work), but because he is someone who does not automatically assume the Hegelian project either, Badiou aims at something else in his *mathematical ontology*. Badiou affiliates himself with Hegelian themes of truth and the subject, (a direct heritage from Lacan's psychoanalysis), but his philosophical construction was first concerned with getting rid of *sutures* which were applied into philosophy itself. Badiou wants to let the void inside philosophy breath and produce a field attentive to the generic procedures (the arts, politics, science and love) instead of being suffocated by it. Badiou changed and developed these points in different ways towards his thinking, but these principles remain, he points out the formal implication of mathematics as a foundation of the subject and of truth and the crucial necessity of picking this up against the poetic, the impasses of language and body. Nonetheless, Badiou aims at both transformation and movement, but under the terms of his own philosophical project.

In Badiou's *Theory of the Subject* (2009) the philosopher introduces his understanding of Hegel's heavy machinery of the dialectical movement as a materialist undertaking. Introducing the good news of Hegel's thinking being a *materialist* and not an idealist. This requires a necessary disentanglement between two processes and two movements which take place in Hegel's dialectics, instead of automatically assuming a subsumption of the "subjective system of knowing" (Badiou 2009, 3). Thus, the "heavy machinery of the global system" advancements, can be understood as "…the very accumulation of these arbitrary local decrees that everywhere gives form to the acute and partial framework of Hegel's materialism" (Badiou 2009, 5). The local decrees which Badiou describes here from Hegel's *Logic*, concern the journey of Whole (which is told as history of the One) and how it can't be anything else but *materialistic*. And yet, in order to think dialectically, a *division* must always be present there. As Badiou explains from Hegel, between "something and something other (*Etwas und Anderes*)" (Badiou 2009, 5), there is a *division*, which keeps away the overall idea that there is something *idealistic* in Hegel's dialectics. It is from the understanding of Hegel's *materialism*, that Badiou formulates the heavy machinery of his philosophy of Being and its relationship with Events.

Badiou's philosophy is far more complex, but to our argument here, it is quintessential. We can affiliate ourselves with the idea that Hegel sustains a materialistic perspective, providing a fundamental perspective upon dialectics and introducing the puzzle of the local decrees and its relation to the exceptions. This precise moment, which is a radically *extimate* (in Lacanian terms) moment, in Lacanian terms, is where I would like to provide a key logical argument towards monstrous materialism. This has nothing to do with figments of our imagination, nor about fantasizing ideals. The approach here suggested concerns being attentive of a series of elements which struggle to be subsumed in dialectical terms and being careful not to suture its away above it or upon it, as Badiou suggests. It is through this specific perspective that monstrous materialism, under more Hegelian terms, is being defended here.

3.3 Žižek and the contours of monstrosity

Žižek himself describes his theoretical developments as a knotting between Lacan, Hegel and Marx through a *Borromean knot* (in the Lacanian sense of its knotting use, which means that if one gets untied all others fall apart) (Žižek 1992, 2). This notion guides Žižek's philosophical project of intertwining psychoanalysis, philosophy and politics; nonetheless, the *weight* given to these theoretical realms (much like Lacan development of his RSI) have changed over time. Noticeably, his *philosophical* endeavours always were committed to a Hegel which is not *caged* or *domesticated* philosophy; he keeps close to traditional philosophical literature and usually establishes the German Idealist. The same goes for his *political* reflections challenging orthodox Marxism to *wake from its dogmatic slumber*; and finally, his *psychoanalytic* render of Lacan that goes against all attempts of numbing and renormalization discursivity, cautioning psychoanalysis against becoming another hermeneutics of the bourgeoisie. An important feature which remained consistent over time in Žižek's philosophical framework as a *Borromean knotting* articulation, follows Lacan's own articulation of RSI in this knotting, where you can see movements, in which the prevalence of one realm (or author) rises above the remaining ones. Thus, you notice his thinking moving towards the borders of one of its realms, but that does not mean that the remaining ones aren't also present there.

Žižek's philosophical work is composed by many works and different moments, but the three internal elements of his thinking never change: philosophy, psychoanalysis and politics (under the proper names: *Hegel*, *Lacan* and *Marx*). This section has no intention of summarizing Žižek's vast and intricate philosophical work, but it does aim at benefiting from the contours it provides to *monstrosity*. From his philosophical attention towards psychoanalytic paradoxical impasses of (in)humanity, to his *theory of ideology*[6] and implications of *enjoyment* at the political level, Žižek has been consolidating consequences of this articulation for the past few decades. One of these theoretical *consequences*, is the formulation of the outlines of *monstrosity* under the terms to which we are here advocating for, which is how Žižek approaches Lacan's *homological* bond between the uncanny and anxiety in the formulation of *object a* in many different moments of this theoretical construction. The attempt of systematizing such *contours* of monstrosity within Žižek's theoretical thinking, provides an unavoidable argument towards (in)humanity and its impasses. Nonetheless, this very own *movement* towards *negativity* and understanding of *monstrosity*, as presented by Žižek, introduces a radical scope beyond *identification* and beyond *normativity* to think psychoanalysis, philosophy and politics, especially concerning how monstrosity dialectically sustains the deadlock of (in)humanity and an attempts to traverse it (not in a naive sense, but rather as an attentive comprehension of providing grounds towards *new signifiers*, consequently a *new subjectivization* and emancipatory modes of collectivization).

The effort of systematizing (some) of Žižek's philosophical developments here is an openly *biased* effort. Focusing strictly on how monstrosity is outlined by his theoretical thought, the key points to what monstrosity circulates and why its dialectical materialism articulation dimension is crucial against impasses and contradictions of our (symbolic) reality. Thus, this section does not pretend to encapsulate or exhaust the entirety of Žižek's multiple theoretical developments, it simply traces and articulates the fundamental points for an understanding of *(in)humanity* and the impasses of monstrosity. Let's start by addressing what "monstrosity" is not, according to the philosophical standpoint of Žižek: monstrosity is not about *moralisation*, is not about *psychologization*, is not about *substantializing* and it is not about *physiological abnormalities*, monstrosity under Žižekian terms concern fundamental *impasses of formalization* of (in)human reality (Žižek 1989, 1992). The Slovenian thinker's theoretical articulation of monstrosity is a closer approach towards the inherent negative condition of the subject of the unconscious, that is, its relationship with the lack of symbolic coordinates in his or her troubles with the Real in the demand for *new* signifiers.

Žižek's monstrosity is a call for inventing a *third way* in the face of a given antagonistic impasse. Much like a symptom in psychoanalysis subverts the causal-effect relation, *monstrosity* follows a similar articulation of a demand (that does not *fully* know its consequences when is being articulated) but it sustains a connection to the Real that the demand itself covers up (It is the *veil* itself which provides the illusion – like it is the hidden demand which is always in plain sight. We are too busy trying to lift the veil thinking the Real is backstage that it is only once it is lifted that we realize two things: there is nothing under the veil – the true monstrosity – and that we were always already situated within the Real while we were in the act of lifting it – the horror of this realizing fright. We were never where we thought we are or should be – so for Žižek, it is the veil which is the ideological mechanism for the Real). Thus, the justification behind this approach of monstrosity under Žižekian terms affiliates *dialectical materialism* to *counter* the current (re)enchantment of reality so popular in rising ontologies of the current philosophical field and gives room to alterity within us as a monstrous materialist impasse.

Žižek's more direct arguments on *monstrosity* appear in the following books: *The Ticklish Subject* (2000, 46), following which *The Monstrosity of Christ* (2009), he presents afterwards a shift within his dialectical materialism propositions on *Less Than Nothing* (2012) and *Absolute Recoil* (2014) to finally "stop" at *Disparities* (2016b). The claim that the Žižekian contours of *monstrosity* ends with *Disparities* (2016b) is mostly because it is where a more emphatic theoretical dedication of *monstrosity* within Žižek's thinking through German idealism, (new) directions of dialectical materialism and Lacanian thinking under his own terms appears. Žižek engages with *monstrosity* not in a direct *descriptive* way but he leaves entries about it throughout many different works. The preset effort aims at the general contours of monstrosity for the Slovenian thinker instead of an *exhaustive* systematization. The attempted cartography of monstrosity aiming at the conceptual web that accommodates *monstrosity* for Žižek goes as follows: (a) an exception and a point of excess; (b) self-engendering impasses of the (un)ethical Act; (c) pre-sexual dimension; (d) negative dimension of the subject (Kant *avec* Stephen King); (e) Parallax view of the Object-Thing (Antigone's Act) and the troubles with neighbours ("other" in psychoanalysis); (f) monstrous automaton (the uncanny); (g) totally alien dimension; (h) revolutionary monstrosity; (i) the ideological romanticization of monstrosity; (j) Frankenstein and monster. Our point here is to take a closer look at this cartography of Žižek's philosophy and not his entire philosophical commitments.

The Žižekian contours of monstrosity spell out the impasses of *(in)humanity*. Instead of a humanistic appeal to be abstractly "more human," the developments of thinking *monstrosity* surface from impasses of our constitutive negative core of (in)humanity, from the impasses of subjects (of the unconscious) and to our contradictory Enlighted attempts at emancipation that got us here. The overall idea of highlighting monstrosity lies in understanding it as an impasse of *monstrations* as Zupančič summarizes (2017, 69), it is a certain point where *equivocity* requires formalization and manages to invent something new. Where the singularities demand a better political identification to turn radical difference into a new common. It is not about "the illusion of the Real, but the Real in the illusion itself…" as Zupančič (2017, 68) argues. It is a point of identification which entails a logical requirement of traversal through social identificatory traits and conditions towards something ethically new.

In *The Ticklish Subject* (2000), Žižek dedicates an entire section to the theme of *The Monstrous* (2000, 46), precisely while debating the deadlock of transcendental imagination (on Kant's synthetic imagination), suggesting an important provocation concerning Kant:

> …when Kant claims that, without the minimal synthesis of transcendental imagination, there would be no 'phenomena' in the proper sense of the term, only 'a blind play of representations, that is to say, less than a dream', docs he not thereby evoke the monstrous 'chaotic aggregate', the 'not-yet-world', the pre-ontological *chora*, which forms the background of the experience of the Sublime?
>
> *(2000, 42)*

What Žižek sustains in his Kantian (re)articulation on the dialectics of the Sublime is not a retroactive reading of Kant, but a defence that the theme of the Monstrous ("the heart of the transcendental aesthetics") (2000, 42) from the third Critique was already operating in the first Critique, precisely at the crucial point where "the experience of the Sublime reaches the border of this 'chaotic aggregate' of the senses to retreat from it into the suprasensible dimension of the noumenal Law" (2000, 42). Here, Žižek questions the role of transcendental imagination (in its synthetic function) as a defence against this "chaotic aggregate," a formulation which allows Žižek to place Kant peculiarly close to Hegel, as he states:

> Are not the spectral appearances of partial objects mentioned by Hegel in the quoted passage about the 'night of the world' precisely such a pre-synthetic, pre-ontological 'blind play of representations', which is 'less than a dream'? The wager of the Kantian Sublime is that another synthesis, not that of the ontological synthesis accomplished by the temporal self-affection of transcendental imagination, can save us from this abyss of the failure of imagination.
> *(2000, 42)*

Žižek's approximation of Hegel's "night of the world"[7] and the "appearances of partial objects" (2000, 42) invites a better look at these "spectral appearances" as pre-synthetic, pre-ontological elements and on Kant's attempt to resolve this impasse (Beauty–Sublimity–Monstrosity) through yet another synthesis. Žižek's Kantian reading concerns a violent clash occurring in two levels: between imagination itself ("our senses are stretched to their utmost and bombarded with images of extreme chaos") (2000, 42) and from imagination against Reason ("which compels our faculty of imagination to exert all its powers and then to fail miserably, since it is unable to comprehend Reason") (2000, 42). He formulates that "[e]very imagination is already violent in itself, in the guise of the tension between apprehension *[Auffassung]* and comprehension *[Zusammenfassung]*: the second can never fully catch up with the first" (2000, 42). This formulation has another consequence: "…temporality itself, 'as such', involves a gap between the apprehension of the dispersed multitude and the synthetic act of the comprehension of the unity of this multitude" (2000, 42). Thus, the "mathematical sublime" regards the limits of our faculty of imagination to deal with an object too large to be counted, when our faculties fall short to integrate too many unities to be synthesized. A comprehension of time arises here as Žižek indicates: the affirmation that "there is time" can only derive from "not having enough time," or, to know that there is not enough time from the mathematical sublimity affirms an (im)possibility of time. From this Kantian point, Žižek affirms:

> temporality *as such* is sustained by the gap between apprehension and comprehension: a being able to close this gap and fully to comprehend the

> apprehended multitude would be a noumenal *archetypus intellectus* no longer constrained by the limitations of temporality.
>
> (2000, 43)

To reality itself have any ontological consistency, a certain *violence* against pure temporal dispersal takes place. For Žižek, a transcendental schematism between the pure pre-synthetic temporal dispersal and its (violent) subordination to the synthetic activity of the subject, "whose definitive form is the application of the discursive categories of Understanding to intuition" (2000, 43), occurs. Such schematism propels our temporal experience in homogenous terms, in linear succession (past and future subordinated to the present, as Žižek argues), yet, nonetheless, "what transcendental schematism prevents us from thinking is precisely the paradox of *creatio ex nihilo*" (2000, 43). This point is important, since:

> In schematized time, nothing really *new* can emerge - everything is always-already there, and merely deploys its inherent potential. Sublime, on the contrary, marks the moment at which something emerges out of Nothing - something new that cannot be accounted for by reference to the pre-existing network of circumstances. We are dealing here with another temporality, the temporality of freedom, of a radical rupture in the chain of (natural and/or social) causality... The feeling of the Sublime is aroused by an Event that momentarily suspends the network of symbolic causality.
>
> (2000, 43)

Here lies an important aspect of the Kantian Sublime. It concerns a feeling aroused by an Event which suspends the network of symbolic causality (at the symbolic order). Obviously, Žižek sets this debate orientated towards politics at the Imaginary, while the act lies at the Symbolic (and relying on a Hegelian horizon to organize this argument). Nonetheless, Žižek summarizes one of Kant's main philosophical points: "The central tenet of Kant's transcendental idealism is that it is the subject's 'spontaneous' (i.e., radically *free)* act of transcendental apperception that changes the confused flow of sensations into 'reality', which obeys necessary laws" (2000, 44). Or rather, in (Kantian moral philosophical) terms, in order for the subject to acknowledge her/his freedom, she/he can only: "...get to know (to conceive of) our freedom...via the fact of the unbearable pressure of the moral Law, of its *necessity*, which enjoins us to act against the compulsion of our pathological impulses..." (2000, 44)[8] and freedom almost as an imaginary affective condition, a sort of particularized jouissance, which can only be experienced as such within limits. What Žižek points out is how "necessity" as "the symbolic necessity that regulates our lives" (2000, 44) "relies on the abyssal free act of the subject, on his contingent decision, on the *point de capiton* that magically turns confusion into a new Order" (2000, 44). So, there is a freedom not yet captured by necessity and the name of this abyssal freedom is found in Hegel's "night of the world" (2000, 44).

This pondering upon this abyssal freedom which Žižek engages here with was a stance raised by Kant's transcendental subject, but this was not neglected by German Idealism. Thus, Žižek finds in Fichte, who is the "first philosopher to focus on the uncanny contingency at the very heart of subjectivity" (2000, 44) and also a thinker who sustains a different perspective concerning Kant's subject, that is, "the Fichtean subject is not the overblown Ego=Ego as the absolute Origin of all reality, but a finite subject thrown, caught, in a contingent social situation forever eluding mastery" (2000, 44). The Fichtean notion of *Anstoss*[9] [obstacle] which is not an *obstacle* where "the absolute I posits to itself in order to stimulate its activity" (2000, 44) but "something that *resists* the boundless expansion of our striving; and an impetus, a stimulus, something that incites our activity" (2000, 44), it is a primordial impulse which displays creative power. Following Žižek's line of thinking, there is a crucial distinction about Lacanian Real to be made: *there are emissaries of the Real which are not to be confused with the Real itself.* Žižek affirms this refinement when he says: "If the Kantian *Ding an sich* corresponds to the Freudian-Lacanian Thing, *Anstoss* is closer to *objet petit a*, to the primordial foreign body that 'sticks-in the throat' of the subject, to the object-cause of desire that *splits…*" (2000, 44–45).

Žižek's debate on the uncanny objects propels the instigating perspective of a necessary parallax of this constitutive negative gap. His understanding on *monstrosity* derives from Kant's transcendental imaginary deadlock, but it gains another thrust through Žižek's Hegelian lenses – translating a further paradoxical look into *uncanniness* but setting the record straight with the metaphysical remainders within it – the *spectral* Real and the symbolic *reality* under a dialectical materialist perspective. The *uncanny* as (dis)orienting experiences for the subject (of the unconscious) are placed in a more accurate logic assumed in relation to the Real. Žižek's monstrosity denotes how *uncanniness* is the ultimate *extimate* experience for the subject (of the unconscious), and moreover, how it has two levels of occurrences (not necessarily contradictory, if negativity is adequately understood under dialectical materialism): there is *Anstoss* (concerning *object a*) and *das Ding an sich* (the Thing itself). Such differentiation promotes a further perspective on the radical encounter with such pre-ontological remains of the Real that monstrosity captures. The external that lies within us displacing ourselves, this strangeness is experienced through the uncanny. Thus, monstrosity is the philosophical investigation of the realism of (death) drive, realism of desire (Zupančič 2005) and realism of *jouissance* (Žižek 2016a, 12) which deals with the impasses of monstrous uncanny.

3.4 For a non-Heideggerian Lacan (a Žižekian approach)

Žižek's sustains a Hegel which is not "dead and buried" and the same can be said about his Lacan. Žižek's approach to negativity through both thinkers sustain their actuality to our impasses. One of Lacan's influences is Martin Heidegger and Žižek makes a good case to rid Lacan of his Heideggerian traps. This certainly does not mean to diminish Heidegger's importance to philosophy, especially in France over the 20th century (Badiou 2012) and to early Lacanian psychoanalysis. Lacan did engage with Heidegger's thought (Capobianco 1995), but it seems *troubling* to assume Lacan *is* a Heideggerian. Lacan approached Heidegger's because of language and ontology (Richardson 2003), but this certainly did not *reshape* Lacan's psychoanalysis which had no intentions of making room to fit Heidegger's ontological project of subjectivity (the *Dasein*). Žižek (2016b)[10] argues against the understanding of Lacan as a Heideggerian through the distinction between neurosis and psychosis (as different relations with the *objet petit a* through language).

For Lacan, the truth has the structure of fiction and Žižek notices how symbolic fiction presents two reactions towards a lie: either a furious rejection or a "sub(li)mation into a "more elevated" truth. Such reactions for psychoanalysis are analogous to the difference between *Verwerfung* and symbolic transubstantiation (2016b, 8). This point developed by Žižek concerns a clinical questioning from François Balmès about psychosis, specifically about *verwerfung* ["foreclosure"] which cannot be understood simply as the expulsion of a psychotic subject out of language altogether. Basically, psychotic structured subjects participate in language, however, the point is that the psychotic structure does not participate under the same terms of symbolic efficiency (as neurotic or perverted do so) (2016b, 9). Balmès introduces a distinction proposed between *Bejahung* (a certain "positive" primordial subjective gesture of assuming a place within language) and *Verwerfung* (a more fundamental, primary symbolization from the Real – "...the almost mythic zero level of direct contact between the Symbolic and the Real that coincide at the moment of their differentiation..." (2016b, 9) the *negative* procedure of the primary surfacing of the battery of signifiers which expels the Real towards the pre-symbolic (2016b, 9).

Žižek uses the Freudian case of *The Wolf Man*[11] as an example. Freud's patient who saw their parents *coito a tergo* was symbolized but kept *libidinally neutral* until it was activated later when he was concerned with the question: "where did children come from?" and the arising of his sexual fantasies (2016b, 9). The mnemic trait was *bejaht* (it was historicized) and activated onto his personal narrative to build a place that organizes meaning. Thus, when psychotic individuals integrate language, they give the first step towards the symbolic order, but they are unable to subjectively perform *within* language, unable to symbolically "historicize" their subjective processes or of realizing the *Bejahung*, as Žižek claims. This is why Balmès defends that lack operates in a different way for psychosis. Psychotics "inhabit" the symbolic level of the primordial (maternal) Other, not assuming the symbolic castration (as neurotics do) as a "rewarding" lack, a liberating loss, which conditions "things to appear in their (meaningful) being" (2016b, 9). In this way, psychosis is a loss which is strictly private and only translates being deprived. Following Žižek, in a more speculative articulation, Lacan attaches this "primary" symbolization ("accessible to psychotic subjects and prior to their subjective engagement") (2016b, 9) to Heidegger's distinction between: "the original dimension of language as opening to Being and the dimension of speech as carrier of (subjective) significations or as means of intersubjective recognition..." (2016b, 9). Heidegger's procedure concerns an originary level of speech *as* demonstration (*Sagen* as *Zeigen*) "where the difference between reference and signification disappears, a word that says something does not 'mean' this thing, but it constitutes/demonstrates it in its Being opening the space to its existence..." (2016b, 9). This original dimension of language is the "level of 'appearance' as such, not appearance as opposite to its underlying reality, as a 'pure' appearance which 'is' entirely in its appearance...'" (2016b, 9) and Lacan denounces the metaphysical clamour of reducing appearances to its foundations.

Žižek investigates Lacan's debate on psychosis through Lacan's debate on the "thing representation" (*Sach-Vorstellung*) and "word-representation" (*Wort-Vorstellung*) in Freud as inherent to the symbolic order. This provides a distinction between primary symbolization "establishment of the unconscious battery of original signifiers" (2016b, 10) and the second symbolization (between the conscious/preconscious language systems), therefore, the (paradoxical) condition of psychosis: "a psychotic [subject] is not, as generally assumed, someone who regresses to a more 'primitive' level of thing-representations, who treats 'words as things'; he is, on the contrary, someone who precisely has word-representations without thing-representations" (2016b, 10). Thus, a psychotic inhibit language, what is missing is any connection with an unconscious background, which would "provide libidinal resonance to the words that we use, its core and specific subjective weight" (2016b, 10). Žižek refines this impasse, translating how it is not necessary to postulate between different phases of symbolization:

> first the symbolization, the surface of the primary battery of signifiers through the expulsion of the Real, and afterwards the expulsion of a signifier. Both processes are one and the same, and psychosis comes on later, at a secondary stage when - or if - the signifier which represents the incomplete-inconsistency of the Other, which inscribes its incompleteness, is foreclosed.
>
> *(2016b, 11) (our translation)*

Following Žižek, the precise sense which is forecluded by the symbolic returns in the Real can be found in phenomena of the verbal hallucination for psychotic (unbarred) subjects, which have symbolic content as emissaries of the Real. How does this work? There are two traits which make such phenomena real: *isolation* and *certainty* (2016b, 12). These hallucinations, as Žižek explains, are foreclosed for the subject, that is, they do not "exist" for the subject; nonetheless, they "ex-sist, persist and impose themselves out of the symbolic fabric; they are completely isolated of its symbolic context, which by definition is the context of trust and supposition…" (2016b, 12), they depend on a minimal level of trust at the symbolic order to be operative in order for any wager to take place. Any symbolic assumption comes with the risk of trusting that the Other (knowingly barred) has our "symbolic" secured, while in psychosis, is not so much about believing what these voices are saying, but the belief of "knowing" these voices to be real (even if they do not *trust* them) (as Žižek explains, deriving from Balmès) (2016b, 12). The underlying question concerns the relationship between the real, the symbolic and the lack (2016b, 12). For Žižek, Lacan oscillates between the thesis that the "symbolic introduce the 'lack-of-being' at the Real… and thesis that Being arises strictly with the Symbolic – there cannot be a Being prior to the Symbolic" (2016b, 12) and here, Lacan wisely subtracts from repeating the Heideggerian procedure of partializing being into separate modes: "[b]eing in the ontological sense of openness at the interior from where all the things arise, and being in the ontic sense of reality, of existing entities in the world…" (2016b, 12) and finds a rather elegant stance (as claims Balmès): "Lacan…understands the question at stake as the response" (2016b, 13). And Žižek explores the consequence behind Lacan's procedure of avoiding following Heidegger:

> This means that being and lack-of-being coincide, are the two sides of the same coin — the space of the horizon in which things fully "are", or exists, arise only from the condition that something gets excluded ("sacrificed") for it, that something in it is "absent in its own position." More precisely, what characterizes a symbolic universe is the undermost lack between the elements and the places which these occupy: the two dimension do not coincide directly, as it is the case in the shallow positivity of the Real, reason why, at the differential order of the signifiers, lack itself can be considered a positive trait… And Lacan's basic "ontological" hypothesis is that, it must occur this undermost lack between elements and their structural positions, *something — some element — must be radically (constitutively) excluded*; the name given by Lacan to this object which is (by definition, structurally) missing from its own place, coinciding with its own lack, is, evidently, *objet petit a* as the object cause of desire, or surplus-enjoyment, the paradoxical object which embodies the very lack-of-being. The *objet petit a* is that which must be excluded from the frame of reality, that which its exclusion constitutes and sustains the foundation of reality.
>
> *(2016b, 13) (our translation)*

This is a key difference between psychosis and neurosis, described by Žižek, while in neurosis this object gets *excluded*, in psychosis this object is *integrated* in reality as a hallucinatory object ("a voice or a gaze which haunts the paranoid and etc.") (2016b, 13) and such inclusion logically leads towards the dissolution of reality or a sense of disintegration of reality for the subject (2016b, 13). And Žižek explains, Lacan transforms Heidegger's theme of language as the dwelling place of being, language is not an instrument and a creation of man, it is man who "inhabits" language – "Psychoanalysis must be the science of language inhabited by the subject" (2016b, 13). More than an imprisonment, Lacan twists this screw and calls it the "torture-house of language," in order to describe the constant re-editing of this original lack between subject and language through corporeal symptoms which persistently inscribe themselves (on different degrees and qualities, also accordingly with the kind of defence structurally inscribed on the subject at stake) and signalling another trait of the Freudian *wo es war soll ich werden*, in how "man can never be at home in its own home" (2016b, 14). (Let's make this clear, the theme of the uncanny (homely/unhomely) is a key articulation for the theme of Lacan's *object a* and this is a key element to always have in mind here.) From this point, the distinction between Lacan and Heidegger becomes clearer, but also how Lacan's negative ontology is sustained. There is certain dialectics of negativity of becoming within language, which can be clearly posed as Lacan's (negative) "ontological" formulation (what Zupančič calls realism in psychoanalysis) (2017). The regime of beliefs in which we invest our animistic reminders occurs through language and the uncanny organization of this negativity is our monstrous (in)human process of subjectivization in society.

3.5 The monstrosity of Christ: Žižek's mapping of "spectral materialism"

In "The Monstrosity of Christ: Paradox or Dialectic" (2009), Žižek explains what he means by *monstrosity*. Applying Hegelian lenses to the theological debate on the *monstrosity* of Christ's *Incarnation* and Christ's *full* humanity (2009, 40). Žižek investigates Christianity through a Hegelian triad appraisal (Universal–Particular–Singular) between Orthodoxy, Catholicism and Protestantism (each new term is a subdivision *and* a split from its previous unity). Noticing how each perspective addresses a different relationship between the *body of believers* of God's Word and subsequent aspects of alienation (2009, 28). To solidify his Hegelian approach on Christianity, Žižek mainly investigates G. K. Chesterton and Meister Eckhart. His Hegelian (re)articulation provides remarkable appreciations on crucial theological impasses, for example, when debating Chesterton's God's *abandonment* of himself, arguing that: "Chesterton is fully aware that it is not enough for God to separate man from himself so that mankind will love him—this separation has to be reflected back into God himself, so that God is abandoned *by himself*" (2009, 40).

For Žižek, Hegel's philosophy cannot be "deflated" from his own "ontological-metaphysical commitments, reduced to a general theory of discourse, of possibilities of argumentation" (2009, 26). Žižek offers a Hegelian perspective against Chesterton (who is critical of Hegel), raising a "core question of Hegelian Christology: why the idea of Reconciliation between God and man (the fundamental content of Christianity) has to appear in a single individual, in the guise of an external, contingent, flesh-and-blood person (Christ, the man-God)?" (2009, 73). This thought derives from Hegel's lectures on the philosophy of religion,[12] where a *double formulation* of *reconciliation* is investigated by Žižek: a subject who pursues reconciliation through pious actions and a community aiming at bringing heaven on Earth. But what Žižek articulates here on *monstrosity* concerns another point: Hegel's *minimal gap* or the direct passing from In-Itself to For-Itself (a point previously developed in *The Ticklish Subject* (2000) and now further articulated). Žižek pursues how Hegel's remark here can be assumed under two levels: the individual's divinization or the pursue towards spiritual perfection and the collective actualization of the divine community (where a community tries to live in accordance with the divine law) (2009, 73). Žižek explains how this leads Hegel to anticipate questions that resonate with Marx, he questions:

> ...why cannot we conceive a direct passage from In-Itself to For-Itself, from God as full Substance existing in itself, beyond human history, to the Holy Spirit as spiritual-virtual substance, as the substance that exists only insofar as it is "kept alive" by the incessant activity of individuals? Why not such a direct dis-alienation, by means of which individuals recognize in God qua transcendent substance the "reified" result of their own activity?
>
> *(2009, 73)*

Here, Žižek sustains his Hegelian reading of *monstrosity* deriving from this gap between In-Itself to For-Itself which is *impossible to be directly traversed*. Hegel relies on the dialectic of positing and presupposing[13] to answer these questions and he sustains how:

> Christ as God-man is the externally presupposed Unity/Reconciliation: first the immediate unity, then the mediate one in the guise of the Holy Spirit—we pass from Christ whose predicate is love to love itself as subject (in the Holy Spirit, "I am where two of you love each other...").
>
> *(2009, 73–74)*

Žižek does not merely assume Hegel, but counters Hegel against Hegel himself (2009, 74) (a usual philosophical procedure applied by Žižek against the (re)normalization of Hegel towards more radical implications of Hegel's thoughts). Thus, Žižek takes the particular case, considering a circuit of positing-presupposing *as* a substance-subject circuit, where the spiritual substance of the Holy Spirit is kept alive through the (re)actualization of living individuals, its effective existence relies on the communal effort to sustain it. This captures the key point of Hegel's understanding that "spiritual substance is properly virtual" (2009, 74), that is, its existence relies on subjects acting *as if* it exists (2009, 74), precisely like the push behind ideological causes like "Communism" or Nationalism, as Žižek explains. Basically, the "'spiritual substance' of individuals who recognize themselves in it" (2009, 74) composes the grounds to their entire existence, it becomes the ultimate coordinate for any horizon of meaning in their lives, a perspective in which individuals devote and commit their whole life to and are ready to give themselves completely to such perspective. But, as Žižek denotes, the only thing that "actually exists" are the individuals and their activities, which means "this substance is actual only insofar as individuals "believe in it" and act accordingly" (2009, 74).

Žižek almost formulates a *subject supposed to believe* here, defending how such positing-presupposing circle is the substance-subject circle (which maintains the Holy Spirit "as a spiritual substance" alive, effectively existing) through the actuality of living individuals. But still, Žižek's question remains: why can't we pass directly from "spiritual Substance as presupposed (the naive notion of Spirit or God as existing in itself, without regard to humanity) to its subjective mediation, from the awareness that its very presupposition is retroactively "posited" by the activity of individuals?" (2009, 74). Basically, because this is where the troubles with *monstrosity* start. Following Žižek, it becomes clear how Hegel defends that reconciliation cannot take place directly, how it first must be generated or "appear in" a *monster*:

> …twice on the same page Hegel uses this unexpectedly strong word, "monstrosity," to designate the first figure of Reconciliation, the appearance of God in the finite flesh of a human individual: "This is the monstrous [*das Ungeheure*] whose necessity we have seen." The finite fragile human individual is "inappropriate" to stand for God, it is "*die Unangemessenheit ueberhaupt* [the inappropriateness in general, as such]"—are we aware of the properly dialectical paradox of what Hegel claims here? The very attempt at reconciliation, in its first move, produces a monster, a grotesque "inappropriateness as such." So, again, why this weird intrusion, why not a direct passage from the (Jewish) gap between God and man to (Christian) reconciliation, by a simple transformation of "God" from Beyond to the immanent Spirit of Community?
>
> *(2009, 74)*

The monstrous [*das Ungeheure*] here introduced by Hegel, basically translates the impossibility of *immediate* reconciliation, but as Žižek notices, there is a further dialectical paradox at stake – the very own attempt at reconciliation produces a grotesque "inappropriateness as such" (2009, 74). Žižek discusses that only through the "Hegelian relationship between necessity and contingency" (2009, 74) this "inappropriateness as such," this monstrous dimension can be adequately approached. What Žižek takes from Hegel, is how their "encompassing unity is necessity, i.e., that necessity itself posits and mediates contingency as the external field in which it expresses-actualizes itself — contingency itself is necessary, the result of the self-externalization and self-mediation of the notional necessity" (2009, 75). Žižek supplements this unity with an "opposite one," with contingency as the encompassing unity of itself, elevating necessity into a structuring principle, as he defends, the contingent realm of multiplicity deriving from a contingent act, this is the outcome of the struggle for hegemony required from contingency (2009, 75). As Žižek describes (and this is key), this shift corresponds with the shift from S to $, that is, from substance to subject (2009, 75)

> The starting point is a contingent multitude; through its self-mediation ("spontaneous self-organization"), contingency engenders-posits its immanent necessity, just as Essence is the result of the self-mediation of Being. Once Essence emerges, it retroactively "posits its own presuppositions," i.e., it sublates its presuppositions into subordinated moments of its self-reproduction (Being is transubstantiated into Appearance); however, this positing is retroactive.
>
> *(2009, 75)*

The procedure of posited retroaction is central to deal with the consequences of contingency. Retroacting allows for a creation deriving from something new fruit of contingency. And this implies a shift between positing-presuppositions and presupposing the positing, while the first one concerns the limit of the Feuerbachian–Marxian logic of dis-alienation[14] (where "the subject overcomes its alienation by recognizing itself as the active agent which itself posited what appears to it as its substantial presupposition") (2009, 75) what Žižek further locates is the missing aspect of the properly "Christian gestures" to supplement this logic and also, how the proper Hegelian perspective goes beyond the Marx–Feuerbachian in a more radical sense. Basically, to posit the presupposition, where to "humanize" God or to reduce him to an outcome of human activity or expression, or like Žižek explains, "*the (human-subjective) positing itself should be "presupposed," located in God as the substantial ground-presupposition of man, as its own becoming-human/finite*" (2009, 75). The point for him, is that the subject's constitutive finitude, the discontent of facing finitude itself, calls for a movement of full positing of presuppositions propelling a fully "retroactive positing/generation of its presuppositions" (2009, 75) which leads to a subject "absolutized into the full self-origin" (2009, 75).

What Žižek's speculative Hegelian thinking ponders upon here, concerns the excessiveness in the monstrosity of Christ, an "excess which prohibits simple recognition of the collective Subject in Substance, the reduction of Spirit to objective/virtual entity (presup)posed by humanity…"(2009, 76) which also operates illustrating the passage of what Hegel called "objective spirit" (OS) to "absolute spirit" (AS). As Žižek explains, through Christ's mediation objective spirit (OS) turns into absolute spirit (AS). Thus, the Holy Spirit *needs* the obliterated body of Christ, otherwise it misses the two poles: "the Universal (the virtual infinity/immortality of the Holy Spirit (OS)) and the Particular (the actual finite/mortal community of believers (SS))" (2009, 76) that is mediated through Christ's monstrosity singularity, as Žižek points out (2009, 76). The attempt at a fidelity for the Event of Christianity, persists in filtering the entire reality through only this perspective and silencing the multiplicity of other worlds and perspectives.

Žižek criticizes the "Feuerbachian–young Marx pseudo-Hegelian approach" to understand the passage of OS to AS, which assumes a passage from objective spirit to absolute spirit through a subjective appropriation of the "reified" objective spirit by the collective human subjectivity (2009, 76) where "the subjectivity recognizes in OS its own product, the reified expression of its own creative power" (2009, 76), as a simple reduction of the objective spirit to subjective spirit (SS). Nonetheless, Žižek also warns that such passage also cannot be done by assuming another objective "spirit beyond, even more In-Itself, absolute entity that encompasses both SS and OS" (2009, 76). The only viable passage from OS to AS is through *dialectical mediation* between OS and SS, as argues Žižek. This dialectical mediation takes place, from including the gap which distances "OS from SS within the SS" (2009, 76), which makes that OS as a "reified" entity by the SS itself, leading to an "inverted recognition" where the subject does not reference an In-Itself of the OS, but where subjectivity itself dissolves, liquefies and collapses (2009, 76).

Žižek then moves towards what this all means concerning dialectics of ontology and epistemology, noticing that the encompassing unity between necessity and contingency *is* necessity, which means it had to be there all along, just waiting to be figured out, "discovered," constructed through subjective means. This necessity figured out through our subjective means, takes place through the "Notion of the phenomenal contingent multiplicity" and its gradual process of figuring out by the subject. As Žižek defends, Hegel's central idea about this point can be found in the Introduction to the *Phenomenology of Spirit*, where the pathway towards truth constitutes truth itself, is a part of truth itself, but if it "is canceled, i.e., we regress to the standard metaphysical notion of Truth as a substantial In-Itself, independent of the subject's approach to it" (2009, 77). Therefore, "[o]nly if the encompassing unity is contingency can we claim that the subject's discovery of necessary truth is simultaneously the (contingent) constitution of this truth itself…" (2009, 77), only through this process the return and rediscovery of eternal Truth *produces* this Truth, as Žižek debates Hegel. Thus, a "dialectical reversal of contingency into necessity, i.e., the way the outcome of a contingent process is the appearance of necessity: things retroactively 'will have been' necessary" (2009, 77).

This dialectical perspective where "the very return to (rediscovery of) eternal Truth generates this Truth" (2009, 77) sets how the "appearance of necessity" and a certain *nachträglichkeit* (retroaction) illustrate a certain "Hegelian performative" action (2009, 78) sustained by the reversal of determinate reflection into reflective determination. Indeed, Žižek goes the extra mile to translate the Hegelian understanding of *monstrosity* of Christ and adding the critical edge of speculative thinking countering Hegel with Hegel, Žižek finds not solutions but *consequences*. From this point, the *monstrosity* of Christ can be understood as an Evental truth and Žižek illustrates a detailed explanation of *how* this occurs. There is a point of excess which assumes Christ as *the* (im)possible figure of Reconciliation (through an Evental singularity) and Žižek brings forward the proper dialectical relation between the OS to AS and the role of SS, to examine this (another) perspective concerning monstrosity of Christ.

The Hegelian logical comprehension behind monstrosity (of Christ), which Žižek brings forward here, concerns the price to be paid to "render the Absolute in the medium of external representation"(2009, 80), to sustain the medium of religion. Nonetheless, the very own logic of *monstrosity* is not reserved to religion and for Christianity. Understanding monstrosity's radical excessiveness and how its Evental truth provides meaningful philosophical insights (which Žižek bounds with ethics and political discussions[15]) provokes the symbolic rupture with the texture of reality and has also something to do with the intricacies of *Incarnation*. Žižek refines the "monstrosity" of Christ to sustain its differentiation with the Greek gods who are theologically known to have walked amongst humans. Žižek separates "spectral materialism" as opposition between idealism/materialism and how "true materialism," as defended by Žižek, assuming the "disappearance of matter," to the fact that there is only void (2009, 92). This where real abstraction takes place and Žižek further sustains this point by arguing towards "open" ontology and of ontological inconsistency in accordance with the "disappearance of matter," that is, as true materialism.

For Žižek, the psychoanalytic claim on sexuality posits a critique to Badiou's Evental philosophy, who misses

> ...the simple fact that there is no human animal (governed by pleasure and reality principle, bent on survival, etc.) — with humanity proper, animality is derailed, instinct is transformed into drive, and it is only into such a distorted animal that an Event can inscribe itself.
>
> *(2009, 93)*

A debate concerning the troubles of the duality of human animal and the subject, as Žižek defends the excessiveness of drives to explain this Evental trait over individuals, where "...in order for the Event to inscribe itself into the human animal's body, and thus transform the individual into the subject, this human animal itself has already to be derailed/distorted by drive, by what Eric Santner calls its "too-muchness" (2009, 93). Žižek aims at a Hegelian way out and wages

> that only the materialism of void and multiplicity, going well beyond the commonsense assertion of "external" material reality as the only thing that "really is," is the materialism that, as Hegel would have put it, reaches the level of its notion.
>
> *(2009, 94)*

Finally, Žižek argues that

> [t]he difference between multiplicities and the void is thus a pure difference, not the difference between two ontic entities, not even between Something and Nothing (as if there are multiple Somethings surrounded by the void of Nothing, as in ancient atomism), but rather, "ontological."
>
> *(2009, 94)*

In this way, Žižek's arguments deriving from Badiou's "ontology" permit a distinction between the materialism(s) which do not suffice to go beyond bodies and languages and to meet what in Hegelian terms is a *notion*. The monstrosity of Christ propelled by Žižek through many different incursions, indicates the radical *excessiveness* of an Event,[16] is this crucial discussion about radical materialism, that should paradoxically reject "...naive reliance on external reality as the vulgar-materialist obverse of idealism" (2009, 98) and this does not mean a rejection of the world, not a vulgar idealism, but the importance of including into the symbolic texture of reality the Hegelian perspective of the "night of the world" (2009, 98), the core of negativity that propel us to transform. Here Žižek emphasizes an "undecidability" of the Real in an Event,[17] but his uptake is radically different from the deconstructionist defence of undecidability. Žižek defends how Badiou's point of the "self-relating" nature of an Event, in its undecidability since there is no neutral "objective" criteria for an Event, which means that the "rules" to measure an Event must immanently come from the Event, because the previous "objective" standards cannot fit to *measure* it, since these previous coordinates are loss. This means that there is a crucial moment of monstrosity, under Žižek's terms: the undecidability of the "minimal difference" in-between a parallax gap, or as Žižek states:

> [t]he "minimal difference" which sustains the parallax gap is thus the difference on account of which the "same" series of real occurrences which, to the

eye of a neutral observer, are just part of ordinary reality are, to the eye of an engaged participant, inscriptions of the fidelity to an Event.

(2009, 99)

3.6 Žižek's disparities: the further examination of the "minimal difference"

Žižek's examination on monstrosity is solidified in the book *Disparities*[18] (2016b), where Žižek investigates the section: From the Sublime to the Monstrous (2016b, 238) engaging with Karl Rosenkranz, a Hegelian scholar and author of the *Ästhetik des Häßlichen* ("Aesthetics of the Ugly") (1853), concerned with the abandonment of the unity True, Good and Beautiful: "not only can something ugly be true and good, but ugliness can be an immanent aesthetic notion, that is, an object can be ugly and an aesthetic object, an object of art" (2016b, 238). Following Žižek's argument, Rosenkranz maintains the long tradition started by Homer of associating physical ugliness with moral monstrosity. However, his investigation on ugly as *das Negativschöne* (the negatively-beautiful) (2016b, 239) distinguishes between a "healthy" and a "pathological" mode of enjoying the Ugly in a work of art. As Žižek summarizes: "in order to be aesthetically enjoyable and, as such, edifying and permissible, ugliness has to remain as a foil of the beautiful; ugliness for the sake of itself is a pathological enjoyment of art" (2016b, 239). Žižek's adds to Rosenkranz sustaining that every concept in its self-development immanently contains its opposite within itself. Thus, Ugliness is immanent to Beauty and to embrace ugliness as a middle ground between *Beautiful, the Ugly and the Comical* (2016b, 239) but the dimension of the Sublime requires the three. Deriving from this discussion, Žižek investigates three key points: (a) could the ugly (in all its chaotic and blunt monstrosity which instigates the (re)conciliation of the subject threatened by its opposite short-circuits the fact of Reason and moral law) be conceived as the Sublime? (2016b, 239); (b) how the notion of the Ugly as obverse for the appearance of the Beautiful is fundamentally ambiguous (2016b, 240) and (c) what happens when the reversal of the Ugly into the Comical (or the Sublime) doesn't takes place? (2016b, 241)

The dimension of the excessive-monstrous (which can traverse into a *ridiculous* state) can only operate if placed under the Beauty–Sublime–Monstrous triad; otherwise, there is no way to assume the proper dialectical torsion (and subsequent inversions) between them. The obliteration of the Sublime attempted by Rosenkranz, does not adequately fit to examine the inherent movement on the immanent inversion which such aesthetic objects demand, much like the Sublime which can become ridiculous as illustrated in Chaplin's late films, as Žižek argues (2016b, 240).

Rosenkranz's appropriation of the Ugly, as Žižek defends, can be read under two main perspectives (a Hegelian and an Adornian one): the first (in Hegelian terms), the Ugly is a subordinated aspect of the interplay of the

Beautiful with itself, operating as an immanent self-negation which established the (back)ground for its full appearance, or the second (the Adornian version), where if could be assumed literally, as Žižek defends, the Beautiful arises from the background of the Beautiful which precedes it (2016b, 240). And finally, the third articulation which Žižek debates (the reversal of the Ugly into the Comical (or the Sublime) derives from Herman Parret (reinstating Kant to the debate under some Hegelian appreciation), who investigates an alternative to the Kantian Sublime: "if the overwhelming pressure of the Ugly gets too strong, it becomes monstrous and can no longer be sublated/negated into the Sublime" (2016b, 241). Thus, implicating in a question of *limits*, which Parret discusses when Kant moves from the *colossal* to *monstrous*, annihilating the faculty of presentation.[19] Žižek notices from Parret's point how the monstrous dimension (in its inexpressible and abyssal properties) does violence to subjectivity, for going beyond the sublimity permitted limits which are still sustained by the subject, and as Parret's continues:

> [t]he Sublime pleasure is a pleasure in unpleasure, while the Monstrous generates only unpleasure – but, as such, it provides enjoyment. In short, this is Kant's point: the distinction between pleasure (Lust, regulated by the pleasure principle makes us avoid all painful excess, even the excess of pleasure itself) and enjoyment (*Genuss*, jouissance).
>
> *(2016b, 241–242)*

Žižek takes from Parret's investigation on Kant the link between enjoyment and disgust,[20] and highlights an ontological designation in the weird *Genuss* (enjoyment) which propel us dive into its self-destructive vortex (2016b, 242). But, instead of arguing for either culture or nature, after noticing that this concerns an "unnatural" excess derailing nature, Žižek risk the articulation with a different Kantian development: the "unnatural" savagery (*Wildheit*) or "passion for freedom" (2016b, 242) a supplement from Kant's *Anthropology*. Žižek takes interest in the scream (*Geschrei*) especially of a newborn human being in its primal explosion of rage, in a moment where the baby reacts to the discovery of his limited freedom under the constraints of his body (2016b, 225). Žižek defends that there is nothing supernatural in the freedom which explodes in this rage, how this rage signals the conflict between "phenomenal bodily reality and the noumenal Real of wild freedom that precedes moral Law" (2016b, 225). The appearance of this "weird 'savagery' is passion" (2016b, 225) or a particular option so intense it suspends a rational examination of other viable choices (2016b, 225); and it goes without saying that such passion is purely *(in)human*: animals do not have passions, just *instincts*. This Kantian designation of savagery is noticed by Žižek as "unnatural," and it concerns the specific sense which appears to break and suspend the usual causal chain that sets all natural phenomena, "…it is as if in its terrifying manifestations, noumenal freedom transpires for a moment in our phenomenal universe" (2016b, 226). At this particular object of enjoyment which is by definition disgusting, which Žižek explains that what makes it disgusting is a weird superego injunction that appears to emanate from it, a call to enjoy it even if (and precisely because) we find it ugly and desperately try to resist being dragged into it (perhaps an echo of what Kristeva calls the *abject*, as Žižek enunciates) (2016b, 226)

From this consideration on the abject (deriving from the weird superegoic injunction and a call to enjoy it) Žižek addresses the heart of disgust, "the object of disgust 'threatens the stability of our corporeity'," concerns this object that destabilizes the borders which "separate the inside of our body from its outside" (2016b, 227). In a way, Žižek is addressing the borders which separate inside of our bodies with the outside which gets violated: as in the case of blood or excrement. The homely/unhomely of the body getting violated in its Inside/Outside frontier, can articulate disgust[21] (2016b, 227). This is what Žižek argues as a key dimension that differentiates man from animals: it is not so much that excrements bothers us because of bad smell, that will leave a territorial mark which could harm our probabilities of hunting or any anthropomorphism of such nature… what actually bother us is that excrements came out from our innermost. The shame felt by excrements, as Žižek defends, concern how it exposes and externalizes our innermost intimacy (2016b, 227).

Žižek examines Freud's debate on death drive, on the relation between organic and inorganic, from the concise passage from Ray Brassier, where the gap between "organic interiority and inorganic exteriority" is fought at the cost of a part of the organism itself, and that death provides a protective shield… "Thus, individuated organic life is won at the cost of this aboriginal death whereby the organism first becomes capable of separating itself from the inorganic outside" (2016b, 228). If disgust comes from the "dead" barrier shattered between the organic interiority penetrating the surface, as Žižek defines, "the ultimate object of disgust is bare life itself, life deprived of the protective barrier" (2016b, 228). Basically, the birth of a human being is a *monstrous* event (something extremely intimate which is radically exposed), as Žižek defines. Continuing with this investigation on the intricacies of the disgust, which is a domain where excrements, spits, pus, bodily fluids, belong to. The author discusses how feces which disappear after being flushed, how they vanish away, enacts a "metaphor for the horrifying sublime Beyond of the primordial, preontological Chaos into which things disappear" (2016b, 229). Where we rationally understand what is going on with the vanishing excrements, but the imaginary mysteries about it persists. Since, the excrements are an object of excess, are an abject, that does not fit into our reality, Žižek will rise a Lacanian point to sustain what happens in this situation when we pass from animals to humans, he notices the specific moment where excrements start to bother animals, becoming a problem and excess which annoys. And for humans, we can rationally *know* that the excrements do not actually disappear, that they are in the sewage network, the central point is the topological "torsion" or the "role" that seems to "curve" the space of our reality – we *imagine* that the excrements disappear, they vanish into another dimension which is not part of our everyday life, which is not a part of reality itself, as Žižek explains (2016b, 230).

Žižek's *monstrosity* re-enforces the Beauty–Sublime–Monstrosity dialectical perspective, which seems clear when he (re)articulate it with Kant but additionally introduces further complications deriving from his anthropological perspective. In this way, Žižek does not directly articulate the "spectral materiality" or with the Hegelian "night of the world" via knotting his debate with the preontological elements surfacing into reality which are at stake here, but this is his very point. Žižek introduces a deeper perspective to the disgust along with the dialectics of monstrosity,[22] as an "ontological" realm of the excess, implying a key facet of uncanniness: the violation of Inside/Outside frontiers at the level of the body.

Žižek investigates this dimension under three versions of the abject (the ugly, creepy and disgusting), but supplementing speculative layers towards the uncanny objects and the "spectral materialism" (2009, 92). The background of this debate concerns a proper materialism oriented by "ontological incompleteness" and the role of radical negativity for Žižek in politics. This all now brings more clarity to the Hegelian debate of what constitutes the minimal difference between the In-Itself and the For-Itself (as previously addressed). For Žižek a true materialist perspective addresses the multiplicity of the multiple and not the spectral orientation of the spiritual tendencies that sustain hidden deviations within their "materialism." A true materialist perspective lies in the debate of uncanniness, if dialectically articulated in terms of the triad of Beauty-Sublime-Monstrosity. This Žižekian understanding, organize impasses on the violations between the Inside/Outside, providing valid arguments to what Freudian uncanny leaves out in the open; nonetheless, Žižek really does exhaust the uncanny here, but also furthers its logical operations and inevitably its precision concerning this (in)human dimension.

Žižek furthers versions of the abject (the ugly, creepy and disgusting) which emphasize the *horrors in-between* the tragic and the comedy (2009, 239), going beyond the given moralist and the essentialist perspectives towards something else. Following Žižek, the crucial appreciation of monstrosity denotes the *murmurs of the Real*, that is, encounters which cause disgust can be creepy or deemed ugly. These are layers of the uncanniness which compose the grammar of monstrosity itself. Examining Kristeva's abject,[23] Žižek investigates what happens when we are stumble upon a decaying human corpse or "disgusting" elements (e.g., feces, saliva, vomit) (2009, 242), but also, when we witness brutally torn-out nails or eyes (which are the uncanny example *par excellence*) (2009, 242) encounters that disintegrate the ontological coordinates which would allow someone to place an object into external reality "outside" (2009, 242). For Žižek, uncanny objects concern "spectral materiality" (informed by true materialism), designating the implications of ontological incompleteness under suitable terms.

Žižek argues for Lacanian extimacy based on Kristeva's phenomenology of the abject. Since the abject must be external to subject, it manages at the same time, to be radically external to the space where the subject differentiates itself from the reality "out there" (2009, 242). The Lacanian neologism "extimate" seems suitable here, as Žižek argues: "the abject is so thoroughly internal to the subject that this very overintimacy makes it external, uncanny, inadmissible" (2009, 242). This dimension of the subject's overintimacy made external (uncanny) signals the "extimate" dimension that composes the subject. In a möbius strip like torsion, the most intimate to the subject (of the unconscious) appears externally. From such proximity, Žižek sees the ambiguity that the abject raises especially in terms of the pleasure principle; how attentive and mesmerizing such moments can be, as the philosopher states. Basically, the repulsive, shocking, horror inducing and disgusting, exerts simultaneously an unavoidable fascination which compels our gaze to its horrific dimension. This explains how "…many victims of the abject are its fascinated victims – if not its submissive and willing ones" (2009, 243) as Kristeva defends and Žižek agrees, there is a combination of horror and pleasure fitting to the realm beyond the pleasure principle, the realm of jouissance, where Žižek quoting Kristeva explains, it is a realm where unknowingly without desiring it, one enjoys [*on en jouit*], the realm where a passion assumes in all its pain and violence (2009, 243).

The scope of the *realism of jouissance* presented by Žižek, explores how the abject enacts something of Lacan's *object a*, embodying "the 'indivisible remainder' of the process of symbolic representation which functions as the always-already lost object-cause of desire" (2009, 243). However, Žižek crucially *distinguishes* one from the other, and defends that these should *not* be confused; while the *object petit a* "as the object-cause of desire is, in its very excessive nature, an immanent part of the symbolic process, the spectral/eluding embodiment of lack that motivates desire sustained by the (symbolic) Law…" (2009, 243). While the *object a* function within meaning as its constitutive blind spot or stain, the abject stands for radical exclusion. As Žižek argues (based on Kristeva's work) the abject manages to indicate the point where meaning collapse, precisely for that fact that it is excluded from the symbolic. It draws attention to this point. Basically, the abjectal dimension refers to the reminders of the pre-objectal condition where a body gets violently detached from another body. Thus, following Kristeva and Žižek, the abjection is a primordial condition to impasses of culture and nature, prior to internal and external, inside and outside, of repression and the repressed, and so on. In short, the abjection does not concern a certain immersion into nature, an attempt at re-establishing a 'primordial Mother', but it indicates "the very violent process of differentiation, it is the 'vanishing mediator' between nature and culture, a 'culture in becoming' which disappears from view once the subject dwells within culture" (2009, 243).

This *distinction* teaches us that the abject concerns the pre-objectal relations. It is an emissary of the immemorial violence of *differentiation*; more specifically, the "vanishing mediator" which vanishes itself once the subject "arises" towards "culture." Once the condition of the symbolic edifice grounds the subject (of the unconscious), it signals to the *minimal difference* realm which monstrosity designates this is what Žižek's speculative thinking addresses. Although the *abject* does set out to "disturb identity, system, order," because it does not respect limitations, "borders, positions [or] rules," it inevitably does so. It relates to the 'fragility of the law' (as a *vanishing mediator*), not for some ("supernatural") connection to the "natural" flow of things, neither to the "cultural" designations, as Žižek interprets from Kristeva's definition. Rather, the disturbance of the abject concerns the "fragility of the law" – since it renders palpable the very own fragility of the laws itself, even the laws of nature, which is why the attempts to be symbolically normalized in the radical pre-ontological realm through any "culturalization" falls short. Thus, the encounter with the abject provokes fear, but it is not the fear usually attached to a particular object (e.g. cockroaches, snakes, heights, clowns and so on). The abject invokes a primal fear of the irruption from what "separates us from external reality: what we fear in an open wound or a dead body is not its ugliness but the blurring of the line between inside and outside" (2009, 244). Žižek is reenforcing how the "abject," if treated under a (Lacanian) psychoanalytic uncanniness perspective, manages to render a deeper dive into the angst of the blurred lines between inside and outside (2009, 244).

For Žižek the intricacies of monstrosity concern the *realism of jouissance*, it combines modes of jouissance and the extimacy dimension. The ultimate incompatibility between myself and my own jouissance which is forever an extimate intruder (the monstrosity we persist to enjoy). But much more revealing is how one attempts to solve such a deadlock, the "projection of the core of its jouissance onto an Other, attributing to this Other full access to a consistent jouissance" (2009, 259). In this way, Žižek is mapping a crucial impasse concerning social bonds and identificatory traits, both of which are mixed into this mechanism of the subject (of the unconscious).

The distinction made here is that the abject and the subject relate to one another through *excessiveness*, the abject being on the side of "inside of a living object" while "creepiness" resides inside of subject. For Žižek, creepiness is "today's name for the Freudian 'uncanny'" (2009, 271). This excessive dimension of the extimate deadlock of the neighbour. And Žižek argues how the uncanny translates this extimate innermost aspect of the subject (of the unconscious), but monstrosity *is* the proper dimension of the impasses which creates. Instead of "substituting" the uncanny with creepiness, one could argue towards these uncanny features as a development from the Lacanian extimate:

"contradictory" situations where a subjective transformation could occur to the subject. Here creepiness does not preserve the Lacanian torsion (in a möbius strip) characteristic reserved to such dimension, it rather quickly (and perhaps unnecessarily) moralizes it. Another strategy to be put to work here, is to take Žižek's further investigation as a refinement of the Freudo-Lacanian uncanny. For example, sustaining the "Lacanian distinction between the object of desire and the object-cause of desire, that which sustains our desire for the object..." (2009, 272) where the uncanny surfaces

> when we perceive that the subject in front of us is doing what he is doing directly for the object-cause of desire, remaining indifferent towards the object of his desire – in short, when there occurs a kind of short circuit between the object and object-cause, the object directly becomes the object-cause.
>
> *(2009, 272)*

To assume the uncanny strictly as creepiness misses the short-circuit of the most radical depths: Žižek is far too generous here by reshaping the "creepiness" into the more meaningful dimension of the uncanny, his defence of the radical negativity stance and its impasses concerning spectral materialism under proper materialistic terms are the precise point.

For Žižek to make creepiness into a monstrous event, he would need to intervene by (de)moralizing it, by having to disambiguate from its more misleading approach, and defer to Freud and Lacan as having "consistently emphasized that perversion, far from being subversive, is the hidden obverse of power: every power needs perversion as its inherent transgression that sustains it" (2009, 273). This is especially since the proper subversive discourse lies within the hysterical position where "...the $ over a stands for the subject who is divided, traumatized, by what for an object she is for the Other, what role she plays in Other's desire" (2009, 273). In a way, Žižek articulates how the uncanny has the potential of furthering a crucial subversive[24] trait within symbolic reality itself by its distinct disturbance from the void of the $ like Antigone's "between two deaths."

3.7 Žižek on Antigone and the Lacanian "two deaths"

Lacan's investigates Sophocles' Antigone and being *between two deaths* as an ethical stance. And in "The Sublime Object of Ideology" (2008), Žižek discusses how such situations between two deaths are a privileged *topos* where death drive *meets* the symbolic order (Žižek 2008, p.145) (or, as one could defend, one of the pillars of the discussion of *monstrosity*). Žižek summarizes Lacan's approach to this connection (between death drive and the signifier) in three different moments of his teaching: (a) the Hegelian approach

> (Hegelian phenomenological idea that the word is a death, a murder of a thing: as soon as the reality is symbolized, caught in a symbolic network, the thing itself is more present in a word, in its concept, than in its immediate physical reality…)
>
> *(Žižek 2008, 145)*

where there is no way of an *immediate* return to reality, from word to thing; (b) the accent towards language

> (the accent is shifted from the word, speech, to language as a synchronic structure, a senseless autonomous mechanism which produces meaning as its effect… The death drive is now identified with the symbolic order itself: in Lacan's own words, it is 'nothing but a mask of the symbolic order'.)
>
> *(Žižek 2008, 145–146)*

where an opposition between the imaginary and meaning takes place; and finally, (c) where "the main accent of Lacan's teaching is put on the Real as impossible, the death drive again radically changes its signification. This change can be most easily detected through the relationship between the pleasure principle and the symbolic order" (Žižek 2008, 146). And Žižek reminds us, this had everything to do with Lacan's attempts at defining the ultimate psychoanalytic cure, but it brings forwards different accents towards this point between Symbolic and Real.

For Žižek, up until the 1950s Lacan considered the pleasure principle identified with the imaginary level, while the symbolic order was deemed as the realm "beyond the pleasure principle"(Žižek 2008, 146), but around the Seminar on *The Ethic of Psychoanalysis* (1959–60) there is a contrasting shift in Lacan's accent, where

> the symbolic order itself which is identified with the pleasure principle: the unconscious 'structured like a language', its 'primary process' of metonymicmetaphoric displacement, is governed by the pleasure principle; what lies beyond is not the symbolic order but a real kernel, a traumatic core.
>
> *(Žižek 2008, 146)*

This is how Lacan integrates Freud's terminology of "*das Ding*":

> the Thing as an incarnation of the impossible *jouissance* (the term Thing is to be taken here with all the connotations it possesses in the domain of horror science fiction: the 'alien' from the film of the same name is a presymbolic, maternal Thing par excellence).
>
> *(Žižek 2008, 146)*

Žižek is quite precise with Lacan when he underlines his tone to *jouissance*. Right at the first class of his seventh seminar (*L'Éthique* or The Ethics from 1959 to 1960), Lacan introduces general lines on the ethics of psychoanalysis engaging in a conversation with Angelo Louis Marie Hesnard about the *"l'univers morbide, dit-il, de la faute"* (Lacan 1992, 2) [1960] "the morbid universe [of transgression], he said, of 'fault'" ["blame"]. This brief passage translates an *uncanny* tone, which is furthered by Lacan at its monstrous dimension and signalling this shift of perspective addressed by Žižek. Certainly, the *morbid* aspect is a quintessential monstrous element which lurks behind the Sublimity and Ethics, and the key point of "between two deaths" debate argues for that. So, the dimension of the "morbid universe" is the proper dimension of monstrosity and a point which Žižek certainly notices in his analysis.

As Žižek continues, while the Symbolic order aims at a viable balance, at its kernel lies a "strange, traumatic "element which cannot be symbolized, integrated into the symbolic order – the Thing" (Žižek 2008, 147). Here is precisely where Lacan coins the neologism: l'extimite (external intimacy). And Žižek places a fundamental question to this point: what is death drive at this level (for Lacan)?

> Exactly the opposite of the symbolic order: the possibility of the 'second death', the radical annihilation of the symbolic texture through which so-called reality is constituted. The very existence of the symbolic order implies a possibility of its radical effacement, of 'symbolic death' - not the death of the so-called 'real object' in its symbol, but the obliteration of the signifying network itself.
>
> *(Žižek 2008, 147)*

Žižek's interpretation of this shift in Lacan's psychoanalysis concerns death drive and the ethics of desire. It becomes clear that such an operation introduced by Lacan, realizing the shift of emphasis from the symbolic to the Real, provides all sorts of debates about what does "knowledge in the Real" means (Žižek 2008, 148). The idea of Antigone as an agent of death drive, unconditionally persisting, sustaining the demand for a symbolic ritual, a symbolization that does not compromise or does not satisfy with half-measures, is the pinnacle of Lacan's formulation of drive or as Žižek summarizes, "the subject unconditionally insisting on a symbolic demand" (Žižek 2016b, xv). And this is where being *between two deaths* finally meets its proper monstrous dimension:

> The problem with Antigone is not the suicidal purity of her death drive but – quite the opposite – that the monstrosity of her act is covered up by its aestheticization: the moment she is excluded from the community of

> humans, she turns into a sublime apparition evoking our sympathy by complaining about her plight.
>
> *(Žižek 2016b, xv–xvii)*

Here, the pair Sublime–Beauty meets the Monstrous dimension of her ethical stance in its tragic configuration. And as Žižek reminds us, it is because of monstrosity that Lacan chooses yet another heroine to build his argument further, the analyst finds in Paul Claudel's *L'otage*, the character of Sygne de Coûfontaine with her repeated tic

> that momentarily disfigures her face. This feature which spoils the harmony of her beautiful face, the detail that sticks out and makes it ugly, is the material trace of her resistance to being co-opted into the universe of symbolic debt and guilt.
>
> *(Žižek 2016b, xvi)*

This "hysteric twitch of the lips" is a grimace which disturbs the unity of her face (Žižek 2016b, xv).

The Slovenian thinker, after a brief engagement with the Sublime Beauty of Antigone and Sygne, delineated the proper dimension of monstrosity following the footsteps of Lacan's Seminar *The Ethics of Psychoanalysis* (1992) and Žižek moves on to engaging with Christianity, basically addressing how the dying Christ is, actually, on to the side of Sygne and not on the side of Antigone: "Christ on the cross is not a sublime apparition but an embarrassing monstrosity" (2016b, xvi). But most importantly is Žižek separation between Antigone and Sygne:

> Antigone is thus to be opposed to Claudel's Sygne de Coufontaine: if Oedipus and Antigone are the exemplary cases of Ancient tragedy, Sygne stands for the Christian tragedy. Sygne lives in the modern world where God is dead: there is no objective Fate, our fate is our own choice, we are fully responsible for it.
>
> *(Žižek 2016b, xvi)*

For Sygne, there is no external pressures, only her innermost freedom and her pursuing love all the way to the end, sacrificing her "ethical substance, for God, for His pure Otherness" (Žižek 2016b, xvi); when Sygne is deprived of any ethical substance or of any remaining respect, there is no Fate for her to blame for, as Žižek explains (Žižek 2016b, xvi). It is under this scope that Sygne's tragedy is far more radical than that of Oedipus or Antigone. Žižek raises Sygne's figure of monstrosity as similar to Christ's, denoting her gesture of defiance and where no love is possible, as radical abandonment as its utmost possibility.

Although Žižek follows Lacan's steps to build up Antigone's demonic/ uncanniness (Žižek 2016b, xx), he also finds that it is not necessary to rely on European modernity to do so. Already in the Ancient Greek universe, Žižek finds in Sophocles' Electra another example of a "more human, full of empathy but also of pragmatic conformism" (Žižek 2016b, xviii) and which the living dead dimension is perfectly portrayed. But still, Antigone is the defying figure *par excellence* as defends Žižek and especially because of her uncanny monstrosity:

> ...her defying act expresses a stance of de-measured excessive insistence which disturbs the 'beautiful order' of the city; her unconditional ethics violates the harmony of the polis and is as such 'beyond human boundary'. The irony is that, while Antigone presents herself as the guardian of the immemorial laws which sustain human order, she acts as a freakish and ruthless abomination; there definitely is something cold and monstrous about her, as is rendered by the contrast between her and her warmly human sister Ismene. This uncanny dimension is signalled by the ambiguity in the name 'Antigone': it can be read as 'unbending', coming from 'anti-' and '-gon/-gony' (corner, bend, angle), but also as 'opposed to motherhood' or 'in place of a mother' from the root 'gone', 'that which generates' ('gonos', '-gony', as in 'theogony')."
>
> *(Žižek 2016b, xx–xxi)*

The monstrous contours are a key insight concerning experiences deriving from the Real, which cannot be completely captured by the Symbolic, resisting to be symbolized at all costs and monstrosity is the name of the realm which such elements of (pure) negativity pertain to. The uncanny (under Žižek's treatment) denounce the emissaries of the Real (in its *murmurs* or its *encounters*) implicating in a certain dialectical logics of its (im)possible topology, along the lines of Žižek's speculative endeavours on the "minimal gap" (2016b, 244) deriving from *between the two deaths* (2008, 144) and having radical implications concerning what does it mean to approach "knowledge in the Real" (2008, 145). To deal with this realm concerns facing the crucial implications of radical alterity as what really matters (or at least, what should matter...) and to be attentive to this dimension, means that it must be able to *hear it*, so that is recognized, remembered (symbolized) and transformed.

3.8 The ontological contours of monstrosity under Žižek: the living-dead logic

Žižek addresses the (non)relation established between the subject and the object through a topological torsion around a void (the realm of *monstrosity* as the core of our inhumanity that negatively makes us "human"). Or as Žižek summarizes: "…the Kantian break toward this new dimension is with regard to the changed status of the notion of the "inhuman" (2006, 21). The Kantian transcendental turn is not an easy "way out" from negativity, but an affirmation of negativity "as such." Žižek explains how Kant defines a new dimension behind the notion of the "inhuman" through the distinction between *negative* and *indefinite* judgements:

> the positive judgment "the soul is mortal" can be negated in two ways: when a predicate is denied to the subject ("the soul is not mortal"), and when a non-predicate is affirmed ("the soul is non-mortal")—the difference is exactly the same as the one, known to every reader of Stephen King, between "he is not dead" and "he is un-dead. The indefinite judgment opens up a third domain which undermines the underlying distinction: the "undead" are neither alive nor dead, they are precisely the monstrous "living dead." And the same goes for "inhuman": "he is not human" is not the same as "he is inhuman"—"he is not human" means simply that he is external to humanity, animal or divine, while "he is inhuman" means something completely different: the fact that he is neither human nor inhuman, but marked by a terrifying excess which, although it negates what we understand as "humanity," in inherent to being-human.
>
> *(2006, 21–22)*

This logical procedure operated by Kant at the face of antinomic stances sets a negative ontological route to the subject. One of the cultural figures that best illustrates monstrosity at this level are the zombies, since these uncanny creatures negate positive judgements in a different manner. The negative potency of the "undead" as the monstrous "living dead" responds to the binary stance of being either dead *or* alive indicating an alternative towards something else. Zombies integrate a terrifying excess which negates the possibility of assuming an understanding of "humanity" or being-human. The *indefinite judgement* is the driving logic behind this new realm of (dis)orientation of the (in)human condition.

The passage from Kant to Hegel concerns transformative perspectives, the parallax view which logically explains the dialectical transformation propelled by negativity. One could affirm how Žižek formulates his notion of parallax through monstrosity (as refinements of pure negativity). The shift from Kant to Hegel not in terms of an "overcoming" of the Kantian abyssal devisal, but as an "assertion" of it "as such" (2006, 28). This means giving up the need for its "overcoming" placing a "reconciliation" of opposites to gain insight—through a purely formal parallax shift— into how positing the distinction "as such" already *is* the looked-for "reconciliation" (2006, 28). For Žižek, this has nothing to do with Kant's inability of facing the Infinite, but quite the contrary, the key issue about Kant's philosophy is that "*he already has what he was looking for*" in his "very search for a transcendent domain beyond the realm of finite oppositions" (2006, 28). And Hegel's "triad" is a reversal to this very own point. The possibility of asserting a different realm derived from the distinction between negative and infinite judgements (2006, 21), propels Žižek to approach Kant's position of sustaining antinomies (and sticking behind them), that is, his transcendental turn through a *parallax* (which is a Hegelian inspired operation), not neglecting Kant's antinomic position, but assuming this negative potency of the Thing in itself (as such) without forcing a "dialectical synthesis." Therefore, monstrosity is the realm disputed between Kant and Hegel, where the (non)relation with the Real takes place.

Žižek engages with monstrosity (investigating the "pre"-ontological stances of Kant's project) and Kant's transcendental turn, re-framing the question of the subject and the Real. Žižek introduces the theme of the "Night" (debated by German Idealism, especially under Hegel) as the proper background of the Real to the subject, suggesting a dialectical materialist approach. In a way, Žižek's philosophy, ponder upon strategies to handle impasses deriving from such emissaries of the Real and enacts a possibility to (re)approach monstrosity under its proper negativity. Instead of a mystical approach or some naïve spirituality (disguised as materialism), Žižek establishes a critique of spectral materialism (which should be approached under true materialist terms) (2009, 90). Monstrosity is a core investigation concerning (non)relations between the subject (of the unconscious) with the Real through language. The contours of monstrosity provided by Žižek are fruitful philosophical foundations to investigate ontological incompleteness under dialectical materialism.

Notes

1 As Kant (2007) distinguishes:

> A transcendental principle is one through which we represent *a priori* the universal condition under which alone things can become objects of our cognition generally. A principle, on the other hand, is called metaphysical, where it represents *a priori* the condition under which alone objects whose concept has to be given empirically, may become further determined *a priori.*
>
> (2007, 16–17)

As Kant defines:

> ...the meaning of 'an end' in transcendental terms (i.e. without presupposing anything empirical, such as the feeling of pleasure). An end is the object of a concept so far as this concept is regarded as the cause of the object (the real ground of its possibility); and the causality of a *concept* in respect of its *object* is purposiveness (*forma finalis*).
>
> (2007, 51)

2 The thinker explains how for Kant:

> the full emotions effect from the magnitude of the pyramids must neither get too close to them nor stay too far away. For if one stays too far away, then the parts

(the stones of which they are built) are presented only obscurely, and hence their presentation has no effect on the subject's aesthetic judgment; and if one gets too close, the eye needs some time to complete the apprehension from the base to the peak, but during that time some of the earlier parts invariably fade from the imagination before it has apprehended the later ones, and hence comprehension is never complete. The spectator, Kant proceeds, has the feeling that his imagination is inadequate for exhibiting the idea of a whole, a feeling in which imagination reaches its maximum, and as it strives to expand that maximum, it sinks back into itself, but consequently comes to feel a liking that amounts to an emotion.

(Kant 2007 [1987], 108–109; Zupančič 1992, 64–65)

3 Hegel's influence is easily noticed in Germany, France and England philosophical developments. A good example is Alexander Kojève's introduction of Hegel's *Phenomenology of Spirit* in France. Prior to Kojève's efforts, Hegel was deemed as a troubling philosopher in an overwhelming neo-Kantian scenario of France until 1931 and after his efforts to take this work seriously, Hegel's philosophy gained a different attention and provoked re-configuration of the Kantian trend. Amongst the many visitors to Kojève's lectures, we can place: Jacques Lacan, George Bataille, Jean Hyppolite, Raymond Aron, Maurice Merleau-Ponty and even Jean Paul Sartre on a few occasions. But shortly after this reconnection with Hegel's philosophy, the field was met with a blunt anti-Hegelianism, presented by: Derrida, Lyortard, Deleuze and Foucault (to a certain extent) who questioned negativity of the subject as an obligatory reconnection with the Universal (Safatle 2006).

4 Žižek's key point is that Hegel should be read through Hegel's own thoughts and ideas. Thus, it is more suitable to short-circuit Hegel's philosophy with Hegel's writings – making it open enough to current vicissitudes – instead of persisting with a dead Hegel, fixed and trapped into a domesticated normative perspective, which might look academically refined but ineffective in real life.

5 This can be found in Žižek's early works, like "The Sublime Object of Ideology" [1989] and "For they do not know what they do" [1991].

6 Well, the Hegelian perspective of the "night of the world" appears in a few of his works, it informs of what is yet still under dispute, the proper (revolutionary and *negative stance*) as a pre-ontological site where determinations aren't yet fixed or placed under no clarity of definition (as seen in Hegel's Philosophy of Right, for example). It is certainly not like Hegel stops at *indetermination* as such, he indeed seeks out towards determination (nonetheless, the implication of understanding negativity under more Žižekean terms) permits a more interesting perspective even from what one could find in Hegel's Philosophy of History, for example. As Hegel (1977) [1805–6] in *Jenaer Realphilosophie* claims:

> The human being is this night, this empty nothing, that contains everything in its simplicity—an unending wealth of many representations, images, of which none belongs to him—or which are not present. This night, the interior of nature, that exists here—pure self—in phantasmagorical representations, is night all around it, in which here shoots a bloody head—there another white ghastly apparition, suddenly here before it, and just so disappears. One catches sight of this night when one looks human beings in the eye—into a night that becomes awful.
>
> (Hegel 1977, 204; quoted in Verene 1985, 7–8)

This is a core passage in Žižek's work, placing the night of the world as a radical indeterminacy which can be conditioned and frame *as* disputable (im)possibility.

7 The trouble about this very own point, in a Kant *avec* Sade fashion (as prescribed by Lacan) were rigorously discussed by Zupančič and were already introduced earlier (2000, 57).

8 Žižek defines the Fichtean *Anstoss* as follows:

> The *Anstoss*, the primordial impulse that sets in motion the gradual self-limitation and self-determination of the initially void subject, is not merely a mechanical external impulse; it also indicates another subject who, in the abyss of its freedom, functions as the challenge *[Aufforderung]* compelling me to limit/specify my freedom, that is, to accomplish the passage from abstract egotist freedom to concrete freedom within the rational ethical universe – perhaps this intersubjective *Aufforderung* is not merely the secondary specification of the *Anstoss*, but its exemplary original case.
>
> (Žižek 2000, 44)

9 Žižek's "*Why is Lacan not a Heiddegerian?*" (2016a) was translated and published to Portuguese in the Brazilian edition of *The Ticklish Subject* [1999].

10 Sergei Konstantinovitch Pankejeff was Freud's analysand and his pseudonym, "The Wolf Man" derives from a dream he had about a tree full of wolves.

11 Hegel's passage investigated by Žižek is the following:

> Cannot the subject bring about this reconciliation by itself, through its own efforts, its own activity—so that through its piety and devotion it makes its inner [life] conform with the divine idea, and express this conformity through its deeds? And further, is this not within the capability [not merely] of a single subject but of all people who genuinely wish to take up the divine law within themselves, so that heaven would exist on earth and the Spirit would be present in reality and dwell in its community?.
>
> (Žižek 2009, 73)

12 Žižek summarizes Hegel's dialectics of positing and presupposing as follows:

> if the subject were to be able to do it on its own, through its own agency, then it would have been something merely *posited* by it—however, positing is in itself always one-sided, relying on some presupposition: 'The unity of subjectivity and objectivity—this divine unity—must be a presupposition for my positing'.
>
> (Žižek 2009, 73)

13 As Žižek further claims:

> This is why the difference between Substance and Subject has to reflect/inscribe itself into subjectivity itself as the irreducible gap that separates human subjects from Christ, the "more than human" monstrous subject. This necessity of Christ, the "absolute" subject which adds itself to the series of finite human subjects as the supplementary *a* ($+ $ + $ + $ + $... + *a*), is what differentiates the Hegelian position from the young Marx–Feuerbachian position of the big Other as the virtual Substance posited by collective subjectivity, as its alienated expression.
>
> (Žižek 2009, 75)

14 For example, in a few times where Žižek debates an Antigone-like monstrous/ethical gestures enacting such ruptures, like in "Greta Thunberg is no genius – she's an apostle". See more in: https://spectator.us/topic/greta-thunberg-genius-apostle/.

15 It is also the radical excessiveness of the fantasy of an Event – this is where the jouissance (and anxiety of fright) are located.

16 The Real certainly chooses, whether we like it or not, which in a way is what makes an Event to be evental; the undecidability and a certain (non)contingent "relation."

17 As Žižek explains, disparity is a concept designed to discuss the disruptive effects of Kraken's monstruous tentacles in three main domains: ontological, aesthetic and theologico-political (Žižek 2016b, 16–17).

18 As Herman Parret (2009) argues concerning the monstrous and the colossal:

> If the colossal can already be considered a sublime correlate, then it remains certainly inside an acceptable limit; with the monstrous, on the other hand, one has passed beyond the acceptable limit, in full terror and total unpleasure. With the monstrous we are in the margin of the acceptable where the imagination is fully blocked to function. It looks as if the monstrous is the Thing, inexpressible and abyssal. The monstrous does violence to subjectivity without submitting it to any legality.
>
> Herman Parret, 'The Ugly as the Beyond of the Sublime', 4, http://www.hermanparret.be/media/articles-in-print/21_The-Ugly-as-the-Beyond.pdf.

19 Paraphrasing the passage from Parret investigated by Žižek, we understand it concerns the passing from the disgust for the object towards a certain "enjoyment" [Genuss] at the level of sensations, accomplishing a distance between subject and its purposiveness. While pleasure [Lust] is understood in opposition to "enjoyment" in terms of "'pleasure is culture' [wo die Lust zugleich Kultur ist]". Thus, "enjoyment" provokes disgust. And Parret notices how such "enjoyment of losing oneself in the matter of 'charms and emotions'" directly impacts the body: such enjoyment causes disgust and provokes corporeal reactions such as "nausea, vomiting and convulsions. Pleasure/unpleasure [Lust/Unlust] in the feeling of the sublime has nothing to do with that 'enjoyment' [Genuss] destructive of culture and generative of disgust."

20 As Žižek explains the Hegelian dialectics of abstraction: the proper notion of abstraction under dialectical terms, which allows to conceive Hegel's "concrete universality" infinite lies in the fact that it includes "abstractions" in concrete reality itself, as their immanent constituents. And that the proper philosophical attitude towards abstraction means to avoid the popular empiricist notion of abstraction. Following Žižek, proper philosophical thinking starts from the awareness of "how *such a process of 'abstraction' is inherent to reality itself*: the tension between empirical reality and its 'abstract' notional determinations is immanent to reality, it is a feature of 'things themselves'" (Žižek 2009, 74). From this understanding, a certain anti-nominalist attitude in philosophical thinking develops, one of the examples being Marx's insight that "the abstraction of the value of a commodity is its objective constituent…" (Žižek 2009, 75). Such distinction is a foundation to distinguish between the "true infinity" from the "spurious (or bad) infinity." Following Žižek, while the bad infinity is

> the asymptotic process of discovering newer and newer layers of reality – reality is posited here as the In-itself which can never be fully grasped, only gradually approached, i.e. all we can do is to discern particular 'abstract' features of the transcendent/inaccessible wealth and fullness of the 'real thing'. The movement of 'true infinity' is exactly the opposite one: one includes the process of 'abstraction' into the 'thing itself'.
>
> (Žižek 2009, 74–75)

The idea behind this point is how dialectics must acknowledge how *such a process of "abstraction" is inherent to reality itself* and this is at stake concerning monstrosity in the face of true infinity.

21 Kristeva's abject concerns the human reaction (horror, vomit, blood and wounds) to a symbolic rupture of meaning provoked by the loss of the distinction between subject and object or between self and other. In short, it concerns radically excluded "objects."

22 See more in: Lacan's 'The Subversion of the Subject and the Dialectic of Desire in the Freudian Unconscious' (2006, 671).

23 The Greek term for morbid: "*νοσηρός*" (preoccupied with death) or its derivation (*ιατρικό*) "*νοσογόνος*" (related to disease) share a common root: "*νοσηρή περιέργεια*," translated as "*macabre or obsessive interest in, also roughly translated as curiosity*" (Pring 2001). So, the preoccupation with death and disease presents itself as a (un) human trait which surfaces when questions of "transgression" take place, nonetheless, this must be approached under its proper background, namely: death drive and the symbolic.

24 Žižek illustrates this point with one of Rembrandt's paintings:

> Another aspect of this monstrosity was clearly perceived by Rembrandt, whose 'Lazarus', one of the most traumatic classic paintings, is a depiction of Christ at the moment he is raising Lazarus from the dead. What strikes the eye is not only the figure of Lazarus, a monstrous living dead returning to life, but, even more so, the terrified expression on Christ's face, as if he is a magician shocked that his spell really worked, disgusted by what he brought back to life, aware that he is playing with forces better left alone.
>
> (Žižek 2016b, xvi)

References

Badiou, Alain. 2009. [1982] *Theory of the Subject*. London: Continuum.

Badiou, Alain. 2012. *The Adventure of French Philosophy*. London: Verso Books.

Buck-Morss, Susan. (2009) *Hegel, Haiti, and Universal History*. Pittsburgh: University of Pittsburgh Press.

Capobianco R. (1995) Lacan and Heidegger: The Ethics of Desire and the Ethics of Authenticity. In *From Phenomenology to Thought, Errancy, and Desire. Phaenomenologica (Collection Fondée par H.L. van Breda et Publiée Sous le Patronage des Centres d'Archives-Husserl)*, edited by B. E. Babich, Vol. 133. Springer, Dordrecht.

Dolar, Mladen. Substance is Subject. Filmed December 4th, 2018, in European University – St. Petersburg. https://www.youtube.com/watch?v=UBlOABhRglo

Fugate, Courtney. Kant and Leibniz on Negative Magnitudes. *Estudos Kantianos*, Marília, Vol. 4, No. 2, 149–168, 2016.

Hegel, Georg Wilhelm Friedrich. 1807 [1977]. *Phenomenology of Spirit*, translated by A. V. Miller, edited by J. N. Findlay, Oxford: Clarendon Press, 1977.

Houlgate, Stephen. *Freedom, Truth and History: An Introduction to Hegel's Philosophy*. New York: Routledge, 1991.

Kant, Immanuel. *Critique of Judgement*. 1790. London: Oxford University Press, 2007.

Lebrun, Gérard. *Envers de la dialectique (L'): Hegel à la lumière de Nietzsche*. Paris: Seuil, 2004.

Lacan, Jacques. *Écrits*. New York: W.W Norton & Company, 2006.

Lacan, Jacques. *The Ethics of Psychoanalysis: The Seminar of Jacques Lacan, Book VII. 1959–60*. New York: W. W. Norton & Company, 1992.

Moder, Gregor. *Hegel and Spinoza: Substance and Negativity*. Illinois: Northwestern University Press, 2017.

Pring. *Oxford Dictionary Greek* - English. London: Oxford University Press, 2001.

Richardson, William J. Heidegger and Psychoanalysis?. *Natureza Humana*, Vol. 5, No. 1, 9–38, 2003. http://pepsic.bvsalud.org/scielo.php?script=sci_arttext&pid=S1517-24302003000100001&lng=pt&tlng=en

Safatle, Vladimir. *A paixão do negativo: Lacan e a dialética*. São Paulo: Unesp, 2006.

Žižek, Slavoj. *Absolute Recoil: Towards a New Foundation of Dialectical Materialism*. London: Verso Books, 2014.

Žižek, Slavoj. *Antigone*. London: Bloomsbury, 2016a.

Žižek, Slavoj. *Disparities*. London: Bloomsbury, 2016b.

Žižek, Slavoj. In Defense of Hegel's Madness. *Filozofija I Društvo*, Vol. XXVI, No. 4, 2015. https://doi.org/10.2298/FID1504785Z, http://www.doiserbia.nb.rs/img/doi/0353-5738/2015/0353-57381504785Z.pdf?fbclid=IwAR0LwAkQchMzv7t03kSmZnY_OXtlX7Rwn45Bsp0P_2VsrrTpbXvtFJmAQ5

Žižek, Slavoj. *Less than Nothing: Hegel and the Shadow of Dialectical Materialism*. London: Verso Books, 2012.

Žižek, Slavoj. *Looking Awry - An Introduction to Jacques Lacan through Popular Culture*. London: MIT Press, 1992.

Žižek, Slavoj. *Parallax View*. Cambridge, MA: Mit Press, 2006.

Žižek, Slavoj. *The Sublime Object of Ideology*. London: VersoBooks, 2008.

Žižek, Slavoj. *The Monstrosity of Christ*. Cambridge, MA: Mit Press, 2009.

Žižek, Slavoj. *The Sublime Object of Ideology*. London: VersoBooks, 1989.

Žižek, Slavoj. *The Ticklish Subject*. London: VersoBooks, 2000.

Zupančič, Alenka. The Logic of the Sublime. *The American Journal of Semiotics*, Vol. 9, No. 2–3, 51–68, 1992.

Zupančič, Alenka. Reversals of Nothing: The Case of the Sneezing Corpse. *Filozofski vestnik*, Vol. XXVI, No. 2, 173–186, 2005.

Zupančič, Alenka. *What Is Sex?* Cambridge, MA: Mit Press, 2017.

4

MONSTROSITY AND IMPASSES OF FETISHISM

A Marxist approach (or, a debate towards "monstrous materialism")

4.1 The insidious invisibility of global capitalism and the hauntings impasses of capitalist commodity exchange and troubles in abstraction

Monstrosity has transformed immensely over time and an incursion into its depths has revealed it as a proper *topos*. The following chapter aims at illustrating another important feature concerning monstrosity, one which seems to have travelled through "history," but which requires further examination, the material productive forces and the modes of exchange of commodities over time, the monstrous as an implication of global capitalism.

The philosophical problem of *ontological inconsistency* gains different contours under the scope of *monstrosity*. The classic subject–object gains another dialectical perspective once we consider monstrosity, explaining subjective suffering to contemporary modes of exploitation. The premise behind this chapter is to appreciate how the persistence of "monstrous" ideas has something to do with "those invisible maneuvers of capitalism" and moreover, how the proper dimension of this invisibility does have something to do with the persistence of sustaining capitalism as the only viable force, as the only alternative, maintain its contradiction at the cost of human lives and the brutalization of those who endure it. What I am referring to here is that there is a precise material point behind monstrosity, which does not only rest at the imaginary realm and as figments of our imaginations. This invisible visibility of monstrosity also presents a point of not only idealistic tension but also tension emanating from the conceived limits (and perhaps, also of its ways out of impasses, ways to "traverse" them). Only through this more dedicated perspective does the meaning of the "spectral materiality" earn its proper relevance as a character

DOI: 10.4324/9781003437543-5

of the monstrous, which instead of becoming a (re)incantation of "reality" gains its "monstrous materialism" *topos* (as I would like to call).

This chapter will attempt at appreciating under a Marxist perspective, the appreciation of Marx's *bestiary* and tries to present how "monstrosity" under capitalism gains a much more interesting perspective – not because it suffices with Gothic materialism, to which Mark Fisher advocates, but because with a proper materialistic approach monstrosity has the possibility of presenting further insightful proposition to some of its impasses – and fundamentally, this chapter tries to debate the relevance of this line of argumentation. This literary aspect of Marx is not usually appreciated and certainly there is a scarcity of studies on this regard, nonetheless *this is not the point of this chapter* (or of this thesis for that matter), inviting Fredric Jameson's notion of figuration (which comes from one of his interpretation on Marx), as well as the approach of animism via Karatani's philosophy (2014), the idea is to engage with the role of exchange as the proper indication of a "monstrous materialism" in order to fully express how the thesis of monstrosity can be a fruitful and interesting point of injunction to be ponder upon.

One main inspiration for this chapter derives from Susan Buck-Morss' (2009) work. Her Hegelian reading of Haiti and the Universal History approaches the dialectics of lordship and bondage through the *Phenomenology of Spirit* and the *Jena texts* (2009, 52) in order to present the political *and* economic terms between the master and the slave (2009, 53). However, while developing her argument, the philosopher makes a very fascinating footnote, in which she illustrates a very interesting usage of monstrous [*ungeheueres*] from Hegel. Buck-Morss offers a very tempting strategy of investigating the monstrous, she finds a "turning point" in Hegel's reading of Adam Smith, present in the *Jena Systementwürfe* (1803–4), while debating the "battle for recognition" that breaks with the concept of ethical community (*Sittlichkeit*) and a Hobbesian notion of individual self-preservation (2009, 52). Following Buck-Morss' investigation, at the end of Hegel's discussion (in the "fragment 22"), he addresses the "'absolute necessity' of 'mutual recognition' injury to property must be avenged 'to the point of death'" (2009, 52). How the property-owing head of the family turns into a "slave of the other" [*er word der Sklav des andern*] when he risks a wound instead of life itself (and Buck-Morss emphasizes how Hegel uses two terms *Knecht and Sklav*, establishing a dialectic of mutual recognition. But Buck-Morss raises the fundamental question under Hegelian terms:

> ...what if the "property" is itself the injurer, the slave who rectifies the injury to *his person* by asserting his own freedom without compensation? Hegel does not raise this question but moves, rather, to a discussion of the "customs" of "the people" (*das Volk*) and the common "work" of all. This takes him in a strikingly non-Hobbesean direction, to a critique of the stunting

and repetitive work of modern manufactory labour (the division of labor, exemplified by Smith's pin manufactory); see Hegel, *Jena Systementwürfe I*, 227–228. Hegel then critically describes the uncontrolled and "blind" interdependence of laborers in the global economy, the "bürgerliche Gesellschaft" of market exchanges that forms a "monstrous system" (*ungeheueres System*) of mutual "dependency" (*Abhangigkeit*) and that "like a wild beast needs to be tamed" (*Jena Systementwürfe I, 229, 230)*. Fragment 22 ends (in 1804!) just at the point where Hegel's discussion of "possession" (*Besitz*), as the form in which the generality of "the thing" (das Ding) is "recognized" (*anerkannt*), would have led him to confront the contradiction that the law of private property treats the slave (whose existence is nothing but to labor) as a thing! The slave is the one commodity like no other, as freedom of property and freedom of person are here in direct contradiction. Is it for this reason that Hegel's manuscript breaks off suddenly? The revolt of the slaves in Saint-Domingue, in this context, saved Hegel from the bad infinity (the "monstrous system") of contrast reciprocity by providing the link (via a shift in emphasis from exchange to labor) from an economic system (the infinite system of needs) to politics the founding, through a struggle unto death, of the constitutional state.

(2009, 52–53)

This direction seems to present a very crucial perspective concerning the monstrosity of capitalism that is obvious in Hegel's understanding here. What Buck-Morss highlights is how obvious this becomes and the implications of the monstrosity in persisting reciprocity leads all the way towards a fundamental contradiction, not only to the one's suffering through the capitalist system, but to all those subjected to it in order to persist within it. Hegel was attentive of monstrosity at the level of the capitalist system itself. But the proper monstrous element becomes obvious with Zupančič's (2017) examination on how the truly political lesson of psychoanalysis can be a powerful in order to elaborate on the contradictory stances of capitalism. For her, power *first* appropriates negativity of the symbolic order, its fundamental non-relation and turns it into a narrative of Relation (relations of domination are sustained through this procedure, as she claims). But concrete exploitation, according with Zupančič, concerns the "privatization of the negative" (Zupančič's 2017, 31).

Zupančič argues how capitalism starts off from two revolutionary ideas: "'the economic Relation does not exist' and 'the non-relation could be very profitable'" (Zupančič's 2017, 31). The first one concerns Adam Smith's (the 18th-century economist) who was led by the cynical affirmation, which provokes questions towards the previous "mercantile" doctrine and a belief system which it sustained. As the Slovene philosopher explains, the "mercantile" doctrine paints the picture of a "closed" totality in which a nation only increases its wealth at the expense of another nation, to have more means to take it from somewhere, establishing a relationship of subordination. But the new economic perspective deriving from the Industrial Revolution, as Zupančič argues, is that world's wealth can also increase on its own, "by itself" through a new organization of labour (Zupančič's 2017, 31).

Zupančič is presenting these general points to highlight this specific shift. The first remark presented by her, concerning that "the economic Relation does not exist" and how this mentality of the "closed" totality which the relation sustains a visibility of the difference (in wealth), is the fundamental point of the *monstrous system* which Hegel has pondered upon; and the shift towards the second remark as defended by Zupančič concerns the point of "contradiction" with which Buck-Morss has addressed as a point of disruption in Hegel's writings. This is speculative; however, it seems like a formidable clue to consider the effects of *this* monstrosity and its subsequent consequences. And as Zupančič clarifies this contradictory stance, it concerns the profitability of the non-relation (Zupančič's 2017, 31) which is the key discovery of capitalism and from this came the "narrative of a new, higher Relation, the foundational myth of modern capitalism, known as "the invisible hand of the market" (Zupančič's 2017, 32).[1] Zupančič introduces how Smith's idea of "capital" also furthers itself towards other levels of the social life.

Zupančič argues how Smith's argument falls short to fully capture what is really at stake: at first, it seems that at the core of the most individual enjoyment what can be found is the Other (which sustains a general welfare), but what can actually be found at the core of this Other is a further "masturbatory" self-enjoyment[2] (Zupančič's 2017, 32). Following her line of thinking, Adam Smith fails to apprehend "the dimension of the Other" (Zupančič's 2017, 32) which operates in the selfish pursuit of individual interests, since "we never do just what we think we are doing and what we intend to do" (Zupančič's 2017, 32). Thus, there is a crucial aspect of how the monstrous dimension, which is here being addressed, which is certainly an excessive dimension. This excess requires Hegelian-Lacanian lenses to be fully understood.

Following Zupančič's argument, Adam Smith sustains the idea of forcing "the non-relation work for everybody's profit" (Zupančič's 2017, 32). Even if wealth has increased in absolute (not only relative) terms since the 18th century, what the thinker denotes is how the price of modern economic "higher Relation" is exponential disparity between the rich and the poor "fed by non-relation in its 'higher' form" (Zupančič's 2017, 32–33). Indeed, productivity and profitability reached new highs, but the disparity of wealth between the rich and the poor has only intensified (which is where the price of productivity and profitability has been paid); this disparity is necessary for capitalism, and this will never change in any capitalist society.

Capitalists explore the negativity of the economic system to work primarily for their benefit. In a way, here lies a crucial impact of the bestiality of capital, which Hegel has spoken of (as Buck-Morss previously exposed): this monstrous system of capital's productivity, concerns the paradoxical redoubling of "the point of structural negativity and its appropriation as the locus of the market's "miraculous" productivity" (Zupančič, 33). At the preface of *Capital*, Marx makes this point quite clear: "...in the analysis of economic forms neither microscopes nor chemical reagents are of assistance. The power of abstraction must replace both" ([1867] 1982, 90).[3] Thus, from a Marxist standpoint, the proletariat under capitalism is the "Worker which doesn't exist" (Zupančič's 2017, 334), if it would exist, it would be the monstrous incarnation to what Hegel's defined at the heart of the monstrous system, the proper topos of monstrosity. This is what Zupančič explains about the proletariat not as *one* of the social classes, but a monstrous point of concrete constitutive negativity (Zupančič's 2017, 34).

For Kojin Karatani,[4] Marx's exploration of has called the "substance of the value of each commodity 'abstracted labor' or 'social labor'" (Karatani 2014, 85) and this concerns the precise operation Karatani posits a certain approximation of Marx's *Capital* to Hobbes' Leviathan. Yet, the remarkable Hegelian "monstrous" rendered by Adam Smith's theory, sets a very different "tone" to this "contract"... to take a closer look at this paradoxical redoubling, the efforts of the Marxist British economist, Ian Wright (2020a) about abstraction are crucial. Wright's essay *What is abstract labour, and who does the abstracting?* explains how "money" is a (in)human technology for representing "*numerical quantities*" and Marx's first chapter of *Capital* ([1867] 1982) is an attempt at dealing with the "meaning of money", as Wright explains:

> He [Marx] notes that the exchange of commodities in the market implies there's something equal, or equivalent, about them. For example, if I sell 20 yards of linen for 10 pounds, and then spend my 10 pounds on a new coat, then, indirectly, 20 yards of linen have been made equal to 1 coat by *the act of exchange*.[5]

The importance of denouncing this is that global market prices, although fluctuating, are not necessarily at random. If it was a matter of randomness, such equivalence would be accidental and there would be nothing to be said. The British economist, agreeing with Marx on equivalence, defends that there are exceptions, nonetheless, it is not usual that by selling a pen one would manage to buy a plane. This means that "during any period of time there are definite well-established market prices that determine the ratios in which commodities can exchange, that are equalised, with each other" (Wright 2020a).

In a way, Wright's examination of the "magic" of abstraction in capitalism, invites another look into "spectral materiality" and to the "magic" of commodity exchange. Marx himself deals with the "mystery of commodities" with its "magic and necromancy," as Wrights remembers. The first mystery explained by Wright is abstraction which is "exchange-value refers to a special, common property shared by all commodities – that of being the products of labour" (Wright 2020a). And "[t]he act of exchange abstracts from the individual peculiarities of different labouring activities, leaving something common to all of them" (Wright 2020a) (such commonality cannot be an specificity of any kind of labour, since there are heterogeneous forms, e.g., fishing caviar is different from writing advertising software and so on, says the British economist), which is directly connected with Marx's composition of the economic value of commodities and a certain "embodiment" at stake in this mechanism ([1867] 1982, 129).[6] In order to answer, "how to measure abstract labour?" Marx endeavours to question the magnitude of this value being measured (which is clear in the first chapters of *Capital*) as Marx explains:

> A use value, or useful article, therefore, has value only because human labour in the abstract has been embodied or materialised in it. How, then, is the magnitude of this value to be measured? Plainly, by the quantity of the value-creating substance, the labour, contained in the article. The quantity of labour, however, is measured by its duration, and labour time in its turn finds its standard in weeks, days, and hours.
>
> *([1867] 1982, 129)*

Following Wright's investigation, what Marx addresses here concerns a particular scale of time, but before starting calculating a correlation between time and work, Wright notices in Marx, how Marx does not offer or explain how one can measure quantities of abstract labour, or even less, can it be measured in duration? Wright's point is that "*we* don't measure abstract labour. *Something else measures it*" (Wright 2020a). The redoubling of infernal loops occurs here. For Wright, a "negative feedback control system" (Wright 2020a) takes place in a fully capitalist system,[7] where "profit-income *must* be reinvested in order to make more profit" (Wright 2020a).

The magical power of abstraction turned into a demonic power is the crux of *fetishism* of commodities argued by this section. The monstrosity established between the controller and the controlled, but does the controller (capital), evaluate different concrete activities across all its portfolio under the same rubric? No, "capital *wants* specific kinds of concrete activities, and does not want other kinds. The kinds of activities it wants are those that yield above-average profit. Capital is therefore controlling us. It controls how we spend our time" (Wright 2020a).

Capital has concrete labour under its control (the real labouring activity of the working population) and "*Maximising profit is identically the process of maximising the manifestation of abstract labour out of concrete labour*" (Wright 2020a), since Capital *creates* value through processes of abstraction, as Marx defends. For Wright, the "dialectical relationship between the form of value and its content" under capitalism creates a "negative feedback control system" by assuming that capital is a controller which employs, mediate[8] forms of value through money, consequently, it controls the content of value through labour time; it becomes clear how there is a forceful attempt to link the form and content, under regularities instantiated by generalized commodity production, as Wright explains. What this means is that capital assumed as a control system must have internal representations that "refer" to the world it acts within (Wright 2020a). This is why the British economist assumes that Marx's theory of value is "*fundamentally a theory of an alien cognition that controls us*." This is an interesting point, which explains why Marxists have been engaged with "invisibility" in its truest materialist fashion and also, why Marx's language in order to address and refine certain elements about capital *requires* to appeal to the *necromancy*[9] ([1867] 1982, 169), phantasmagories and monstrous elements.[10] Note how this formulation has *nothing* to do with figments of our imaginations, but on how their formation persist because its symbolic stance is alive, repeated and sustained on the everyday lives of labourers worldwide.

Following Wright, Marx needed a certain *necromancy* of commodity production in order to address a key aspect of "money" (which under the foreignness of capital) is because "only the religious, magical and occult traditions in our history have adequate concepts to express our predicament" (Wright 2020a). The "occult" figure which Wright advocates to translate such operation of capital is an "*egregore*" (Wright 2020a),[11] which translates the

> collective ritual activities of a group yet operates autonomously, according to its own internal logic, to materially influence and control the group's activities. The group creates the egregore, and the egregore creates the group, in a selfreinforcing feedback loop
>
> (*Wright 2020a*)

What makes him affirm how "*capital is an egregore*." As he goes on to explain:

> Not metaphorically, or ironically, but actually. Capital is a being, an autonomous entity, with primitive thoughts about us. Not only 'us' but how we ought to be ordered as a specific collective which serves the function of money – this is absolute concrete labour in praxis.
>
> In this way, money is a procedure for the subject (who has no choice) to serve. Money is what measures us, and how money commands us. Capital is an alien cognition that acts in the world to bind the form of value to its content.
>
> (*Wright 2020a*)

It is precisely at this point that the economist advocates for neither a naive materialism, nor subject idealism (which is a fundamental perspective in order to approach Marx's *necromancy* and ever further, a viable debate on monstrosity under true materialistic terms), and how under this standpoint, Marx's theory of value becomes realized.

It may sound cynical at first, but Wright's argumentation is solid. The idea of capital as an entity operating in reality is a monstrous idea, since capital can be considered a decentralized abstract operator which controls everything it touches and creates more abstractions in order to exist. What is the most material, under capitalism can also be the most monstrous in its dialectical terms. As Wright states, capital is an autonomous entity, with a "cognition" of its own and which is "alien" to anyone. Therefore, the

> abstract labour is *its* concept, not ours. But we can form a concept of abstract labour that corresponds to its concept of abstract labour. After all, we, the controlled, and it, the controller, all live in the same world. And we can both talk about, and represent, an objective property of it.
>
> (*Wright 2020a*)

The redoubling which capitalism produces, provides a materialist explanation to its "invisibility," it concerns value-form, which determines abstract labour and our lives in the process. This is how under the rule of capital, we "are reduced to shadows, mere narrow abstractions, of what we could be" (Wright 2020a). We are a mere ghostly fraction of ourselves. Following Wright's "Prolegomena to a demonology of capitalism" (Wright 2020b), he will argue that the animism[12] used to explain forces of nature that ruled us have migrated to explain capital. Although the material basis for animistic belief system was changed, religious and magical beliefs persist,[13] as Wright correctly denotes. Since there is no rational question to question: "who controls capitalism?" (Wright 2020b). There is an attempt to fill this gap with animistic magical thinking. This is why Marx's argument on "The fetishism of commodities and the secret thereof" is crucial. Marx explains how capitalism "may think of itself as a thoroughly modern, sensible and secular enterprise, but if we look more closely, we find fetish objects with mysterious powers, magical thinking, and everything ritualistically branded with strange numbers" (Wright 2020b). Marxist economics denounce the control of the "occult spirit".

This argument has nothing to do with nihilism, nor does it have anything to do with (re)enchanting reality; this argument does not sustain a naïve perspective of spectral materiality. Inspired by Marx, Wright argues towards an "animistic theory of modern capitalism" *in order to* "constitute scientific progress" (Wright 2020b). Certainly, Wright sustains the *gap* of negativity which does not conform form and content (Wright 2020a), but much deeper than that, it sustains the *gap* of the Hegelian Night of the World, it sustains the monstrosity which the German philosopher had found in Adam Smith in the first place as Buck-Morss addresses (2009, 52–53), Wright does not *ignore* this gap and defends this alternative against those who explore this gap, as Zupančič explains (2017, 33).

4.2 Fredric Jameson's notion of figuration

As previously addressed, a certain (truer) materialist perspective bets on debating modern capitalism benefiting from the perspective of "animistic theories," therefore advocating for approaching a grammar that is not *foreign* to capitalism itself (which is "the" foreign parasite) (Wright 2020b). The idea of "speaking a monstrous language" to address the monstrosity (of global capitalism) is a valid effort to examine the illusions (Pfaller, 2014) that govern us. In Fredric Jameson's "Representing Capital: A commentary on Volume One" (2014), he discussed the notion of *figuration* which helps to examine this monstrous approximation to Capital. As Jameson explains:

> ...[t]he process must then be imagined as a specific proto-narrative form, in which the transformation or recoding of a conceptual dilemma in a new and potentially more manageable way also results in the expansion of the object of study itself: the successive resolutions of the linked riddles or dilemmas lay in place the architecture of a whole construct or system, which is that of capital as such.
>
> *(2014, 12)*

So, Marx was concerned with the theorization of the entirety of the system, not finding quick fixes (2014, 13). Here, Jameson is focused to propose a literary alternative of reading to Capital, one which is not entirely philosophical nor economical and an alternative concerned with the question of representation:

> It is now around the question of representation that contemporary interrogations of truth must turn, as well as those concerning totality or the Real. The problem of representation today eats away at all the established disciplines like a virus, particularly destabilizing the dimension of language, reference and expression (which used to be the domain of literary study), as well as that of thought (which used to be that of philosophy). Nor is economics exempt, which posits invisible entities like finance capital on the one hand, and points to untheorizable singularities like derivatives on the other.
>
> *(2014, 15–16)*

Jameson locates at the problem of representation the key problem of contemporary confusion (2014, 17). He even adds that

> [m]aybe theology could have done a better job with capitalism, consisting as it is of a free play of categories in the void and an exercise of figuration without a referent: an interplay of the dialectics of the One and the Many, of subject and object, of the circumference whose center is everywhere and the *ens causa sui*.
>
> *(2014, 17)*

This is a similar posture adopted by the economist Ian Wright's approach to Capital, nonetheless, one must adapt Jameson's point here: it is not about religion (which is already structured faith) but positing an insightful *animist perspective* which can (re)articulate the symbolic restraints which are prerogative of global capitalist formations. So, what is Jameson's understanding on the impasse of representation? Jameson rescues how representation for Heidegger means the symptomatic consequence of modernity concerning the subject/object split (2014, 18) and how the Marxist tradition in "its critique of epistemology and the contemplative, its denunciation of onedimensionality and of reification more generally – would enrich this analysis with an identification of modernity and capitalism" (2014, 18). Jameson sustains his approach using a Freudian stance:

> I would therefore also wish to stress the relationship between representation and representability as we find it in Freud, where the unconscious construction of the dream scans the signifier for usable elements and building blocks, for the presentation/representation of desire and the drive. Freud's work thus presupposes two features: first, that any full or satisfactory representation of the drive is impossible (in that sense every form of desire is already a representation). And second, that we must always pay close attention in this process to representability, something which has to do on the one hand with the possibility in the drive of some minimal expression, even if as a mere symptom; and on the other with the material available for that expression (in Freud's case, the language and images of everyday life).
>
> *(2014, 19)*

The incommensurability of capitalism is what explains the inherent dialectical aspect of it, in the first place. When Hegel pondered upon Adam Smith's formulation and called it a "monstrosity" (Buck-Morss 2009, 52–53), perhaps this specific dialectic torsion was already at stake for the German philosopher. Jameson makes it clear, this is certainly the reason why representations are unsatisfying under capitalist ruling, these are always somewhat already infiltrated by its notional limitations having to chase their inherent impasses[14] and its incompatibility towards "reality" (mostly because of the inherent reaction to the gap of negativity of the Real, which requires procedures of disparities and parallaxes also at this level, as the text have been trying to sustain). Nonetheless, Jameson states that nihilistic resignation is not a proper alternative. Although capitalism is unrepresentable, this does not mean it is "ineffable and a kind of mystery beyond language or thought; but rather that one must redouble one's efforts to express the inexpressible in this respect" (2014, 22). The redoubling efforts required in order to express the inexpressible contradictions inherent to global capitalism, at least from the perspective which the present texts try to engage with, concerning how figuration helps to translated the monstrous *topos* which represent inherent symptomatic contradictions of capitalism.

In a way, the necessity towards a monstrous grammar, is an effort of trying to refine the animistic perspective to engage with contemporary capitalism. And if Jameson is correct, this seems to be something that Marx attempted with his dialectical approach in Capital (2014, 22). Jameson defines *figuration* as follows:

> For one thing, figuration…is capable of arresting the effects of nomination and reappropriating them for a new moment of dialectical awareness. For another, the very structure of binary oppositions which would seem to condemn thought to a perpetual repetition of stereotypical dualisms contains mechanisms which can be turned against its own traditional ideological dynamic to short-circuit it and produce a more complex and historical awareness in its place.
>
> *(2014, 325–326)*

Jameson's definition of figuration is a short-circuit dispositive between nomination and a new moment of dialectical awareness. It is an interesting dispositive in the face of contradictions and when nomination falls short, thus, requiring an opening towards (re)signification. Well, Jameson's figuration provides a Marxist perspective alternative to the regular imprisonment between the tragic and the comic narratives (2014, 15) we can introduce "figuration" as a tool towards a render of monstrosity (within capitalism). It is a refinement to examining points of inflection, its exhaustion and the requirement towards a "new" dialectical awareness.

4.3 From Marx's *fetishism of commodity* to Karatani's perspective on modes of exchange (or, the material magic of ghostly exchanges)

Karl Marx in *Capital* [1867] explains that "[a] commodity appears at first sight an extremely obvious, trivial thing. But its analysis brings out that it is a very strange thing, abounding in metaphysical subtleties and theological niceties" ([1867] 1982, 163). There is something enigmatic and secret that Marx sheds light in his incursions on fetishism of the commodity. This obscure and strange trait of a commodity analogously relates to "something that should have been kept hidden but that comes to surface" on two different levels.[15] Marx finds no mystery in the conception of use-value through the transformation of nature through labour, that is, the form of wood turned into a table to serve human needs. These two levels of the enigmatic feature of the commodity lies first on how commodities relate to other commodities but also on how commodities encapsulate social traits of labour within itself. As Marx puts it:

> …commodity reflects the social characteristics of men's own labour as objective characteristics of the products of labour themselves, as socio-natural

> properties of these things... Hence it also reflects the social relation of the producers to the sum total of labour as a social relation between objects, a relation which exists apart from and outside the producers.
>
> *(Marx [1867] (1982), 164–165)*

So, the second level of this enigmatic feature of commodities concerns this redoubling of commodities, basically when human labour traverses a commodity, integrating additional layers into a commodity, but once a commodity "emerges as a commodity, it changes into a thing which transcends sensuousness" (Marx [1867] (1982), 163). Hence, the passage from products of labour towards commodities, this shift towards the relation of a commodity towards another commodity in its abstraction attribution concerns the embodiment of social relations shaping commodities.

What Marx articulates as the uncanny feature of commodity-form, which gains full meaning as the "fantastic form of relation between things" (Marx [1867] (1982), 165) of the development of value-relation in exchange-value, surpassing the "physical nature of the commodity and the material [*dinglich*] relations arising out of this" (Marx [1867] (1982), 165), translates this haunting autonomous trait of commodity. This much visible illusion integrated into the result of the process of labour, which translates itself as an excess of the commodity-form in capitalism, is what Marx defines as fetishism. So, the remarkable component here is social relations and how it infiltrates commodity-form in such a way that Marx had to find support in metaphysics and theology for his materialist approach (Marx [1867] (1982), 163). Thus,

> the mysterious character of the commodity-form consists therefore simply in the fact that the commodity reflects the social characteristics of men's own labour as objective characteristics of the products of labour themselves, as the socio-natural properties of these things.
>
> *(Marx [1867] (1982), 164–165)*

For Marx, fetishism is presented as follows:

> There the products of the human brain appear as autonomous figures endowed with a life of their own, which enter into relations both with each other and with the human race. So it is in the world of commodities with the products of men's hands. I call this the fetishism which attaches itself to the products of labour as soon as they are produced as commodities, and is therefore inseparable from the production of commodities.
>
> *(Marx [1867] (1982), 163)*

Fetishism arises in the world of commodities "from the social character of the labour which produces them" (Marx [1867] (1982), 165), as Marx states. Certainly, the abstract operation in which capital reinforces a relationship between commodities, takes place once objects of utility turn into commodities and "[which] are a product of the labour of private individuals or who carry on their work independently of each other" (Marx [1867] (1982), 165). Marx debates how the relationship behind fetishism of commodities concerns an excess, which is carried out in an exchange relationship, and which takes place in the very act of exchange itself (Marx [1867] (1982), 167). Or as Marx puts it:

> ...the labour of the individual asserts itself as a part of the labour of society, only by means of the relations which the act of exchange establishes directly between the products, and indirectly, through them, between the producers. To the latter, therefore, the relations connecting the labour of one individual with that of the rest appear, not as direct social relations between individuals at work, but as what they really are, material relations between persons and social relations between things.
>
> *(Marx [1867] (1982), 167)*

Thus, the mystery or the mystical excess which seems to "take over" only does so in the act of exchange. Nonetheless, it becomes clearer that Marx is noticing the profound marks which the act of exchange implies, and, in a way, it is important to notice that there is nothing strictly "magical" in a naïve sense, but something profoundly "animistic" in the sense of the act of exchange (Karatani 2014). There is a profound redoubling which takes place in the very own act of exchange, when a commodity becomes a commodity, which imprints a certain symbolic consequence to the producer, but in the same way, it also does so for the commodity and the social status which it represents, as values, to the various forms of existence as objects of utility. Isn't this precisely the point previously addressed by Ian Wright's discussion on the abstraction of capitalism taking place (Wright 2020a)? Or, as Marx states:

> This division of a product into a useful thing and a value becomes practically important, only when exchange has acquired such an extension that useful articles are produced for the purpose of being exchanged, and their character as values has therefore to be taken into account, beforehand, during production.
>
> *([1867] 1982, 166)*

The German economist is straightforward here "only by being exchanged that products of labour acquire a socially uniform objectivity as values, which is distinct from their sensuously varied objectivity as articles of utility" ([1867] 1982, 166). In a way, the crucial remark on fetishism of commodities by Marx, is that it invites this dimension at the act of exchange and this figuration (Jameson 2014) integrates a two-fold dimension in a certain topological

Möbius strip like torsion (Marx does not state this literally, but the logic behind this movement seems to be fairly approximal here). The definitive aspect which must be disambiguated here is that the act of exchange, is in a way a "charged" act, it comes with an additional excess, that may seem at first sight, like the apparition of "magic" but what is actually taking place is an invitation to a complex relationship with our symbolic reality (Karatani 2014). Only through this standpoint, the concept of labour of the individual producer that "acquires socially a two-fold character" as Marx states ([1867] 1982, 166) can make full sense. Concerning this short-circuit of the two-fold character, says Marx:

> On the one hand, it must, as a definite useful kind of labour, satisfy a definite social want, and thus hold its place as part and parcel of the collective labour of all, as a branch of a social division of labour that has sprung up spontaneously. On the other hand, it can satisfy the manifold wants of the individual producer himself, only in so far as the mutual exchangeability of all kinds of useful private labour is an established social fact, and therefore the private useful labour of each producer ranks on an equality with that of all others. The equalisation of the most different kinds of labour can be the result only of an abstraction from their inequalities, or of reducing them to their common denominator, viz. expenditure of human labour power or human labour in the abstract. The twofold social character of the labour of the individual appears to him, when reflected in his brain, only under those forms which are impressed upon that labour in every-day practice by the exchange of products. In this way, the character that his own labour possesses of being socially useful takes the form of the condition, that the product must be not only useful, but useful for others, and the social character that his particular labour has of being the equal of all other particular kinds of labour, takes the form that all the physically different articles that are the products of labour, have one common quality, viz., that of having value.
>
> *([1867] 1982, 166)*

This is exactly where the appeal towards the cognitive relation between the exchange act imprints on people's mind, but not that this operation occurs in a directly conscious way. It is a dimension which invites unconscious action of this very own operation, not for lack of knowledge on the interested parts, but because of the monstrous incommensurability at stake infiltrates this very own dimension. Therefore, the operation of conceiving an animistic theory to deal with modern capitalism, concerns this occult spirit of capital and the crux interior of its continuity.

This unconscious dimension concerns precisely the double mechanism of the foreignness inherent to capital, its inherent abstracting capabilities (Wright 2020a) and the exchange circulatory operations which take place within it (Karatani 2014). Marx debates how "figuring out" the secret social fabric behind our own products means to figure out the "stamp [of] an object of utility as a value, [which] is just as much a social product as language" ([1867] 1982, 167). Marx denotes how foreign a commodity is to us, in the same way noticing how language is also radically foreign to us. It is tempting to place them at the same level, but certainly this is not the case (and in a way, the two-level operation of figuration described by Jameson (2014) tries to bring forward this hieroglyphical mystery which takes place on different levels).

Yet, Marx's argument concerning the secret mystery behind the act of exchanging commodities concerns the symbolic mist which infiltrates this very own process ([1867] 1982, 167), this does not mean that Marx advocates for a (re)incantation of reality, but that there is a certain symbolic fabric of societal operations which holds this together. Basically, the foreignness of capital benefits from this infiltration and to approach its monstrous dimension, a monstrous "language," a proper *grammar* to reach it is required (Wright 2020a) – not in a spiritualization of the world around us, but as an attentive theorization of the animistic remainders which are embedded in our uncanny symbolic reality. Back to Marx ([1867] 1982, 167), the basic "motor" operation of capital, assumed as an "abstraction which abstracts" (Wright 2020a) relates to the "equalization" of human labour turned into a product informed by the form of value.

In a way, what Marx apparently did not fully anticipate was the powerful grasp which the mystery of commodities, all its magic and necromancy, perfects itself in order to perpetuate its own mist and keeps the obscurity of its spirit hidden (even though it hides in plain sight). The monstrous invisibility of capital keeps on persisting through its "magic and necromancy", which is perfected, refined and re-instituted not only at the level of ideology, not only at the level of alienation, but in its abstract redoubling operation relation between form and content (Wright 2020b) through the disguise by money form in capitalism. The symbolic consistency attributed to capital (e.g., Adam Smith's invisible hand argument) holds on to an illusion of self-regulating markets operating on its own, there is nothing more magical and necromantic than this and yet, a large majority sustain adoring such deity without a sheer of doubt in their minds. The far reach of the tentacles of Žižek's Kraken (2016) are deeply infiltrated into symbolic reality and to tear down such symbolic fabric, it requires a refinement that engages with the foreignness of capital, one aware of its foreignness, through its alien and more radical monstrousness (which is why Wright's intuition of the animistic theory of modern capitalism is so compelling and in a way, something which this chapter aims at). Žižek (2016) provides an important addition to this debate, he argues how Marx's *Capital* demonstrates how the self-production of capital operates under the logic of Hegel's "dialectical process of substance-subject which retroactively posits its own presuppositions" (233). But more importantly, he emphasizes how Hegel *did not* noticed this dimension, that Hegel's notion of an industrial revolution was similar to Adam-Smith's manufacture labour (a work process combining individual using tools), which is not yet the labour in factories where "the machinery sets the rhythm and individual workers are *de facto* reduced to organs serving the machinery, to its appendices" (Žižek 2016, 233). Žižek argues that Hegel did not conceive the rule of abstraction for developed capitalism. For Hegel, as Žižek explains, such abstraction lies not only under the misconception of "social reality" spread in our current the speculative financialized world, but that "it is 'real'" since it determines the very own structure of the material social processes, where the fate of entire countries and populational organizations can be rule by "the 'solipsistic' speculative dance of capital, which pursues its goal of profitability in a blessed indifference to how its movement will affect social reality" (Žižek 2016, 233).

Žižek is correct, defending that Hegel was not *fully* aware of the intricacies of capital, nonetheless, as Buck-Morss defends (2009, 52–53) he was certainly not *oblivious* of its monstrous dimension. But it is Žižek himself who adds to this monstrous point and certainly, explicates the fetishistic character of commodities operating in capital in its more monstrous sense and how capital's goal is to seek profitability in a "blessed indifference" of its consequence (Žižek 2016). Žižek, rather elegantly, denoting this "blessed indifference" is positing the bourgeois persistency of capital, perhaps because of the breadcrumbs of "improvement" which are noticed if one ought to compare our lives right now with how things were in Middle Ages (in terms of relative and absolute accumulation), but much deeper than this, Žižek's precise postulation of the "blessed indifference" (or Zupančič's "market's 'miraculous' productivity" (Zupančič 2017, 33)) relates directly with the point of structural negativity and its appropriation by capital; nonetheless, its perpetuation, the symbolic bond which capital ties up together – it is tied up symbolically by all States together (after 1980s, after the collapse of Soviet Union and the falling of a countering narrative to global capitalism), as well as by every person submitted to capital (willingly or unwillingly), providing consistency to an inconsistent entity (an entity which certainly has effects, nonetheless). It might sound counterintuitive, but an animistic approach is *required* because the "magic" which is symbolically embedded in *exchange*, and which holds the significant symbolic fabric of capital's together, can only be *fully* approached under this animistic perspective (Karatani 2014). The symbolic fabric which holds capital together, its invisible cloth over the world, requires a monstrous grammar to reach its foreignness. The mysterious hieroglyphs investigated by Marx, in the fetishism of commodities, attests to how values and time in a capitalist system short-circuit each other and impose a logic of operation which is out of our immediate reach. So, in order to actually reach any critical point, to actually confront the monstrous dimension of a foreign entity against its perpetuation, instead of furthering the mathematization of the financial systems (which as the language which serves to persist mystifying capitalism itself and hiding its implications to the large majority of people who actually paid the price for its operation), perhaps finally listening to a crucial point advocated by Marx himself, concerning the inherent foreignness of capital. Our (in)human subjective capabilities are certainly captured by the grasp of capital's monstrosity, as Žižek said earlier, the "blessed indifference" describes this figuration.

Karatani argues how reciprocal exchange operates within a single community, but also, between communities as an activity of peace keeping. The "power of the gift" (Karatani 2014, 50) and reciprocal exchange once it becomes institutionalized turns into "an obligation imposed by the community" (Karatani 2014, 50). Karatani debates Marcel Mauss' investigation of the aboriginal Maori tribe and their belief in *hau* (magic power) attributed in the gift-object, as well as Claude Lévi-Strauss critique, that

> [t]he gift creates a cycle not because of the hau that resides in the gift object, Lévi-Strauss maintained, but rather because the gift is like "an indeterminate value of signification," a floating signifier akin to an algebraic symbol in a mathematical structure.
>
> *(Karatani 2014, 50)*

However, Karatani agrees with Lévi-Strauss that an already-established community and it's operating structure, is a functioning system within any given community; but if one ought to take a step towards the "process by which one community creates anew, or actively renews, a sense of communality with another community through the reciprocity of the gift, we cannot ignore the power of the gift" (Karatani 2014, 51). Karatani's investigation of gift-giving, presenting an alternative perspective to Marx's fetishism of the commodities, which does not exclusively rely on the theory of reification. As he explains:

> In commodity exchange, right of ownership is transferred from one party to the other. Accordingly, to possess money is to possess the right to acquire ownership over other things. For this reason, the desire to accumulate money arises – the perverse desire (fetishism) for money instead of things. This does not happen with the gift. In the gift, rights of usage are handed over, but not rights of ownership. The gift-object functions as a kind of money, but unlike actual money, the gift-object does not possess the right to own other things: to the contrary, it brings with it the obligation to give things away (the obligation to make a countergift). In sum, whereas money promotes stockpiling and expanding possession, hau functions as a force that rejects ownership and desire.
>
> *(Karatani 2014, 51)*

From this argument, Karatani's investigation of magic and reciprocity from a Marxist perspective, allows the thinker to notice how some reciprocity exchanges differentiate themselves from the commodity exchange, and the power of the gift and the obligation to make a counter gift, as an imposition of retribute with a gift but not sustaining the sense of accumulation or strengthening possession. Thus,

> Magic is the attempt to control or manipulate nature or other people by means of the gift (sacrifice). In other words, magic in itself already includes reciprocity. Like the reciprocity system, magic is not something that existed from the start. At the stage of nomadic bands, magic had yet to develop. Its development began with the adoption of sedentary settlement.
>
> *(Karatani 2014, 52)*

Indeed, the proper precedent to magic lies someplace else, it lies in *animism*[16] itself. Animism permits the appearance of magic to take place in the first place and without animism preconditioning and forming the condition of possibility, magic would never have surfaced into existence. Nonetheless, as Karatani explains, animism is the foundation of magic, but "it does not itself bring about magic" (Karatani 2014, 52) it requires religion to organize it.

Karatani notices how consequences of this mode of exchange did not only permit a possibility of peace but also allowed animism to embark on the symbolical complexity of reciprocity exchange, which permitted fixed settlements and along with it, different types of problems (e.g., coexisting with the dead). Nonetheless, Karatani's debate with Freud does not stop there. Another discussion is brought to surface by the philosopher concerning Freud's *Totem and Taboo* (1955), specifically on Freud's theory dealt with "the problem of how within primitive society the bonds of brotherhood were established and maintained. To summarize, Freud was interested in how tribal society produced the equality and independence that characterized clans" (1955, 54–55). Although Freud's theory is ignored by today's anthropologists, "[t]his does not, however, render meaningless Freud's understanding of the murder of the primal father and of its subsequent ritual repetition. Freud's real interest lay with the question of how the brotherhood system was maintained" (1955, 55). However, Karatani suggests a correction to Freud's approach, since "[i]n a nomadic band society, there was no primal ur-father. To the contrary, the bonds uniting the band and family were fragile. In this sense, the theories that Freud relied on were mistaken" (1955, 56). Therefore, the possibility of fixed settlements brought with it the appearance of inequalities, as well as the "ur-father" or a certain arising of the state, and clan society, or the brotherhood, was established from suppressing this alternative – reading from this perspective, Freud's standpoint remains valid, as the philosopher defends.

If Karatani is correct, the return of what was repressed and forgotten, does not appear automatically as a fond memory from past times, but as a menace or a threat. It is certainly not farfetched to consider how Freud's development of the uncanny ([1919] 2003) has a further dimension to what it is previously accounted for, specifically concerning the non-surmounted elements which (re) appear in reality. The animistic root which Freud has inserted within the uncanny ([1919] 2003, 385) would lead towards the intricacies of castration complex, approaching the uncanny to Karatani's perspective: who understands animalistically that "the return of the repressed" concerns nomadism (freedom), wouldn't it provide a crucial refinement to uncanny encounters having a paradoxical stance between two sides of the same coin: prohibition/law and freedom. In a way, the traversal of uncanniness could prove itself a freeing possibility, not only for the relief of getting rid of it, but because it allows for a proper (re)signification towards a new elaboration.

4.4 Gothic figures and Marx's critique of capitalism: about vampires, zombies, werewolves and Frankenstein's monsters

The idea of philosophically translating the impasses of shared reality under the scope of a certain *in-between* the monstrosities (of Capital) and (in)humanity is far from being an original project. In a way, such a perspective has been taking shape (and shaping reality) through many different epochs and under different *figurations* (Jameson 2014). The idea of inviting monstrous figuration to debate capitalism, is nothing but a possibility of dealing with its foreignness under foreign terms. This thesis offers a consolidated approach which benefits from many previous efforts towards the direction of a monstrous materialism, which started with Marx himself. Basically, in order to fully engage with the foreign dimension of Capital, Marx needed to plead for the debate of necromancy and magic ([1867] 1982, 169) and yet, he also does so by inviting other monstrous figurations, adding to the bestiary of capital. This theme should not be approached as an illusory naïveté, but a reedition of the animistic stance which capitalism (in terms of a mode of commodity exchange) operates with under a financialized language, which hides under its veil the proper mystical animistic belief that holds the very own system operating.

Thus, the interesting approach to Marx's bestiary concerns the possibility of presenting and consolidating how such "creatures" touch in the foreignness of capital, and which required from Marx an invitation of monstrous literature to cover for the animistic powers which were invested. And the idea of taking these monstrous contributions *seriously* does not mean to pretend to find these monstrous things empirically out there, but to understand how these monsters are *symbolically present*, as monstrous "embodiments" of the negativity that capitalism takes advantage of. Obviously, this also does not mean to go out and try to find a materialized version of imaginary creatures, but to notice how monstrous ideas are very much present in our symbolic reality, how *real abstraction* guides our language and thinking. Therefore, the investigation of the perspective of monstrous dialectical materialism could be an insightful line of investigation.

The *invisibility* of capital and the ghostly dimension of its abstracting operations were defended by Adam Smith's *invisible* hand of the market and criticized by Marx, as previously presented. And if the ghostly dimension of capital wasn't troubling enough in its intricate operation within capitalism, things only get *darker* with Karl Marx's monsters. The monstrous economy of the (living) dead (Neocleous 2003) is carried out by Marx throughout his work, validating rhetorical devices as figurations which adequately dimensions Capital monstrous topos. There are vampires, zombies and werewolves approximated by Marx himself, as literary monstrous references which figurate an attempt to push language towards renditions of the animist perspective, presented in the Gothic (re)approach of animism that invites such dimension. In a way, this is a viable invitation to reintroduce the animistic theorization of modern capital, as a demonization of capitalism (Wright 2020a) by pushing these directions forward. Once again, this is not a simple rhetorical device, but a (re)dimensioning of the impasses of animism translated through an uncanny grammar, a more monstrous grammar, which dares to unapologetically approach the foreignness of capital in its utmost monstrous dimension. Following Marx's "Capital" there are numberless references which advocate for the blood sucking nature of capital, in its most vampire like Gothic capability (Neocleous 2003, 669), for instance in the following vampiric passages:

> Capital is dead labour which, vampire-like, lives only by sucking living labour, and lives the more, the more labour it sucks. The time during which the worker works is the time during which the capitalist consumes the labour-power he has bought from him. If the worker consumes his disposable time for himself, he robs the capitalist.
>
> *([1867] 1982, 342)*

> The prolongation of the working day beyond the limits of the natural day, into the night, only acts as a palliative. It only slightly quenches the vampire thirst for the living blood of labour. Capitalist production therefore drives, by its inherent nature, towards the appropriation of labour throughout the whole of the 24 hours in the day. But since it is physically impossible to exploit the same individual labour-power constantly, during the night as well as the day, capital has to overcome this physical obstacle. An alternation becomes necessary, between the labour-powers used up by day and those used up by night.
>
> *([1867] 1982, 367)*

> In the market, as owner of the commodity 'labour-power', he stood face to face with other owners of commodities, one owner against another

> owner. The contract by which he sold his labour- power to the capitalist proved in black and white, so to speak, that he was free to dispose of himself. But when the transaction was concluded, it was discovered that he was no 'free agent', that the period of time for which he is free to sell his labour-power is the period of time for which he is forced to sell it, that in fact the vampire will not let go 'while there remains a single muscle, sinew or drop of blood to be exploited.
>
> *([1867] 1982, 415–416)*

> If money comes into the world with a congenital blood-stain on one cheek…capital comes dripping from head to toe, from every pore, with blood and dirt.
>
> *([1867] 1982, 926)*

Neocleous (2003)[17] investigates each one of these passages. Following his investigation on Marx's vampires, Neocleous (using Hyman's[18] discussion on the horrors of capital) debates how such horrors are presented by Marx in "Capital" which can be summarized under three main points: first, the bloodthirsty legal pursues against vagabond (resuming the efforts of pushing agricultural people from their homes) (Neocleous 2003, 668); second, the colonialist horrors of capital and all efforts to enlarge capital throughout the world (Neocleous 2003, 668); and third (which is the vampiric horror point, added by Neocleous): the Western bloodthirst of the bourgeois class over the working class, where the property-owning class has a desire of consuming the like of the working likes with a vampiric attitude (Neocleous 2003, 668). As Neocleous defends, a lot of attention is usually given to the invisible reach of capitalism and its spectral dimension (the "ghostly" or "spectral" debates), but not enough attention was given to its vampiric horrors – which are more present and significant, for Marx himself, than ghosts, as the author explains (Neocleous 2003, 669). Investigating the previous passages from Marx's *Capital*, Neocleous notices that further these direct references, a closer look to the text can easily reveal viable passages which nod to the vampiric aspect of capital[19] (Neocleous 2003, 669). Neocleous risks a larger textual license with *Capital*, noticing how Marx while addressing the working day compares the labour in factories with different forms of domination through history (e.g., "Athenian aristocracy, the Norman barons, the American slave-owners and the feudal *corvée*") (Neocleous 2003, 669). Marx uses the Wallachian peasants performing forced labour on behalf of Wallachian *boyars* as a key example denoted by Neocleous, and the source used by Marx is É. Regnault's *Histoire politique et sociale des principautés danubiennes* (1855), which reveals that the "Wallachian boyar" mentioned in his text is Vlad the Impaler: Vlad Dracula (Neocleous 2003, 670). Another example debated by Neocleous, comes from Marx's *Grundrisse*, when the German economist states how capital is "'constantly sucking in living labour as its soul, vampire-like', or as 'sucking its living soul out of labour'" (Neocleous 2003, 670) or in the "Inaugural Address of the International Working Men's Association" (which was given while Marx wrote *Capital*, as Neocleous remembers) (Neocleous 2003, 670) where Marx describes the British industry as "vampire like" (Neocleous 2003, 670).

But back to Marx's Capital, Neocleous locates how Marx uses the "vampiric" aspects of those who act cowardly in silence exploiting workers, he notices Marx expands from the vampiric reference turning to werewolves at some point, highlighting the drive to extend the working day as a "were-wolf like hunger for surplus labour" (Neocleous 2003, 353) which denotes the personification of the monstrous dimension of capital in the exploitative attitude of capitalists[20] (Neocleous 2003, 353). Then, Neocleous moves on towards additional works from Marx, where the economist engages with the vampiric motif presence in *The Class Struggles in France, Civil War in France, Eighteenth Brumaire, Holy Family* and the unfinished text *The Correspondent from the Mosel*, denoting the blood-sucking parisitary attitude of the bourgeois in different moments of the class struggle in recent history (Neocleous also mentions how Engels himself had mentioned the idea of "vampire property-holding class" in Marx's Capital) (Neocleous 2003, 671)

As Neocleous formidably consolidates the vampiric references in Marx's work and the author speculates about the possible point behind Marx's usage of the "metaphor" of the vampires, trying to "situate" the vampire (Neocleous 2003, 672). So, Neocleous investigation certainly helps further appreciate how Jameson's "figuration" as a valid operation to pursue such "metaphors" not only as textual references but points of inflection, which traverse language and scientific investigation with an excess that cannot be ignored. It would be too dull to consider that Marx would be bringing forward such examples for the sake of rhetoric and not trying to notice the proper dimension of how intricate these references are in his theory. Nonetheless, Neocleous' investigation defends a closer look at the vampiric (and eventually all other monstrous figurations) but still captured under a certain literary device being applied (Neocleous 2003, 672), not so much as a philosophical operation.

Certainly, the interpretation of monsters in Marx's work finds no consensus and Neocleous presents arguments from Robert Paul Wolff, who notices how Marx's work comes with historical, philosophical and literary allusions embedded in his economic debate (Neocleous 2003, 672). A similar line of argumentation can be notices in Marshall Berman, who defends Marx's "modernism" in such figures, but there are also interpretations, such as Stanley Hyman who assumes that the best way to approach Capital's essence is not through science, social sciences, but as fantastic literature (Neocleous 2003, 672). Which is another way of seeing such monstrous allusions, one that still framed it as mere rhetorical devices and nothing else. From these numerous perspectives, Neocleous affiliates with Wylie Sypher[21] and Andrew Smith,[22] who translated

Marx's use of the vampires as an "occult trope" that recognizes the importance to translate the imaginative account of things (Neocleous 2003, 672). However, Neocleous adds a second perspective to this: Marx's usage of these metaphors under the gothic background of 19th-century[23] (Neocleous 2003, 673) and perhaps, Neocleous procedure here, could be interpreted as a certain affiliation of embracing Marx under the realm of Gothic Materialism (along the lines of Mark Fisher and Donna Haraway). As he further explains, the cultural and literary attributes of the vampire are rather complex, since these creatures translate a certain "Otherness." Inspired by Donna Haraway (much like Mark Fisher) the vampire's unheimlich translates a fundamental ambiguity that does not allow them to be easily encased in labels. Thus, Neocleous emphasizes how the vampire is the "harbinger of category crisis" (Neocleous 2003, 673), its otherness detains a fluidity that prevents well-defined lines separating nature and man. For him, the vampire's disruptive trait as simultaneously inside and outside, breaks the barriers of guarantees of any given politics of identity, because it represents a form of difference (Neocleous 2003, 673).

In a way, this is a very fruitful passage for our debate on monstrosity, it certainly validates the proper monstrous realm of capital in its utmost monstrous capabilities, but it also validates the designation of how such creatures are adequate designations of elevating a point of excess to symbolization. Indeed, the *unheimlich* feature of the vampire nods to a certain embodiment of capital, nonetheless, this cannot be stuck at the level of rhetorics and metaphors, it requires a further implication of the animist perspective which can dispute this very own point of contradiction emitted by capital itself (*the* actual monster) (Wright 2020a). The designation of a monstrous materialism simply concerns the attention of trying to push such renders towards a proper animistic render, which can notice ways out from the binary signifier stances. And Neocleous' Gothic materialist line of argumentation notices how many cultural studies argue how this *difference* actually concerns *poverty*; it concerns difference at the level of class. Basically, the oppressed and marginalized shares of the population in different moments of the capitalist history had turned into the scapegoat of this difference. Neocleous finds in René Girard, a connection between the monster and the shapeshifting aspect of the scapegoat (e.g., the Jew, the homosexual, female sexuality and the travellers from far) (Neocleous 2003, 673), reassuring how the vampire embodies radical "otherness" following material transformations in societies (Neocleous 2003, 674).

In a way, the assumption of the "monstrous" simply assumed as metaphor of difference, (which is the go-to motto of Gothic Materialism) does not suffice to understand the predicament of global capitalism (Wright 2020b). Basically, because it raises the "situation" as a symptom *of* capital, but not as its proper possibility of traversal of such symptom. If Wright's argument about the animistic perspective is correct, this means that Marx's examination at this "figurations," concerns a proper consequence of the monstrous *topos* of capitalism itself. Of course, Marx situates a monstrous dimension which requires further investigation.

Back to Neocleous (2003) discussion on Marx's vampires, the author engages with the proper background of the vampiric tales which were current in Marx's epoch and introduces how this monstrous creature suffered distortion because of Count Dracula (a male character), while prior to John William Polidory's "Vampyre" (1819) who popularized this monstrous lore, the proper reference of the blood-sucking creatures were generally of female vampires and that an ideological inversion took place here. The political aspect of sexuality is key to understand this shift, since women more independent, autonomous and interested in sex were deemed vampiric, as detaining a vampiric nature and the vampire was first identified with the oppressed and outlawed, explains Neocleous (Neocleous 2003, 674). It was the Count Dracula that became a certain figure which could represent female sexual oppression, a predator only concerned with the fulfilment of his own desires: no matter the costs.

This is very interesting notion, since it provides an appreciation of the ideological (re)shaping of narratives, but even more curious, the ideological argument can be flipped to its opposite side, yet the proper monstrous topos of the blood-sucking creature, the forever lasting and who preys at others to survive, remains the same. Once again, the point of this concerns the proper monstrous foundations of capitalism itself, the "occupiers" of the sides can vary as much as they like, the proper monstrous creation of creating monsters does not change under capitalism. The only possible way of understanding global capitalism is through its inherent operative monstrosity. Neocleous continues his investigation noticing that Marx's usage of the vampires (which is completely unsuited to contemporary films and popular culture) was a proper philosophical choice (Neocleous 2003, 674), in his social argumentation Marx does not use terms like "parasite" or "leech," he uses *vampire*. And Marx does not use the vampire under the scope of politics of gender nor to discuss religiosity (e.g., in "On the Jewish Question") his social critique of Otherness concerns the predatory never-stopping drive that vampires represent (Neocleous 2003, 674).

One must agree with Neocleous, Marx was far from being a postmodern cultural theorist and even less an existential thinker. Neocleous introduces yet another approach to translate Marx's vampires, one deriving from Terell Carver who notices that the vampire metaphor was a current discussion of 18th-century Enlightenment thinkers. Thus, Marx's engagement with the vampire is not only a rationalist trait but it was also rooted in philosophy and under philosophical terms (Neocleous 2003, 674). He argues that Marx's philosophical approximation to vampires could be deriving from an inherited philosophical debate between Voltaire and Rousseau, but this is insufficient to translate Marx's usage of vampires as well as the image of the vampire as relating to the pre-capitalist world (Neocleous 2003, 676) which is also insufficient. As Neocleous notices, Marx's metaphorical usage of the vampire is not a ridicule, cynical, superstitious or mystical engagement, his philosophical usage concerns the *embodiment* of the vampiric attitude of human beings under capitalism (Neocleous 2003, 676). In other words, vampires can actually "exist" but not quite how we imagine, not like the fantastic creatures walking around outside, but vampires can "exist" when humans *symbolically* embody the vampiric attitude in their actions, they can exist in the way humans relate to other humans personifying the vampire bloodthirst for exploitation. When humans actualize the concept of vampire in real life.

Indeed, Marx's approach to vampires (or other monsters for that matter) are far from ridicule or just pure dismissiveness towards superstitious beliefs, thus, there is a proper designation behind these monstrous references approached by Marx. Neocleous argues that Marx's usage of the vampires resonates more with the emblematic philosophical background, but under different terms. While Rousseau referenced vampires to address institutions of authority in a metaphorical manner, Marx will use it to personify the authorities *as* vampires. There is a difference in the metaphorical usage of the vampire between Rousseau and Marx, as Neocleous argues (Neocleous 2003, 676). We could argue that the proper dialectic between master-slave in more vampiric terms lies in Marx's render which derives from Rousseau's discussion (Neocleous 2003, 677).

Thus, Marx is presenting something else with his vampiric referends, as Neocleous argues. Taking his research further, Neocleous debates the usual attribution of vampires as allusions of representatives of a feudal aristocracy (Neocleous 2003, 677) but he reaches the conclusion that it is more common to see the vampire personifying capital and the bourgeoise (Neocleous 2003, 677). He agrees with Franco Moretti's essay on the dialectics of fear, which dissociates the vampire from aristocracy. Basically, Moretti's analysis portrays how uses Stoker's Dracula who lacks all the usual traits of an aristocrat. Dracula is decrepit, does not cover himself in luxury, has multiples servants and so on. For Moretti, as Neocleous defends, Dracula's bloodthirst serves as a metaphor for capital's desire for accumulation (Neocleous 2003, 678). The more blood he consumes, stronger he gets and those who he preys upon are weak around him. Moretti's remark is central: by approaching the vampire to capital's accumulation, the point of convergence between the two becomes clear: the vampiric thirst for blood knows no limit and capital's monstrous expansion and eager for accumulation is also unlimited. The vampire translates capital without shame of its own exploitative parasitic features (Neocleous 2003, 678).

Moreover, Neocleous embarks on the overall approach of Marx's vampires as a Gothic metaphor, which implies a certain "projection" of the ruling capitalist economy, placing the "vampire" as a "sanguinary capitalist" (Neocleous 2003, 678). Still agreeing with Moretti, the author defends that following Marx's work it is more compelling to assume the vampire as capital than any other category (e.g., the aristocrat, Jew, homosexual or some "Other") (Neocleous 2003, 678). But Neocleous develops this point further, for him,

Marx's vampires relate to "dead labour": how dead labour starts to reign over the living. How under capitalist production the living turns into a mean to realize dead labour, how it infiltrates humans emptying out sensibilities and substitutes it with the logic of productivity. The vampiric aspect of the capitalist domination over the worker which turns humans into instruments and materials for profit, convincing that humans must enact like dead machinery, should work like dead-meat for the blood sucking desire of the capitalist (Neocleous 2003, 680). Neocleous is emphatic, it is a fight for the soul of the workers against the vampires (Neocleous 2003, 680). The workers produce the living labour and without them the machines will stop. The living detains the power to transform reality and to produce use-values, but they must break free from the vampiric fangs that hold them down.

For Neocleous, the proper way to investigate vampires comes from the perspective of "living labour" and the "dead" (as "accumulated") labour embodied in capital, the vampiric desire of the capitalist is accumulation and if the working class works itself to death in the process, that's just the vampiric logic of capitalist labour operating (Neocleous 2003, 681). In a way, Neocleous is noticing how accumulation has a certain "deadness" inherent to it, but Wright (2020a) would defend how this is more than the embodiment of those who accumulate, this is a monstrous operation derived from the monster itself. Neocleous' argumentation appreciates how Marx approximates the vampire figuration to capital as dead labour. The insidious vampiric-like hunger of capital, which Marx describes, denotes the way in which capitalism invades each and every second of the workers' life, the vampire wants every single cell, muscle and drop of blood from the living life of workers to produce under his control (Neocleous 2003, 681).

Following Neocleous line of argumentation, it becomes clear that another aspect of "necromancy" is present to Marx, and into the "magical" realm which infiltrates in the fetishism of commodities. For Neocleous, "necromancy" concerns the interpretation of dead labour taking over in capital, which is a much-appreciated refinement that validates the importance of approaching such "necromancy." But certainly, Neocleous presents the Gothic materialist appreciation which relies on the standpoint of production and how he pursues the usual Marxist appreciation of political economy to present this argument. This does not change in any way the argument presented by Karatani's approach to modes of exchange (2014), this does not change in any way Wright's arguments on the animistic approach to modern capitalism (2020a, 2020b), if anything, this certainly validates such points concerning the "magical" realm and the necessity of investigating the deadness of capital. Nonetheless, this should be considered not as an ending point, but as a starting point for this debate. Neocleous further adds to the debate on the "necromancy" of capital, addressing Marx's famous quote on the fetishism of the commodity and the "metaphysical subtleties and theological niceties"

(Neocleous 2003, 683), to defend how the "spectral," the "magical" has something to do with the dead. And Neocleous highlights a crucial point: "Because capital is dead labour, the desire to live one's life through commodities is the desire to live one's life through the dead" (Neocleous 2003, 683). The *necromancy* identified by Marx on products of labour which explains the horrors of fetishism, concerns the conjuring of the dead within commodification, as Neocleous states. This "fantastic" trick operated in labour production driven by dead labour explains how "the inorganic realm of the dead … makes the dead appear alive" (Neocleous 2003, 684). And Neocleous defends how the vampire is the perfect "embodiment of the rule of the dead over the living", how its *undead* nature detains a dialectical feature that perfectly encapsulates this mechanism of capitalism between fear and desire (Neocleous 2003, 684).

Finally, Neocleous' argument concerning the rule of the dead (of capital) presents the validity of the metaphor of the vampire, which as a monster:

> …is of course connected to the root of that term: from *monstrare*, meaning 'to show forth', *monstra*, meaning to warn or show, *monstrum*, meaning 'that which reveals', or 'that which warns', and *monere*, meaning 'to warn'. The vampire as monster both *demonstrates* the capabilities of capital and acts as a *warning* about it.
>
> *(Neocleous 2003, 684)*

Nonetheless, isn't this the proper crux of the argument of the monstrosity of capital? The Jemesonian direction of "figuration" certainly translates *this* precise sense. But more interesting than that, couldn't we find Neocleous' crucial investigation of the vampiric monster in Marx, be read as a crucial defence of the proper monstrous trait of capitalism itself? Because if the "situating" of the vampire has any proper meaning in this investigation, it certainly has something to do with a proper understanding which must go beyond a rhetorical or a textual metaphorical sense, it must have a material validity of raising an excess of capital itself. Certainly, going beyond the possible embodiments allocated *onto* such monstrous topos (of capital) within capitalism (which *does not* diminish the bodies which are allocated to it), but it denounces the vampiric monstrous capabilities which go beyond them, which is indifferent to it. The interest in the vampiric stance within global capitalism, is to take a further look at the operating logic of the monstrous topos itself of capitalism.

Neocleous' arguments of these vampiric examples cannot be understood as merely "rhetoric" allusions, and if we ought to understand them as implicated figurations (Jameson 2014), the further consequence of pursuing a *monstrous materialism* is a pertinent perspective. Or to better put it, from this standpoint, on how the "necromancy" of capitalism denotes a point of excess, where words and concepts seems to fail or lack to adequately translate the rawness of contradictions at stake and the monstrous *figurate* by "bringing forward" an impasse of formalization (in materialistic terms). So perhaps, the proper dimension of monstrosity may prove itself useful in terms of "monstration" (Zupančič 2017, 64), not as a mere linguistic "allusion" but as a proper invitation to a point which needs a further symbolic investigation towards the intricacies of its efficiency. In a way, the attempt at an "animistic theory to modern capitalism" (Wright 2020a) only makes sense if undertook under a proper monstrous materialistic term, one which is not stuck at the metaphysics of the spectral, but one that notices the monstrous inherent to the monster itself (capital). This is the proper dimension of real abstraction.

Mark Fisher's efforts on *Capitalist Realism* (2009) must not be left behind or go unnoticed. Following the steps of Žižek and Badiou, he engages with the active role of the monster (of capitalism) and its (gothic) centrality – basically, defending the need for responsibility, to think and problematize the operations of domination within reality, proposing different alternatives for our economic predicament. As Fisher defends:

> To reclaim a real political agency means first of all accepting our insertion at the level of desire in the remorseless meat-grinder of Capital. What is being disavowed in the abjection of evil and ignorance onto fantasmatic Other is our own complicity in planetary networks of oppression. What needs to be kept in mind is both that capitalism is a hyper-abstract impersonal structure and that it would be nothing without our co-operation. The most Gothic description of Capital is also the most accurate. Capital is an abstract parasite, an insatiable vampire and zombie-maker; but the living flesh it converts into dead labor is ours, and the zombies it makes are us. There is a sense in which it simply is the case that the political elite are our servants; the miserable service they provide from us is to launder our libidos, to obligingly re-present for us our disavowed desires as if they had nothing to do with us
>
> *(2009, 15)*

The dimension of the meat-grinder of capital goes along the lines of Neocleous (previously addressed) argument towards the monstrosity of capital and its zombie-maker capabilities. And yet, this is a first approach to the level of capitalist production, which still requires another step towards its "circulatory" dimension, which seems to be Karatani's (2014) development towards modes of exchange and over the fact that modes of exchange that keep the Other (its symbolic stance) operative. Another author who has engaged with the monstrous dimension of global capitalism is David McNally in *Monsters of Global Market* (2011). The entire work is dedicated to the exploration of the zombie-like productions of capital, and he refines a capitalist "monsterology" (2011, 2) which sharply approximates with Wright's thesis (2020b) of a demonology of capitalism. While pondering upon the *incommensurability* of global capitalism, how it infiltrates and insidiously encompass our symbolic reality, McNally defines it as *monstrous* (thus, developing a similar line of thinking defended by the present book). McNally starts with the puzzling aspects of capitalism which is its (very out in the open) "*invisibility*," investigating the famous formulation by Adam Smith (the "invisible hand of the market") as a macroeconomic biased perspective of capitalism's self-regulatory functioning, which "molests" as all with its invisible hand. This particularly ghostly burden can only haunt us all. For as long as capitalism persists, this "invisible magic" (and fetichism) seems to be the symbolic fabric which requires to be ripped. However, this is too simplistic, and McNally neatly formulates how this haunting invisibility comes out in the open only because it is *paradoxical* "… monsters are both everywhere and nowhere" (2011, 2), as he defends. Obviously, the point here is not to engage with metaphysical niceties or with new ontologies, what is at stake is the usual suspects: bourgeois stupidity. What McNally argues is that:

> …the very insidiousness of the capitalist grotesque has to do with its invisibility with, in other words, the ways in which monstrosity becomes normalised and naturalised via its colonisation of the essential fabric of everyday-life, beginning with the very texture of corporeal experience in the modern world. What is most striking about capitalist monstrosity, in other words, is its elusive everydayness, its apparently seamless integration into the banal and mundane rhythms of quotidian existence. This is why the most salient representations of the capitalist grotesque tend to occur in environments in which bourgeois relations are still experienced as strange and horrifying. In such circumstances, images of vampires and zombies frequently dramatise the profound senses of corporeal vulnerability that pervade modern society, most manifestly when commodification invades new spheres of social life.
>
> *(2011, 2)*

McNally's capitalist *monsterology* (2011, 2), argues how in today's liberal bourgeoisie ideology people are put at ease watching and consuming horror in culture, folklore, and film, instead of facing the horrific scenes of everyday life (2011, 4). McNally addresses the exploration of human bodies as commodities, rescuing how such monsters of the market are bound to *occult economies* which they inhibit (2011, 4), translating any open space to be explored must be explored. In his rereading of Marx's "Capital" oriented by the monstrosities of the market, he raises Marx's classic *Gothic* references[24] of the vampiric thirst which drives capitalism to a whole other level. Another much valid point from McNally's (2011) book concerns how "mainstream social science" found grounds on Max Weber's *disenchantment thesis* in order to satisfy their "critical" categories and place all tales from the "peripheries of the world" as "premodern superstitions" (2011, 5), assuming that such categorization for itself suffices (and perhaps it does for the European-North American Imperialist axis), all too quickly dismissing the monstrous. As he argues:

> Mainstream social science has a long tradition of characterising such tales as premodern superstitions that refuse to accommodate the disenchantment of society that is integral to modern life. Yet such dismissals enact a mystification, denying as they do the systematic assaults on bodily and psychic integrity that define the economic infrastructure of modernity, the capitalist market-system.
>
> *(2011, 5)*

Following McNally, one can easily understand how fallacious this understanding about the social symbolic composition of reality can be. Our point is that we cannot fall short onto disenchantment of reality but also avoid a romanticized (re)enchantment of reality, that would also miss a crucial aspect of how such narratives enact disturbances against "the naturalisation of capitalism", as McNally puts it (2011, 5). The structures of denial that dominate conscious life in modernity are so habitual, the intellectual and cultural web that normalises the repression of unconscious desires so intricate, that only images with explosive power can break from the web of mystification. Furthermore, McNally reminds us that Marx had already advanced the "essential features of capitalism… are not immediately visible" (2011, 6) and that "…many of their effects can be touched and measured. But the circuits through which capital moves are abstracted ones…" (2011, 6); therefore, *invisibility does not necessarily mean that there is nothing taking place there*. Well, McNally's point is solid and clear: the *invisible* abstract regulation of the markets is *fantastically real* (2011, 7), thus, to turn towards the grotesque through the fantastic could be impactful in terms of "mimicking" the "absurdity" of capitalist modernity (2011, 7). And a way to go against *occult capitalism* and its bewitching images of accumulation of wealth, McNally aims at psychoanalyzing those images as dreams in order to find transformative alternatives that decode the structural forces of domination. McNally aims at

> …mining a popular imaginary populated by vampires, zombies and malevolent corporations that abduct and dissect people… to construct shock-effects that allow us to see the monstrous dislocations at the heart of commodified existence. And, because modern bourgeois consciousness was decisively shaped by its colonialist horror over African peoples and their customs….
>
> *(2011, 7–8)*

Certainly, this text agrees with the overall basis behind this thesis, especially concerning "mining" of popular imaginary stances and its monstrous figures, which can prove itself fruitful against the normalization of capitalist structures, nonetheless, there needs to be more than just disputing the imaginary: a certain symbolic operation which allows the infiltration of imploding these very own edifices is also required. While McNally analysis provides a critical scope, heavily relying on the Frankfurt School and their critical interpretation of psychoanalysis which rather quickly became a certain hermeneutics of the bourgeoisie (which renormalizes any radical potential to keep things as they are...), by adding Lacanian psychoanalysis to supplement this critical endeavour can provide further fruitful endeavours towards *monsterology*.

McNally's project concerns how these imaginings of monstrosity have ties to movements of capitalism around the world, from the *Imperialist* exploitation of Africa towards the rising of Industrial capitalism from England in the late 19th and 20th centuries, translating how such hauntings figures accompanied the transformations of the globalisation of capitalism. In a way, these haunting images enact a response to a demand from the bourgeois modes of production alerted by Marx and Engels at the preface of "The Manifesto of the Communist Party" ([1848] 2011) concerning the bourgeoisie's desire of constant expansion of the market:

> The bourgeoisie, by the rapid improvement of all instruments of production, by the immensely facilitated means of communication, draws all, even the most barbarian, nations into civilisation. The cheap prices of commodities are the heavy artillery with which it batters down all Chinese walls, with which it forces the barbarians' intensely obstinate hatred of foreigners to capitulate. It compels all nations, on pain of extinction, to adopt the bourgeois mode of production; it compels them to introduce what it calls civilisation into their midst, i.e., to become bourgeois themselves. In one word, it creates a world after its own image.
>
> *([1848] 2011, 9)*

This very own demand of imperialism under the name of "civilisation," portrays bourgeoisie's imposition of its mode of production throughout the world, as what truly is: imperialist exploitation. But with it, come along a structural aspect of self-recognition[25] which cannot be quickly dismissed. And more than mere "relics" of an (not so) ancient past, the very own re-telling and transmission of such monstrous figures in our culture are more than just an illustration and more an adequate portrayal of the inner contradictions of capitalist domination, serving there are simultaneously a shocking sight against its very own normalization ([1848] 2011, 9).

To take monsters seriously means to also be able to go beyond the strict *imaginary* articulation, to go beyond its obvious understanding as philosophical *impossible objects*, that much like *unicorns* are entities nowhere to be found empirically, but their regulatory idea is well established as such, that one knows how it would look like if it were found empirically (Zupančič 2017, 22), the point is not to *perfect* a regulatory Idea under Platonic terms (ideal essences) (Zupančič 2017, 22) but to approach monstrosity as a need towards another *grammar*, because although such monsters are not empirically *out there*, as long as there is capitalism, *their monstrous topos will always be there*. Back to McNally, the overall point here is not (1) to pay homage to the (re) enchantment of reality, which would be trying to romanticize what such figures with their underlying logics try to tell us, nor to (2) reproduce something that McNally already criticized about bourgeoisie consumption of these monsters through cultural commodities – which only leads towards further *numbness* and *immobilism* in our symbolic reality Following McNally's argument on the etymological translation of the word *monster* from its Latin root: *monere*, as *to warn* (2011, 9) not as *foretelling*, but of something which is already *happening* (2011, 9). But something is missing concerning monstrosity in a fitting philosophical discussion. Digging a bit further into this etymological debate, we can introduce Margo Hendricks and Patricia Parker (1994) supplement to this translation, and according to them: "Janis Pallister, [who]... notices the derivation of "monsters" both from the root of warnings or "signs" (monere + *-strum*) and from the sense of bringing forth to "show" (*monstrare*)" (1994, 165) (Neocleous 2003, 684), which accommodates the implications of such debate.

Back to McNally's investigation (2011), the author denounces the absurd embracing which normalizes the monster from using tropes of monstrosity (2011, 10), or an attempt to celebrate the monster in an overcompensatory stance, which merely valorizes the monstrous in a postmodernist limited view. Or as he puts it: "Rather than seeing the arena of monstrosity as a site of contestation, instead of recognizing that monster-images are multi-accentual, the postmodern celebration of the monstrous flattens out a field in which different social accents and values contest one another" (2011, 10). For McNally "not all monsters are equal..." (2011, 11). Thus, modern horror (of capitalism) must be perceived as a painful and traumatic process which hides the prior modes of exchange, as well as the subsequent modes of sociability built through it, but which lies still present within our own capabilities and possibilities. As McNally defends:

> ...the painful and traumatic processes through which non-capitalist social bonds are dissolved, individuals subjected to market-forces, and impersonal economic relationships created between the dominated and the dominant. In such circumstances, images of monstrosity track the intertwined experiences of corporeal fragmentation and social apartheid that characterise modern capitalism. Something is decidedly lacking, therefore, in an approach that cannot differentiate distinct forms of monstrosity, and which cannot grasp the ways in which subaltern groups in capitalist society attach

> images of monstrosity to oppressive powers, not just subversive ones. Lacking a critical theory of capitalism, much of cultural studies is hampered when it comes to explaining the intertwining of monsters with markets, and the genuinely traumatic (monstrous) experiences of subjugation and exploitation that occur when people find themselves subordinated to the market-economy.
>
> *(2011, 12)*

McNally's investigation centres on two key figures: vampires and Frankenstein's Creature. He centres them because of their literary emergence with industrial capitalism, but also, because they "continue to haunt the modern imaginary" (2011, 12). Following the author, these monsters are as much a fruit of the early 19th century capital industrialisation in Britain as the anxieties which they register (2011, 12). The author defends that Marx's appropriation of monsters concerns a "strategic-theoretical purpose," as he states:

> As Marx searched for a means of depicting the actual horrors of capitalism – from child-labour to the extermination of North America's indigenous peoples, from the factory-system to the slave-trade – he reworked the discourse of monstrosity that emerged with the rise of capitalism.
>
> *(2011, 14)*

The horror-story and mystery tale tone transpire through Marx's rendition of popular and literary debate, but the proper "strategic-theoretical purpose" is certainly the point and without such references the language of monstrosity itself gets lost (2011, 14).

Nonetheless, McNally investigates Frankenstein's Creature as a certain translation of the fear and anxiety generated in workers by the terrors of over-exploitation even to the level of body parts. Certainly, the horrors of "separation and dismemberment" (2011, 13) which characterize the workday of workers and their labour, once reduced to commodities which start competing against each other on the market. All in the name of the production of surplus-value. As McNally summarizes: "As a result, radically different concrete work processes are reduced to a single standard: commodity-producing, profit-generating labour"(2011, 14). The debate on Marx's *abstract labour* and how capitalism is organised around its basis is understood by McNally in the literal sense of the word:

> To abstract [Latin: *abstrahere*, 'to draw away'] is literally to separate, detach, cut off. And capitalism abstracts (detaches, cuts off) labour and its products from the concrete and specific individuals who perform unique productive acts, treating all work as effectively identical and interchangeable.
>
> *(2011, 14)*

Thus, capitalist systems of production and exchange operate by homogenizing all forms of work and reducing them into a "pure quanta of qualitatively undifferentiated human labour in the abstract," (2011, 14) which is the proper zombie-making or the proper meat-grinder of the capitalist system and its process of *real abstraction*, in the "world of universal market-exchange governed by money" (2011, 14). The author will defend that one of the aspects of "deadness" operating in capitalism, in its more Frankenstein's Creaturelike trait, takes place through "commodified abstract labour" which is "thus effectively *disembodied*, detached from the persons who perform it. This detachability of commodified labour allows capitalists to break up and dissect work-processes into their component parts, confining individuals to the repetition of a limited number of human movements" (2011, 14). In order to cover the incommensurability behind the processes of rhythms and processes of work, which would potentially spread out globally (as Marx and Engels had already predicted in their Manifesto), Marx needed to appeal to a foreign approach, he needed a monstrous language in order to approach the proper monstrosity of capitalism (McNally 2011, 15). Indeed, as McNally remembers:

> Capitalist manufacture 'mutilates the worker', he writes, 'turning him into a fragment of himself'. Describing capital's appearance in the form of the modern automated work- place where machines dominate workers, he refers to it as 'a mechanical monster whose body fills whole factories', and he denounces its 'demonic power' over living labour.
>
> *(2011, 15)*

Certainly, the approach to the Frankenstein's monster is adequate here. The monstrous-like machinery of factories and the way automation took over industries, embodies the dismemberment which the Frankenstein's Creature so vividly translates. Insightfully, McNally rescues that Marx's cunning perspective "was to discern that capitalism could not be understood merely in terms of new techniques for producing goods" (2011, 15), which would be falling into the trap of fetishism, or the naïve rendering of the transformations in human social relations *as* mere relations amongst things (machines and commodities) (2011, 15). The operation of commodified labour is a "profound and thoroughgoing restructuring of human experience: people's sense of their very bodies, of their capacities and creative energies, of the interrelation of self and things, and of self and others – all of these are utterly transformed by commodification" (2011, 15). And McNally's engaging Marxist lenses permit a different perspective to Mary Shelley's Frankenstein's Monster, one which highlights the monstrous topos of the commodification of abstract labour and a point which certainly should not be ignored.

McNally's examination of monstrousness is certainly the most interesting effort towards a dialectical materialism of the monstrous. Certainly, the effort towards monstrous materialism benefits directly from his contributions. Nonetheless, McNally's development of the monstrous should not be restricted as a rhetorical utilization or a metaphor of the grotesque in order to prove a point, there is more to it than just a textual reference and McNally makes this point very much clear by not siding with postmodernist approaches. Following the author's development on the fetishist aspect of the global market in capital, all the way, towards his reflections of African zombies in a global capitalist society, provides enough grounds to sustain the importance of taking monstrosity seriously.

4.5 About Badiou, the monster and monstrosity

Does the philosopher Alain Badiou debate anything about *monstrosity*? He does. Certainly, within the perspective of his philosophical system (specifically concerning politics which is one viable site for the generic truth-procedure to take place), but he does, nonetheless. Badiou did not only engages with "the monster," but he also actually coined the term itself to *explain* global capitalism:

> I think that, today, any political decision, at the level of the state, depends strictly on what I would call a monster, namely global capitalism, with its inequalities, its crises, and its wars. It is not true that a government, today, can be an autonomous entity. From the very outset, it is tied down within an all-encompassing determination, and it must affirm that what it does, and even more what it can do, depends upon its adhering to the laws of this determination, which are the laws of the monster. And the monster becomes more monstrous every day.
>
> *(2019, 16–17)*

The French thinker summarizes a central aspect of our predicament: the autonomous entity is to the side of capitalism. Badiou explains how the *lack of alternatives* within today's global capitalist reality came to be, focusing on one of the latest victories of global capitalism back in the 1980s. Briefly summarizing how the failure of socialist states (first Russia, then China) also took with itself a central aspect of theory: Marxism which became a relic of thought from a "forgotten" past. But Badiou flips this logic around, since Marx actually introduces something much new and the kind of accumulation that we actually witness in our highly contemporary reality is a proof of how we are still stuck at the Neolithic age:

> namely the organization of all wealth and of the entire means of production under the legal form of private property, protected by the police and their power, and conceived of as the very heart of social life and of humanity.
>
> *(2019, 12)*

Thus, requiring another *break* towards rejecting the domination of private property towards an existence which faces inequalities, aiming at collective organization of production and exchange (2019, 13). There are two other points from Badiou's brief summarization of "how did we get where we are?" which makes sense to take advantage of. First, the discussion about *lack of alternatives*, which is the consolidation of the Global capitalist hegemony under the (neo)liberal narrative: "The power of the liberal capitalist way lies in declaring itself to be the only way" (2019, 14). And second, his *psychoanalytic* appreciation of *symptoms* (2019, 43) as a way to present *how monstrosity* surfaces as manifestations of Global capitalist contradictions into our reality in the 2 level: (a) monstrous inequalities amongst people (p. 17, 56) and (b) in the form of political *plutocrats and oligarchs*: "The symptom of the crisis is the appearance of strange persons who are very difficult to understand: they are politicians, but they are in some sense like new gangsters" (2019, 53).

And Badiou argues for the necessity of *invention* against these monstrous *symptoms*: "I think that we must absolutely find something on the side of universality and equality; we have to create something new. We cannot repeat; we have to invent" (2019, 56). In a way, maintaining something of the *psychoanalytic logic* of providing solutions towards *repetitions*, much like analysands under psychoanalytic treatment sometimes repeat something without fully grasping the reason why and Badiou applies this notion towards some of the repetitions within history:

> In some sense, all political words are corrupted. History is a great corruption of everything that is present in history itself. But a name is only a name. What we lack is an Idea, a great Idea. What do I call an idea? It's a philosophical term, a mediation between individual subjects and the collective and political task, movement, or organization. An idea is the possibility of action across and with very different subjectivities.
>
> *(2019, 56–57)*

Here, Badiou advocates for the necessity of coming up with an Idea, in order to mediate between subjects and collectives, the *fidelity* attempted towards an Idea that goes beyond itself and reaches more subjects, engaging them towards a transformation (under the political form here, but there are similar fidelities towards other truth-procedures in Badiou's philosophy). And concerning *what* to do with the problem of the monster of Global capitalism Badiou provides an answer and he stops at the *how*:

> collectivism against private property, polymorphous work against specialization, concrete universalism against closed identities, and free association against the state. I would emphasize that these are only principles, not really

> a concrete program; but with these principles we can judge all political programs, decisions, parties, and ideas.
>
> *(2019, 57)*

In a way, these principles arise against the construction over time of the State, which was concerned with the accumulation of wealth and that protects inequalities and sustains the *monster*. So, it is valid to argue that Badiou takes the monster and its monstrosity seriously.

Badiou has an approach to *monstrosity* which is key to be considered. It is far from a fundamental aspect of his philosophy, nonetheless, he engages with it, when he is describing global capitalism and the monsters it creates (2019). For instance:

> In fact, I think that, today, any political decision, at the level of the state, depends strictly on what I would call a *monster*, namely global capitalism, with its inequalities, its crises, and its wars.
>
> *(2019, 16) (our highlight)*

It almost seems like Badiou sustains a fidelity towards the Gothic influence of Marx here, when he invites the monster to adequately translate global capitalism. As if such re-incorporation of global capitalist impasses linked him directly to Marx's critique. Yet, Badiou moves on, supporting the diagnosis already formulated by other thinkers concerning the troubling hauntings of a reality *lacking an alternative to global capitalism*. As he states: "[t]oday the dominant idea is that there is no global choice" (2019, 13) and this is how the liberal capitalist gains its power, from declaring itself as the only alternative (2019, 14). And this brings forwards an important aspect of our discussion, which is:

> ...We can thus define the current moment as that of the imposition of the belief that liberal capitalism, which dominates virtually every country in the world, is the only possible destiny for human beings. And, in the process, we also get a definition of the human subject. What is a human subject in this ruling liberal vision? A human subject is an owner; if he isn't an owner, he had better be a salaried employee; in any case, he must be a consumer; and, if he is none of the above, he is nothing at all.
>
> *(2019, 15)*

Thus, Badiou clearly states how global capitalism, in a way, *defines* human subjects. There is a certain *conditioning* of global capitalism to humanity, that at the level of the political it resonates with capitalist logic itself: a human being can either be *some(thing)* or *nothing at all*. Certainly, the contours of *humanity* are entrenched with global capitalism and its predicative are rooted on its own given possibilities. For instance, when Badiou calls Donald Trump a *monster* of capitalism, inviting a psychoanalytic understanding of "symptoms" in order to fully encapsulate what this means, is Badiou's way of saying that the *topos* of monstrosity (within capital) can provoke not only horrors, but also terrors.

4.6 Groundworks towards monstrous materialism

The present section has presented an unorthodox effort to piece together what seems to be a very insightful way to approach Marx's monsters, one which dares to take them seriously. So, instead of just a rhetorical gimmick or the quick assumption of encountering Marx's introduction of monstrous references as a remainder of "modernism" (Neocleous 2003, 674), more recent efforts have allowed to approach Marx's debate with monstrous in a more crucial perspective, one which provides the proper contours of the monstrous topos in which these creatures emanate from. To take Marx's monsters seriously does not only informs us of the more adequate circumscriptions with which these creature surface in Marxist theory (e.g., vampires and accumulation; Frankenstein's Creature caught between the monstrous machinery of accumulation through technological advancements and the commodification of digital labour; zombies and imperialist exploitation; witches and "invisible" labour and women body's controlled over bourgeoise ideology (Federici 2004)); but further than that, approaching these monstrous creatures informs us of the crucial efforts of developing a comprehensive understanding of capitalist *monsterology* (McNally 2011, 2) or a Demonology of capitalism (Wright 2020b). More than a side discussion or a lateral debate, this section argues how a monstrous dimension is very much present within our symbolic exchanges and imaginary societal prerogatives, one which derives from what controls reality today's in truly monstrous terms: capitalism. The readings on the mysteries of the fetishism of commodities intrigued Marx, they revealed the "magical" attribution commodities embodied within themselves once placed into a system of equalization and circulation. The typical route of investigating fetichism focus exclusively on capitalist production, but the proper background of our world's social trajectory also requires a comprehension of our modes of exchange commodities – the animistic nature of fetishism and its social consequences over our subjectivity requires this additional understanding. The more monstrous self-modulations of capitalism, its infernal loops require our participation to work, but we struggle to be able to break free from it.

In *Elements of the Philosophy of Right*, Hegel states how philosophy has a certain lateness, basically "philosophy, at any rate, always comes too late to perform this function" (Hegel 1832, 23). And the idea of introducing *monstrous materialism* is a philosophical coinage results from the consolidated discussion of the authors presented throughout this section. Instead of embracing

Fisher's *Gothic Materialism* (1999), the idea of monstrous materialism concerns understanding radical negativity and contradiction where (re)incantation and fetichism appears. Of course, this section does not pretend to go beyond dialectical materialism, the idea of organizing monstrous materialism, is just a way to further the debate of the dialectics already present in McNally's work (2011). The perspective which plays a significant part towards this debate is the integration of Karatani's (2014) thesis concerning modes of exchange to better locate how within our symbolic reality, in the very fabric of our symbolic exchanges, the gift-giving and counter-gifts operations still consolidate our primordial bonds. More importantly, Karatani advocates that alternatives towards our capitalist predicament are still possible, these have something to do with the mode of exchange D, which is nothing but the return of mode of exchange A in a higher dimension (Karatani's 2014, 9). This point clearly resonates directly with Jameson's (2014) call for a "theological" perspective to counter capitalist advances, perhaps, the point is not so much a proper theological in terms of religiously instituted possibilities, but a proper animistic perspective should be considered here at this level.

Although this section seems to be speculative, there is a certain possibility that Marx's mysteries behind the magic of the fetishism of commodity and the "necromancy" of capital, could benefit from this line of investigation and from the consolidation of the possibility towards a monstrous materialism. The monstrous topos of capital, when global capitalism dictates reality and make its advances over the inherent void of the subjects. Capitalism has substituted past societies dominating and infiltrating our symbolic and imaginary exchanges, not allowing room for any alternatives. From this speculative argument, the engagement with the Freudian uncanny (2003) ties the link between non-surmounted stance and the animistic grounds explored by global capitalism producing subjective suffering through atomization and displacement. To realize this fundamental aspect of our subjectivity, participant in our collectivity nods to our capacity of reinventing other modes of existence and collectivization as a possibility. It simply does not suffice to ignore the animism which Karatani (2014) highlights through Freudian psychoanalysis in our contemporary society. The symbolic sustainment of human exchanges through commodities through beliefs and illusions as an "invisible" structure in our "reality," dominates the subject (of the unconscious) to maintain capitalism intact: this is ideology at its best. This point signals to the potential of approaching the uncanny as methodologic element to localize a symbolic-imaginary emissary that participates in our everyday life exchanges, simultaneously calling back to prior modes of exchange and pointing out to a creation of something else (Karatani 2014). There are possible alternatives of sociability which could derive from the invention of different modes of exchange and sociability, but only if we re-shape our animistic roots under different forms of collective existence.

Notes

1 As Karatani (2014) explains Marx's point on "power of abstraction" in a preface to *Capital*, where Marx writes:

> "Moreover, in the analysis of economic forms neither microscopes nor chemical reagents are of assistance. The power of abstraction must replace both." We are now in the same situation: to analyse money and capital, we must rely on the explanation that Marx produced through the "power of abstraction" – that is, on the theory of value form found in the opening of *Capital*.
>
> (Karatani 2014, 84)

Marx inherited and developed his theory of surplus value through criticizing Adam Smith and David Ricardo (Karatani 2014, 85), however,

> [t]he problems that attracted Marx's attention from the start were the power of money, its religious inversion, and self-alienation. According to the classical economists, money presented no particular riddle: it was simply an indicator of the labor value born by each commodity.
>
> (Karatani 2014, 85)

2 The expression "the invisible 'handjob' of the market" was borrowed from Aaron Shuster (Zupančič 2017, 32) as the Zupančič points out. Smith's "invisible hand" is a direct testament to the unconscious and monstrous trait of capital's force.

3 As Karatani explains: "in order to analyze money and capital, we must rely on the explication that Marx produced through the 'power of abstraction' – that is, on the theory of value form found in the opening of *Capital*" (Karatani 2014, 84).

4 As Karatani summarizes the discussion in the first chapter of Marx's *Capital* concerning commodity value, it becomes clear how the value of a commodity relates to the use value of another commodity (the simple form of value coined by Marx). Following Karatani's investigation of Marx, when the commodity is turned as the relative form of value, the other commodity becomes the equivalent form. Basically, commodity as an equivalent form serves as money (universal equivalent). Following Karantani, considering this simple form of value, a reversal process starts to take place where the commodity who serves the purpose of universal equivalent manages to buy other commodities, which bounds the commodity sold to also operates as money (equated through this relation) (Karatani 2014, 86). This system in place allows for any commodity finding a way to enact like money. But for money to appear as such, the only way for this to happen, requires that the commodity as equivalent serves a purpose as the value form. Deriving from this simple form of value, "Marx theoretically explains the development through 'expanded form of value,' then 'general form of value form,' and finally the 'money-form'" (Karatani 2014, 86). Thus, Karatani explains that money appears when the commodity which enacts such equivalency

> ...is situated as the value form excluded from all other commodities. When gold or silver take up the position of universal value form and all other commodities are positioned as relative value forms, then gold and silver become money. But an inversion takes place here: even though they have only become money because they are positioned in this way, gold and silver come to be thought of as possessing a special intrinsic exchange value....
>
> (Karatani 2014, 87)

5 And Karatani explains how Marx at this point demonstrates how value it is not intrinsic to the commodity, that value appears through the exchange between commodities (from the value form). Following Karantani's Marxist evaluation,

"the value of a commodity can only be understood in terms of the relationship between it and other commodities..." (Karatani 2014, 85). The role of social labour, the abstract, actualizes the substance of value through a retroactive process deposited on money (as universal equivalent), as Karatani denotes, the subsequent relations produce an equalization between commodities (Karatani 2014, 86). As Karatani argues, "understanding the creation of money does not require the labor theory of value" (Karatani 2014, 86). Mostly because Marx in *Capital* discusses labour value and its relation to commodity just before his explanation of the value form, Karatani defends, this only raised confusion. What must be understood, according to Karatani is that "there is no value – labor value or otherwise – intrinsic to the commodity" (Karatani 2014, 86). The commodity acquires value only through the process of equation with other commodities. Thus, the "value is expressed in the form of the use value of that other commodity. In sum, the value of a given commodity arises from the equivalent form it locates in other commodities – in other words, from the value form" (Karatani 2014, 6).

6 As Marx exposes, following Karatani's approach, without the consideration of the use value of commodities, these are reduced to their shared trait, being products of labour (Karatani 2014, 128). Nonetheless, such products of labour are transformed in our hands, as emphasizes Karantani:

> If we make abstraction from its use value, we make abstraction at the same time from the material elements and shapes that make the product a use value; we see in it no longer a table, a house, yarn, or any other useful thing. Its existence as a material thing is put out of sight. Neither can it any longer be regarded as the product of the labour of the joiner, the mason, the spinner, or of any other definite kind of productive labour.
>
> (Karatani 2014, 128)

The useful qualities of products derive from the useful trait from the multitute of labour embodied by them and the concrete forms of labour, which we don't acknowledge right away. What is common to all of them, is that "all are reduced to one and the same sort of labour, human labour in the abstract" (Karatani 2014, 128).

7 Or as Kojin Karatani (2014) defends, in a society where the dominant mode of exchange (C) becomes the capitalist one (or World money) where M-C-M′(M + ΔM) extracts surplus value (ΔM) in a prominent fashion (2014, 97), remembering that this does not obliterate other modes of exchange A (gift giving), B (the contractual protection of ruling) and D (a transcendent mode of all the previous ones) (2014, x), but translates its dominance above all others. This could sound similar to Mark Fisher's intuition of capitalist realism (2009) but it actually provides a much more suitable argument to explain why such realism took over in the way it did in the first place.

8 Since time and money are primary mediators in Marxist Theory.

9 As Marx defends:

> The categories of bourgeois economy consist of such forms. They are forms of thought expressing with social validity the conditions and relations of a definite, historically determined mode of production, viz., the production of commodities. The whole mystery of commodities, all the magic and necromancy that surrounds the products of labour as long as they take the form of commodities, vanishes therefore, so soon as we come to other forms of production.
>
> (Marx [1867] 1982, 169)

10 This is why Wright advocates for a "Prolegomena to a demonology of capitalism" (2020b) defending his rejection of the idea that nobody controls capitalism and also

rejecting the idea that powerful humans control capitalism. His proposal is the following:

> Instead, I've proposed, unironically, that an occult spirit controls capitalism, and this spirit is the root cause of major social ills. First, we should adopt a form of animism in order to properly invoke the spirit, and see its true form. At this point we may hope to discover its proper name. Once discovered, we may command the spirit to do our bidding, and wield its titanic power as our own. At this point, we will be in control, and we will gain the magical power to consciously direct the world's activities to meet our human needs. The Great Work must be to free ourselves from the despotic rule and insatiable appetite of an inhuman, demonic spirit.

Nonetheless, this cannot be a Deleuzian stance, otherwise, it would fall under a (re) incantation of reality and not a proper dialectical material stance. Quiggin (2010) addresses the return of dead notions into the economy in a somewhat relatable manner.

11 This is *far too close* to Žižek's designation of the Kraken (2016) in "Disparities," which with its obscure tentacles have a much long and deep grasp on our world and reality under global capitalism.

12 As Wright explains: "Animism is the belief that all natural phenomena – such as the weather, geography, plants, trees, animals and so on – are ultimately controlled by an autonomous, living entity with humanlike agency" (Wright 2020b).

13 The overall idea of inviting magic here is a delineated one. First, there is no mistake of inviting any kind of metaphysical element back to our discussion concerning magic. Second, the debate concerning magic here relates strictly to the remainders of animistic traits and the social symbolic elements to which these persist within our relationships and exchanges, affirming the symbolic materiality noticed as "magical" or under magical logic (operative invisibility), is nothing but ingrained symbolic exchanges (imaginary stances and social identificatory modalities, which are symbolically carried out). Third, this is certainly not an attempt at advocating towards re-enchantment of reality (which can easily fall into the false pretenses of positivize empirical perspectives under capitalist ideological intensions).

14 A friendly approach to this proposal is Žižek's Hegelian-Lacanian point:

> The ontological axiom of disparity is that such a disparate structure is universal, constitutive of (what we experience as) reality: reality which we experience is never 'all'; in order to generate the illusion of 'all' it has to be supplemented by a disparate artificial element which fills in its gap or hole, as in a movie set composed of 'real' elements (trees, tables, walls), but with a painted background which creates the illusion that we are in a 'real' external world.
>
> (Žižek 2016, 26)

15 As Jameson (2014) indicates the figuration of "fetishism" for Marx: "This indissoluble relationship between Quality and the body will then make more vivid and sinister everything about the "fetishism of commodities" that smacks of spiritualism and of the abstractions of capitalism as such, which are now to be accounted for by Quantity, here identified, as in Hegel, with mind and "theory" as such. (To be sure, Hegel's idealism inclines his valorization in the other direction.) Yet Marx's materialism is not for all that any simple anti-intellectualism, nor does the categorial opposition between Quantity and Quality, fundamental to his thought in Capital, function as a simple dualism, as we shall see presently, but rather results in some strange new entity beyond the alternations of body and soul, a dimension quite distinct from the vulgar-Hegelian third term or "synthesis" that might have been expected" (Jameson 2014, 49). The figuration which Jameson indicates here,

concerns the opposition of a simple dualism but not falling in the vulgar-Hegelian, but to the negative stance which is inherent operating.

16 For Karatani:

> Animism is a belief system that regards all things, whether created by nature or humans, as being animate (possessing life spirit). It already exists at the stage of the nomadic band: the practice of burying the dead proves this. Yet while animism is the foundation of magic, it does not itself bring about magic. Magic appears only when a relation of reciprocal exchange is established with this *anima* (spirits). This development occurs only after the nomadic band takes up fixed settlement and a clan society is established.
>
> (Karatani 2014, 52)

17 There are numerous readings and renderings of the monstrous motif on Marx's work prior to Neocleous (2003), for example, the investigation of the monstrous realm and the Gothic influences to Marx's thinking was investigated by George E. Panichas' (1985) who focused specifically on Marx's werewolves and vampires regarding economic exploitation. While Panichas' presents a very allegorical sustenance of the theme of monstrosity, one which diminishes the vampires, were-wolves and living-dead as some "random" rhetoric allegories (which is a fairly common approach to this creatures concerning Marx's work); our present appreciation decided instead, to follow Neocleous who dedicates a more in-depth investigation to what Marx's usage of these monsters could actually mean.

18 Hyman, Stanley Edgar. *The Tangled Bank: Darwin, Marx, Frazer and Freud as Imaginative Writers* (New York, 1962), 145. The citations are from *Capital*, 899 and 915.

19 Wylie Sypher, 'Aesthetic of Revolution: The Marxist Melodrama', *Kenyon Review*, 10 (3) (1948), 431–444, 430.

20 Andrew Smith, 'Reading Wealth in Nigeria: Occult Capitalism and Marx's Vampires', *Historical Materialism*, 9 (2001), 39–59, 44, 47.

21 As Neocleous explains, Marx enjoyed reading horror stories and these were popular during the 19th century, but the most popular book about vampire, Bram Stoker's *Dracula*, was only published after Marx's death. This signals that vampires were already popular and spread in culture (Neocleous 2003, 673).

22 As Marx stated:

> Capital is dead labour, that, vampire-like, only lives by sucking living labour, and lives the more, the more labour it sucks. The time during which the labourer works, is the time during which the capitalist consumes the labour-power he has purchased of him.
>
> (1982, 342)

23 About this Hegelian self-recognition aspect, Karatani (2014) defends that a nation must be a nation to another nation in order to recognize itself as such.

24 Mark Fisher similarly appreciates this point through Žižek's *interpassivity* (2009, 15), basically denouncing how delegated enjoyment takes over, but delegated criticism operates in its subversion through cultural consumption. For example, watching a film about ecological criticism provokes an unconscious satisfaction to the subject who has consumed the film, this does not mean the person will afterwards engage in an ecological cause, it is regularly the opposite which takes place.

25 As Badiou presents: "After all, we must recognize that, today, 264 people possess as much wealth, in inheritance and income, as the 7 billion others who make up the rest of the world" (2019, 17).

References

Badiou, Alain. *Trump*. London: Polity, 2019.
Buck-Morss, Susan. *Hegel, Haiti, and Universal History*. Pittsburgh: University of Pittsburgh Press, 2009.
Federici, Silvia. *Caliban and the Witch: Women, the Body and Primitive Accumulation*. New York: Autonomedia, 2004.
Fisher, Mark. Flatline Constructs: Gothic Materialism and Cybernetic Theory-fiction. PhD Thesis defended in Warwick, 1999. http://wrap.warwick.ac.uk/110900/1/WRAP_Theses_Fisher_1999.pdf
Fisher, Mark. *Capitalist Realism*. London: Zerobooks, 2009.
Freud, Sigmund. *Totem and Taboo and Other Works*. Translation by James Strachey. In *The Standard Edition of the Complete Works of Sigmund Freud*, vol. 13. London: The Hogarth Press and the Institute of Psycho-analysis, 1955.
Freud, Sigmund. *The Uncanny. 1919*. London: Penguin Books, 2003.
Hegel, Georg Wilhelm Friedrich. *The Science of Logic*. Translated by George Di Giovanni. Cambridge: Cambridge University Press, 1832 [2010].
Hendricks, Margo; Parker, Patricia A. *Women, "race," and Writing in the Early Modern Period*. London: Routledge, 1994.
Jameson, Fredric. *Representing Capital: A Commentary On Volume One*. London: Verso Books, 2014.
Karatani, Kojin. *The Structure of World History*. London: Duke University Press, 2014.
Marx, Karl. *Capital*, Vol. 1. Harmondsworth: Penguin. [1867] (1982)
McNally, David. *Monsters of the Market. Zombies, Vampires, and Global Capitalism*. Leiden: Koninklijke Brill, 2011.
Neocleous, Mark. The Political Economy of the Dead: Marx's Vampires. *History of Political Thought*, Vol. 24, No. 4, 668–684, 2003. http://www.jstor.org/stable/26220011
Panichas, G. E. Vampires, Werewolves and Economic Exploitation. In *Marx Analysed: Philosophical Essays on the Thought of Karl Marx*, edited by G. E. Panichas Lanham, MD: University Press of America, 1985, 125–145.
Pfaller, Robert. "On The Pleasure Principle". In *Culture: Illusions Without Owners*. London: Verso Books, 2014.
Quiggin, John. *Zombie Economics: How Dead Ideas Still Walk Among Us*. Princeton, NJ: Princeton University Press, 2010.
Wright, Ian. *Prolegomena to a Demonology of Capitalism*, 2020a. https://ianwrightsite.wordpress.com/2020/03/05/prologomena-to-a-demonology-of-capitalism/
Wright, Ian. *What Is Abstract Labour and Who Does the Abstracting?* 2020b. https://ianwrightsite.wordpress.com/2020/06/13/what-is-abstract-labour-and-who-does-the-abstracting/
Žižek, Slavoj. *The Interpassive Subject – Lacan Turns a Prayer Wheel*, 2009. http://www.lacan.com/essays/?p=143#_ftn2
Žižek, Slavoj. *Disparities*. London: Bloomsbury, 2016.
Zupančič, Alenka. *What Is Sex?* Cambridge, MA: Mit Press, 2017.

5

A MONSTROUS GRAMMAR FOR PSYCHOANALYSIS

5.1 The psychoanalytic listening of suffering

Following our debate about the uncanny as *site* of compossibility, the incurrences on monstrosity as its radical consequences or the implications of (in)humanity deriving from the subject (of the unconscious). Thus, the importance of investigating the uncanny as a *site* does not mean to ignore its origins but to acknowledge it (as the previous chapter tried to defend) in a radical fashion. It is certainly not an effort of suture, but an effort of *monstration*. This chapter investigates how a "monstrous grammar" could derive from the uncanny as a *site of* compossibility, *without* forgetting or leaving its psychoanalytic background behind. There are impasses which are somewhat *monstrous* and the attention to such *topos*, signals towards the (in)human logic and the manifestations of *anguish* not restrained to either the comic or the tragic – which is the speculative direction this chapter aims at – the requirements towards a monstrous dialectical materialist understanding and its proper grammar.

The Brazilian Literature professor Célia Guimarães (2003) in *Os Monstros e a Questão Racial na narrativa modernista brasileira* [*The Monsters and the Racial question in the Brazilian modernist narrative*] carefully researches monstrosity in Modern Literature, delineating its notion, its relationship with the fantastic, the gothic and the magic-realist narratives, presenting how such European ideas migrated to Brazil. Guimarães (2003) presents how:

> ...monsters have permeated our imagination since Antiquity and the Middle Ages. They have, initially, a connection with a fertile maternal imagination which falls in love with a weird object, thus transferring to its offspring traits of this work, which simultaneously ruptures with natural law of

DOI: 10.4324/9781003437543-6

appearances in the process of reproduction. The result of this reproduction comes, then, to *demonstrate* ["*mostrar*"] nature's deviation and to *foretell* ["*avisar*"] the proximity of a catastrophe. The monster is, therefore, spectacular and mysterious.

(2003, 129)

Following her journey through literature, Guimarães (2003, 129) explains that the figure of the monster was in the Renaissance, a key figure for Shakespeare, "representing many vices and, particularly, the vice of ungratefulness and rebellion against family ties and with the benefactor" (2003, 129). This notion of monstrosity was devoured by Romanticism, which assimilates it while connecting to "the idea of the artwork as a unique creation, substituting the mother figure for the father figure and erasing the notion of co-production within the creation of the work" (2003, 129). Following Guimarães, it becomes clear how at the end of 18th century and the first half of 19th century, once rationalist basis of knowledge and truth started to be dislocated from its prior basis:

fantastic narrative departures from the causal/effect relation presented by realist narrative, bringing monsters and ghosts as their motif, and, as an effect, the hesitation and the reader's fear facing a indefinite choice between the real and the supernatural as explanations to facts.

(2003, 129)

The author explains how the Gothic narrative derives directly from this. Basically, the British and French Industrial revolutions were the birthplace of the vampires and Frankeinstein's Creature (2003, 129). The author sustains how the vampire translates the "parasitic trope," the sucking blood bourgeoisie and class struggle, and how the blood circulation theme enacts the confusion between life and death, how the beginning and ending are anthropophagic feeding for the art, a certain animistic perspective which (re)introduces itself into literature at this point. About Frankenstein's Creature, Guimarães dedicates attention to the dismemberment and attempt of constitution of a possible unity, which seems to be a common debate derived from Mary Sheley's Frankenstein. Nonetheless, Guimarães defends how in Gothic narratives, both monster characters seem to circulate together such themes and mix their lore with one another, and more interestingly, these figures enact attempts of translating dominant ideology to the context in which they were formulated.

Since monsters have the peculiar ability of being everywhere and nowhere simultaneously, these monsters easily travel overseas and become formulations to figurate alterity (Guimarães, 130). One of the examples raised by the author, is the cannibal which appears in one of the final plays from Shakespeare[1] (2003, 130), illustrating the colonial endeavours and its domination practices, which traversed literature adding excess to fiction and a certain symbolic (re) normalization of domination (2003, 130). As Guimarães explains:

> ...as a possible response to the colonial construct the Brazilian postcolonial narrative finds in magical realism, a literary mode which confuses the domains of supernatural and real, fictionalize this very own difference with the political objective of demarking cultural independence, the possibility of providing new meanings to monstrosity, invigorating or metamorphosing already existing monsters.
>
> *(2003, 130)*

In a way, the approach to the monstrous dimension and actualization of animism in our time resonates in the Brazilian case, but also to all anthropophagic colonized countries (2003, 77)[2] as well, in their attempts to deal with colonial domination and finding an "identity." Guimarães insightfully renders how Brazilian Literary Modernism, which helped spreading psychoanalysis in the country, used Freud's argument of the totemic meal in *Totem and Taboo* (1955) [1913], considering such "cannibalism" as a response against foreign domination. The author explains two different reactions to demonstrate this point: the first comes from Oswald de Andrade, who defends "...the full-frontal attack, inverts the given positions between sameness and otherness, demanding the destruction of the prior in order to affirm the identity of the latter, imitating Frankenstein's monstrosity" (2003, 130). And by doing so, the Andrade took particularities from Brazilian colonial relations in his anthropophagic reaction and in its "digestion," tried to devour away all the inherent colonial differences (especially those sustained by capitalism itself) which end it up making them invisible and normalizing racist narratives along the way. Of course, there were more intellectuals behind this movement who also introduced other ambiguous relations to European monstrous influences.

Another reaction comes from Mário de Andrade, who turned the "vampire" into a "trickster" when debating "parasitism and contamination, both at the level of language as to the post-colonial relations" (2003, 131). Guimarães defends that Mário de Andrade assumed a "war of positions," placing counter-discursive narratives trying "...to localize breaches in and at the colonizer's terrains, infiltrating through them in order to undermine them" (2003, 131). Well, Guimarães argues how Mário de Andrade applies a certain trickster narrative to his own narratives, as a rhetorical recourse to highlight alterity itself, "denoting through the 'not so much' monstrous figure of the trickster to debate racism in Brazil. As the author defends, Andrade's writings in *Macunaíma*, invites the trickster who:

> ...emerges as a "not so much" monstrous construction of Brazilian alterities: a nonanthropophagic trickster, a wild card at the narrative game, the

> erratic object of discourse, the Brazilian vampiric version of writing and representation of our postcolonial culture: a difference which inserts itself at an interstitial paradisiac space, contaminating and letting it contaminate by the other, fooling around with white, black and indigenous identities, in order to finally enact the instability and ambiguity of Brazilian identity.
>
> *(2003, 131)*

Guimarães' approach of monstrosity presented the circumscribed perspective of the European creatures into one of its colonies, denoting the emblematic stance of the anthropophagic and the non-anthropophagic positions (as well as its consequences), which permitted the arising of impasses at the symbolic level. Obviously, Guimarães sides with Andrade and his "not so much" monstrous *strategy* behind the trickster and how this remarkable "monstrous" *trickster*, resonates directly with one of Žižek's (2016) debates on the horror, the tragic and the comedy investigating Hegel's *Aesthetics*. As the Slovenian philosopher states:

> So maybe Hegel, in his tragic vision, was not able to consider the possibility of a horror worse than tragedy and which, precisely for this reason, may give rise to comedy, a laughter which is not done from the position of reconciliation, laughing at the vanity of the conflicts that persist, but a laughter through which the subject's total capitulation and disorientation transpires. In other words, Hegel knew that comedy follows tragedy; what he was not able to imagine is a comedy more horrible than tragedy. So it's not that Hegel jumped too quickly to comedy, to comic reconciliation, and that he should have seen that the tragedy of alienation and antagonism goes on in the modern world. In the modern world, the tragedy passed over to comedy, there is no return to tragic experience, and we should learn to see the horror in terms of comedy, in comedy itself.
>
> *(Žižek 2016, 239)*

Žižek's debate of Hegel Aesthetics[3] explain how Hegel seems captured by the tragic dimensions and does not fully notice the possibility of a "horror worse than tragedy" (2016, 239) and since comedy comes right after tragedy, Žižek explains that horrors must be learned to be noticed under comic terms. This rather paradigmatic stance from Žižek, must be understood not as an obliteration of horrors, but as an argument which sides with Zupančič's (2005) *Reversals of Nothing: the case of the sneezing corpse* (as previously addressed in Chapter 1) – it is not about a reconciliatory *forcing*, but a viable uncanny compossibility which nods to horror. The point is that horror is something which requires a proper politics, it must be learned to be talked about. Thus, the idea is not to take the *monstrous topos* itself, but to consider it as a transitory *experience* mobilized and approachable, and consequently, able to be traversed (if given its proper symbolic and imaginary tools) towards better grounds. However, such traversal does not aim at a naïve possibility of a return to the tragic or a return to metaphysics. The detailing of monstrous topos and its traversal is necessary against the false return to the tragic which is a symbolic (re)incantation, a certain nihilistic absurdity. In this same, *forcing* the comic as a reconciliatory movement is nothing but a step towards the dimension of cynicism. Žižek (1989) argues that neither nihilism nor cynicism are proper alternatives towards the horrific dimension of monstrosity, these only seem to (re) enforce affects of immobility and have no transformative capabilities. This is Žižek's way of defending that in the domain of comedy, there are "no privileged 'great topics' and 'anything goes'" (2016, 240), which does not mean that all capable fruition in Hegel is a big joke: far from it.

What Žižek locates in Hegel's *Aesthetics* is how at the level of comedy, there is a possibility for "absolute subjective personality to move free in itself and in the spiritual world" (2016, 240). The possibility of taking the negative and transform it through comedy, is a transformative capability which seems to be very much present in Hegel's passage examined by Žižek [4] The key point here lies in the *monstrous topos* between the tragic and comedy, which we already appreciated earlier by Žižek's contours on monstrosity itself, but which we could further add supplements and insightful implications to these remarks. An investigation Žižek finds also in Lacanian psychoanalysis as debated here in Chapters 2 and 3.

The point of not conceiving the uncanny as a suture, but as a *topological compossibility*, indicates a place of external shared borders between psychoanalysis and philosophy, where "monstration" produces its requirements to be traversed. The idea of purely applying Badiou's Žižek's or Zupančič's philosophies onto psychoanalysis (which is purely *nonsensical*) is certainly *not* what this text tries to do here. The point here is to appreciate the monstrous debate taken up until now and further articulate it to additional developments in psychoanalysis. Certainly, this is a more speculative effort, and it should not be assumed as *consequence* of clinical endeavour. The direction which this investigation takes now, is to rescue the possibility of taking a further look into the monstrous domains and it short-circuits within Lacanian psychoanalysis (with the help of further articulations).

5.2 Zupančič: The ethics of the Real and the discussion about the monstrous

First, it's crucial to stop at Zupančič's *Ethics of the Real* (2000), specifically on her paradigmatic appreciation of Lacan's investigation on the tragic topos. The philosopher is attentive to the ethical realm during her research, nonetheless, her careful investigation also appreciates the *threshold* of the tragic and its relevance for Lacan's psychoanalysis, that is, his articulation between the tragic and the monstrous for psychoanalysis. As Zupančič explains, Lacan consecrates tragedy as a fundamental realm to conceive his ethics (of psychoanalysis), he starts with "Antigone in his seminar *The Ethics of Psychoanalysis*, Lacan (1992) [1959–60] undertook, in his seminar *Le transfert*, a reading of contemporary tragedy with a discussion of Paul Claudel's Coûfontaine trilogy" (2000, 211). Zupančič takes a closer look at the play "*The hostage*" within the trilogy, investigating Lacan's closer examination of the character of Sygne de Coûfontaine, which helps him solidify the role of tragedy as a proper topos concerning impasses between law and desire in psychoanalysis. However, Zupančič investigates in the section "Ethics and terror," that there is an account between the "'classical' and 'contemporary' tragedy" (2000, 213), which leads up to *two different accounts of ethics*. Although Antigone is Lacan's first tragic character to debate law and desire, as subsequently, the ethical impasse deriving from tyranny (2000, 213), it is only with Sygne de Coûfontaine that Lacan seems to find the horrific dimension of terror as Zupančič explains (2000, 213).

Following Zupančič,

> Lacan describes the situation in which Sygne de Coûfontaine finds herself in these terms: 'The subject is asked to assume with enjoyment the very injustice that he finds horrifying.' These words concisely express what is at stake in terror as opposed to tyranny.
>
> *(2000, 213)*

Thus, the philosopher notices how the classical form of the relation of domination pushed to its extreme (which is tyranny), is described as "a radical '*desubjectivation*' of subjects in relation to the master" (2000, 213). As Zupančič explains, under tyranny, subjects are not really subjects, since they lack the fundamental dimension of subjectivity: "the possibility of choosing" (2000, 213). Terror on the other hand, concerns the opposite direction, the fundamental act of terror, the most terrorizing act,

> ...is when we are *forced* to subjectivize ourselves, where we are forced to choose. It is not only that we are allowed to choose - but we must also do so, and thus demonstrate that we are free subjects, whether we want to or not.
>
> *(2000, 213)*

Thus, there are opposite indications and radical subjective consequences at stake here.

Zupančič investigates Lacan's engagement between Antigone and Sygne de Coûfontaine (specifically, on the "grimace of life") and argues for different implications. While Antigone's tragedy and ethical impasse leads her towards a monstrous act (an ethical stance), placing her "between two deaths" and subsequently in all her sublimity, Sygne takes a step further (2000, 213).

Leading Zupančič towards Lacan's discussion of the "'vel of alienation' at the origin of subjectivation - this *vel* is his 'logical operator' expressing the logic of the forced choice…" (2000, 215) to circumscribe Sygne's choice. As Zupančič defends, such a choice is a "forced" choice, but it is not a choice in terms of "your money of your life!" (2000, 215), Sygne faces a different forced choice. The choice at stake is what Lacan discusses as "life or death" and the ethical implications surrounding it, but under the terms of "phenomenon of terror" which fall under a paradox (as Zupančič explains):

> The phenomenon of terror… can be formulated as follows: terror presents itself in those situations where the only way you can choose A is by choosing its negation, not-A; the only way the subject can stay true to her Cause is by betraying it, *by sacrificing to it the very thing which drives her to make this sacrifice*. It is this paradoxical logic which allows subjectivation to coincide here with the 'destitution' of the subject. While the subject constitutes herself as subject through the act of choosing, the nature of this very choice renders her destitute as a subject.
>
> *(2000, 216)*

Zupančič presents that the tragical form seems to be formulate at the proper background of monstrosity, which seems to be the proper way of understanding that, terror in its most radical manner, all the sudden, denotes "a strange structural homology between *terror* and *ethics*" (2000, 216). Certainly, the proper monstrous topos is here and perhaps, there is no possibility for sublimity without it. Of course, terror is not the same as horror, but terror is certainly a factualization of subjectivization (or desubjectivization) which derives from an impasse which has reached a monstrous topos. Certainly,

> [i]f ethics is always correlative to choice, we might say that the closer we come to the ethical Act, the closer we are to the most radical instance of choice - the one we have designated as the core of terror.
>
> *(2000, 216)*

Isn't the ethical Act, in a way, always a certain monstrous enactment? Zupančič defends how "…her ethical act has an ultimate character, because the only way she can act ethically is to choose to act (to use Kant's words) in a pathological - that is to say, non-ethical - manner" (2000, 216). And her line of investigation of the limits of universal ethics, exemplifies how there are situations where moral law requires its own transgression.[5] Nonetheless, Zupančič highlights the logic of the forced choice between the first example "Your money or your life" ("where we must choose life without money, or lose both") (2000, 217–218) and the second "Freedom or death" (where

I cannot affirm my liberty except by choosing death (2000, 218). As the philosopher defends:

> ...the first type of forced choice supports the classical logic of mastery, and thus classical ethics. It is probably unnecessary to emphasize that the vel 'Your money or your life' sums up the dialectic of master and slave. The slave 'gives in' and chooses life, while the master insists on the maxim which, at its heart, is a maxim of classical ethics: better death than ...! This does not imply, however, that the master can now live in peace for ever after, for sooner or later he will find himself in a situation where he must prove himself equal to his maxim. The occasion for such a proof will arise when he is confronted with the second type of choice.
>
> *(2000, 218)*

Zupančič explains how Lacan was attentive to these two different types of forced choice (2000 218), summarizing that the classic logic of the forced choice concerns a situation which implies the "better death than a life of treason" scenario (in the classic ethical decision in Kantian terms, as Zupančič defends). But the Slovenian thinker raises a different variant of this example, which is when "death would perhaps seem like a relief" (2000, 219), an expression of pure angst. Zupančič's complexifies Kant's ethical logics with additional layers, which are crucial to determine our point here. The philosopher defends that, in a story such as this, if the hero betrays his Cause (without turning into a traitor), the rising alternative (allowing the death of an innocent person) works as a certain "'heroic monstrosity', as an 'inhuman' choice" (2000, 219). For Zupančič, the lesson of these stories is that "one's humanity constitutes the limit of ethics and of one's duty. If the hero cannot carry out his duty except at the price of his 'humanity', he cannot be guilty of moral failure" (2000, 219).

Zupančič determines the (in)human's choice as the proper realm of monstrosity implied in the *Ethics of the Real* (2003). The thinker goes back to Sygne de Coûfontaine to determine the level of "'heroic monstrosity' *against humanity*"[6] (2000, 219), which implies the Kantian law in its purest form and how Lacan refers to it as desire in its pure state (2000, 220). Following Zupančič, Sygne seems to have "escaped" from the typical stories of this genre, (and isn't this precisely our point?): Sygne's monstrous act transcends the tragic dimension through her monstrous act. But there is no possibility of going back to the tragedy afterwards (Žižek 2016, 239–240) and there is absolutely nothing to laugh about this. Lacan denotes the point of excess represented by Sygne, whose capture is different than Antigone's predicament "between two deaths," Sygne translates the dimension of the *monstrous grimace*. As Zupančič explains,

> we find here something that goes further than all duty, something that opens 'a hole beyond faith'. So Sygne finally decides to go all the way, even if this path carries her towards the negation of all that she believes in, towards a 'monstrous' and 'inhuman' choice.
>
> *(Zupančič 2000, 220)*

Thus, the realm of the monstrous seems to be the proper topos of the ethical choice beyond the tragic and prior to the comic. But certainly, not in an automatic fashion, there are complex different conditions to adequately mobilize this dimension. Nonetheless, the excessive aspect of the law, which is the pure dimension of desire, is a "monstrous" excess which can tear up the symbolic fabric of law itself (i.e., as Antigone does), and there is another dimension, which obliterates all subjective beliefs for the subject (of the unconscious) along the way (which is Sygne's excess) (Zupančič 2000, 220). However, Zupančič ask:

> is the limit that Sygne must cross, the limit of ethics itself (thus representing a realm 'beyond ethics'), or is it only beyond that limit - once 'the hole beyond faith' has appeared - that (modern) ethics, properly speaking, begins?
>
> *(Zupančič 2000, 220–221)*

The dimension of horror lies in Sygne's terrorized choice, which enacts her reaction to this dilemma. This dimension explains the importance of considering the monstrous when approaching the ethical. As the thinker conceives, a certain modern dimension of the ethical appears here, one which imposes itself in our thinking and that should not be dismissed as "a 'horror' that only appears in extreme cases." Such, unprecedented dimension must be acknowledged when a discussion of 'modern' ethics is attempted (Zupančič 2000, 221).

As Zupančič discusses, Sygne's sacrifice nods the Freudian dimension of *nebenmensch*, it concerns *the Thing* which compels Sygne, the horrific abyss which is presented in front of her, "is this not precisely the thing before which Freud himself had drawn back in horror: namely the commandment, in all its rigour, to love one's neighbour?" (Zupančič 2000, 221) Pursuing Zupančič's argumentation at this precise point, between Lacan and Badiou:

> Lacan, of course, places the source of hostility, of the aggression which arises in my relation to the neighbour, in the field of enjoyment. It is enjoyment that is always strange, other, dissimilar. Lacan formulates still another argument which agrees with Badiou's interpretation: it is not simply the mode of enjoyment of the neighbour, of the other, that is strange to me. The heart of the problem is that I experience my own enjoyment (which emerges along with the enjoyment of the other, and is even indissociable from it) as strange and hostile. To put it another way: we cannot conceive of radical

alterity, of the 'completely other' (to which Lacan gives the Freudian name das Ding [the Thing]), without bringing up the question of the Same (as opposed to the similar).

(Zupančič 2000, 225)

To this point, Zupančič denotes how Lacan seems to capture the crux of this argument, since concerning questions of recognition of the Same (at the level of enjoyment [jouissance]), Zupančič (following Lacan) denotes how Freud evades this point in his line of thinking. When Freud refrains from the "commandment to 'love thy neighbour', he passed over the fundamental problem of *jouissance* (and the 'evil' to which it is linked)" (Zupančič 2000, 226). From this precise Lacanian reminder, the philosopher approaches Sygne, from another standpoint, to explain how Sygne's act has the "character of an act of 'pure desire' which, as such, leads her beyond desire" (Zupančič 2000, 230). Zupančič raises the pivotal point of the character debating "honour" and "life" in sacrifice, with the other characters in the play[7] and how this dimension, permits an approach towards the "exact nature of Sygne's act" (Zupančič 2000, 231) and its implication between the logic of desire and the logic of the drive.

Zupančič establishes from scratch that Sygne's sacrifice stays inscribed in the logic of desire and that it "represents the ultimate horizon of her 'fundamental fantasy'" (Zupančič 2000, 231), leading towards a paradox. As the philosopher explains, the paradox presents itself in the moment Sygne faces this ultimate horizon, given that she is already "obliged to beyond it, to leave it behind" (Zupančič 2000, 231). As Zupančič explains,

> … even if Sygne's act is situated in the logic of desire - of pure desire - it 'contains' something which leads beyond desire - towards the 'encounter with enjoyment', to use Lacan's words that Sygne's case illustrates so well: 'To encounter enjoyment, desire must not only understand, but traverse [*franchir*] the very fantasy which constructs and supports it.'
>
> *(Zupančič 2000, 231)*

Following Zupančič, it becomes clear how Sygne's tragedy starts from the fact that she has lost her Cause and everything that once belong to her world, only "nothing remains for her [to] save the empty frame, and fidelity to this framed emptiness" (Zupančič 2000, 232). Nonetheless, as the philosopher explains the remainder of "nothing" itself, the empty frame is something Sygne *has*, thus, "something she could give up or sacrifice. If she has it, she can give it up" (Zupančič 2000, 232), the crux of this point about Sygne, explained by the philosopher, goes as follows:

> Will you give up on your desire at the moment when, for the first time, it really counts?' It is not difficult to recognize here the horizon of pure desire,

> in the appeal made to Sygne to sacrifice the last 'pathological motive' which truncates the purity of her desire and her adherence to the Cause.
>
> *(Zupančič 2000, 232)*

This is precisely the articulation of the traversal of fantasy, which Zupančič notices in Sygne's act, since even "if Sygne's act comes inevitably to undermine her 'fundamental fantasy', it is at the same time accomplished precisely in the name of this fantasy" (Zupančič 2000, 232). Zupančič clearly captures the monstrous act of Sygne's articulation within the logic of desire, her story portrays exemplarily the radical dimension of Lacan's imperative "Do not give up on your desire" and how it is connected to the fundamental fantasy of the subject (of the unconscious) (Zupančič 2000, 232). And as Zupančič explains, this connection transforms the previous imperative into "Do not give up on the object-cause which constitutes the support of your fantasy!" (Zupančič 2000, 232), but her point is that,

> ...even if this imperative is linked to fantasy, by means of desire, its ethical value nevertheless remains incontestable. We cannot 'get beyond' the fantasy by giving up on the Cause that animates us but, on the contrary, only by insisting on it until the end. Such a 'traversing the fantasy' [*La traversee du fantasme*] is a step which can be taken only from 'inside' this fantasy. As Lacan remarks, to go beyond the fantasy, it is not enough to know it and to speak of it from a distance. Rather, desire must at the same time 'traverse the very fantasy which constructs and supports it'.
>
> *(Zupančič 2000, 232)*

This is why Sygne's refusal of this sacrifice means the betrayal of her desire and simultaneously, to accept this refusal leads her to "lose the cause of her desire (her 'reason for living')," as Zupančič posits (Zupančič 2000, 232–233). It is through the operation of the traversal of fantasy, that "desire meets its end" and allows the passage towards another register, in the case of Sygne, is her ability of stating the final "no" (Zupančič 2000, 233). As Zupančič disambiguates Lacan's point on Sygne, who takes her as the "figure of a woman deified only then to be a woman crucified?" (Zupančič 2000, 233) Zupančič pursues an explanation to the fact that the splendour of Sygne's martyrdom does not prevent the appearance of her tortured grimace within it (Zupančič 2000, 233) and in order to provide an answer, Zupančič hypothesizes this formulation: once there is no longer any guarantee (Divine or of any other order), "Sygne makes herself the support of this guarantee. In fact, she goes further" (Zupančič 2000, 233). For Zupančič, Sygne's "going further" means:

> She does not sacrifice herself to procure a guarantee of the Divine law. She does not make herself into a support of this guarantee, she 'makes herself'

> this very guarantee, such that this guarantee remains dislocated from that of which it is the guarantee. By so doing, Sygne reveals the necessarily invisible support in the sublime image of the Divine. The value of her final 'no' resides in the fact that she, in so far as she incarnates this guarantee, refuses to disappear and abandon herself to God. The end of the play thus leaves us with an unsettling image, an image in which the Divine law and its sole support occupy the same level; the (Divine) law finds itself face to face with this convulsing flesh that refuses to disappear from the picture, effectively preventing a sublime splendour from appearing in its place.
>
> *(Zupančič 2000, 233–234)*

Zupančič discussion on the Ethics of the Real (2003), provides the contours and the relevance of furthering an approach towards the monstrous implications of tragedy. In a way, Zupančič never diminishes such dimension, nor avoids it, her efforts highlight Lacan's necessary approach to it, in order to fully understand the paradoxical (monstrous topos) between law and desire. Of course, concerning the present discussion of this text, Zupančič's investigation of Lacan invites the necessity of engaging with the monstrous dimension *as* the proper dimension of the impasse (of the Real). The designation of the *monstrations* (proper designation of experiences) (Zupančič 2017, 69), which experiences so crucially seem to surface. In a way, this dimension is crucial to psychoanalysis and the possibility of approaching it has many different directions.

5.3 Conjectures towards a psychoanalytic monstrous grammar

Up until now, the designations of the monstrous realm were in a way an attempt to refine the importance of considering a monstrous *grammar*. The importance of refining the monstrous domain does not mean to reconfigure the structural diagnosis in any way (quite far from it), what it does is permit a different approach to psychoanalysis structures, considering the standpoint of *monstrations*. One rather crucial argument made so far on this, regards the capability of approaching the uncanniness experiences as an articulation which (re)edits the monstrous topos and how its proper investigation can lead towards different implications (e.g., Zupančič's differentiation between Antigone and Sygne). Our point here is that the attentive comprehension of the monstrous dimension provides further insights concerning the symbolic-imaginary stances in dealing with the Real. One of these possible directions comes from the psychoanalyst Christian Dunker who provides an interesting render on monstrosity. His render goes against the naïve approaches to Lacanian structural diagnosis (i.e., the idea that these can be surpassed or substituted) and the psychoanalyst finds interesting advances concerning the symbolic-imaginary debate furthering the monstrous dimension. The (in)human dimension, which seems to be the monstrous point, reaches us through the operation of an *act*, as Zupančič (2000, 232–233) has presented. Nonetheless, the *act* itself is not dislocated from the unconscious operations which drives it, as previously debated in Antigone and Sygne. Therefore, the possibility of investigating them, as well as being able to listen to their logics is an important point to be considered. Basically, Dunker's investigation adds elements to this point, and it nods towards a possibility of "listening" to current monstrous impasses of nowadays (this does not mean that this is the only one, it simply implies one of its possibilities) and to the murmurs of the Real.

Dunker's main premise in his book "*Mal-estar, sofrimento e sintoma*" [*Discontent, suffering and symptom*] (2015) is that modes of suffering have a history and particular conditions which can never be "forgotten." The Lacanian psychoanalyst argues the Borromean knot between three spheres (discontent, suffering and symptom), showing how suffering has re-actualized itself through many different *grammars*, through different narratives structures along the time. Dunker argues how Freud's theory of the unconscious comes as a result of psychological suffering which was ignored. In the 19th century, there were other psychiatric methods at that moment, for example, the description of neurasthenia by Beard (around 1880), Pierre-Marie-Félix Janet (who was a disciple of Jean-Martin Charcot) that held his thesis on *psychasthenia* (1903) which assumed suffering derived from neurotic fragility. What differs psychoanalysis from other methods is the Freudian paradigmatic understanding of suffering in hysteric individuals have an unconscious *logic*, one which introduces a new *grammar* to address (in)human suffering. Freud summarizes how work, desire and language could be more comprehensive if formulated under his methodology. The advancements from Freud's psychoanalysis transformed the understanding of mental health and psychopathology in his time. Certainly, psychopathology studies kept on going since Freud's time, additions and/or subtraction of *concepts* and *types* (normative capabilities) are constantly emerging in the field. Nonetheless, Dunker is attentive to the psychoanalytic field and does not wish to clash against heterogeneous perspectives on this matter.

Dunker (2015) reinforces the crucial validity of Lacan's critique of psychoanalysis concerning psychopathology. Lacan's *return to Freud* makes it clear how mental illness is not strictly "mental" nor is strictly an "illness" – it is a matter of how symptoms enact possible universals of the subject through particular conditions (even when experienced singularly). Or as Dunker (2015) summarizes, symptoms are a nod to a lost freedom which could be either self-imposed or imposed by others; much like the neurotic's individual myth for Lacan, where the symptoms cannot be detached from its modes of expression, social recognition and its inherent symbolic-imaginary settlements. Dunker argues how Lacan manages to distinguish the arrival of new symptoms from what could be new modes of suffering to old symptoms, or as he defends,

> contrary of the common usage found in epistemological and sociological studies, that aim at clarifying the conditions of exercising a practice, the

> objective here [in his book] is to show how a *metadiagnostic* investigation is more than just a contribution to social critic, it can transform and reorganize the practice of the clinic itself.
>
> *(Dunker 2015, 46)*

In a way, Dunker is providing crucial tools not to "create" a wild psychoanalysis, he adds further points from the Brazilian experience with psychoanalysis, translating the possibilities of engaging with freedom and suffering from our local context. Especially because "from a psychoanalytic standpoint, the difference between kinship, of totemic and animistic nature and the modes of exchange particular in civil society, present in educating, governing and desiring" (Dunker 2015, 228) must be contextualized during psychoanalytic treatment. This is why the psychoanalyst defends the possibility of furthering a necessary grammar of recognition in order to face experiences of determination and indetermination experienced in our lives. The psychoanalyst provides the crucial possibility of investigating psychoanalysis further added by anthropological perspectives, which allow the comprehension of animism through the lenses of determination and indetermination, providing symbolic grounds towards possible cures to suffering whose cause lies in societal formations.

There is other two key contributions from the psychoanalyst to this debate, the first one is an overall consideration of how monstrous approaches to suffering[8] (2013), precisely when Lacan's assumption of neurosis as an individual myth (where the tragedy facing the ethics of desire), must deal with new kinds of symptoms from the dissolution of the romantic form, as present in James Joyce. And Dunker states that "if there is any homology between a symptom and the work of art, it must consider each and every new suffering as a creation and response to the transformations at the horizon of an epoch" (2013, 28). Thus, the analyst risks an appreciation of zombies, frankensteins, ghosts and vampires, under this psychoanalytic approach. In order to summarize Dunker's development into a visual (with the aim of facilitating the comparison between the two texts) (Table 5.1):

What Dunker explains is that "clinical types are identifications, i.e., narrative forms, more or less collectivized, through the experiences of suffering which are able to be included in already instituted discourses" (Dunker 2013). This is why further developments in this direction are so crucial, the inclusion in discourse of different modalities of suffering makes room for its recognition, destination and possibility of treatment, as the psychoanalyst defend, much in line with Lacan's own developments for that matter. Still following Dunker (2013), the unrecognized suffering turns into a *silenced truth* and "... suffering finishes the theory of its own cause" (Dunker 2013). So there is something of the Real, something of the truth and something to be known in suffering and love, since they point at new forms of being. Thus, the appropriation of such elements could operate in terms of recognizing transformative impasses

TABLE 5.1 Dunker's (2018) overall investigative model for monstrous narratives of suffering

Key traits	*Preponderant trait of suffering*	*How do they perceive the real?*	*What do they interrogate?*
Zombies Frankenstein creatures	Suffering from the lack of productive experiences of indetermination, where processes of rationalization appear as an indifferent void	Real as impossible	Cultural experiences of identity are not given facts and recognition can be subjected to high levels of indeterminacy.
Ghosts Vampires	Suffer with the excess of unproductive experiences of determination, that is, as if they trusted too much in processes of symbolization and subjectivization that regulate different regimes of truths	Real as contingent	Question the totemic authority.

is fundamental for psychoanalysis. It is how practice can enlarge its toolbox of listening to different grammars, different arrangements and make room for different qualities of suffering. As Dunker continues (Table 5.2):

From this first elaboration, Dunker furthers his analysis in "*Zumbis, fantasmas, vampiros e frankensteins.*" [Zombies, ghosts, vampires and frankensteins] (2018), providing a better scope to the analyst's argument. Overall, the text defends an approach which provides *dignity* to the debate of the living dead under four main monstrous forms. These monstrous figurations derived from the literary genre of horror and the psychoanalyst approaches them in Lacanian terms. He starts by explaining how "terror seems to become stronger and it disseminates itself with the reencounter with the same known combination already established by excitation and freight…" (Dunker 2018, 16) and how the gothic literary tales seem to understand how:

> …an aesthetic is received as a recollection of what was once experienced when we were children, wanting to hear the same tale one time again, with all its sordid details, with witches, wolves, stepmothers and villains. Tales which have at their center the evocation of anguish between two series - the series of threat, allusions, of the void; and the series of realization, of the cut and the presence of the body.
>
> *(Dunker 2018, 16)*

TABLE 5.2 A Lacanian appreciation of monstrous narratives of suffering by Dunker (2018)

Inspired by	*Distinctive feature of the modality of suffering*	*Lacanian directions from these traits*
Malabou	(1) the post-traumatic subjectivity translates its suffering by compulsively repeating in a "zombielike" state and does not engage in a proper tragic narrative (it is a fundamental struggle with naming feelings and selective mutism).	The symptom as alienation to Other's desire, under the current mode of production and consumption.
Žižek	(2) the monstrosity as the inhuman way of experiencing life, as indeterminacy which does not inscribe suffering in a discourse…, [a] permanent state of systematic failure in naming the cause of their suffering and the discontent in the world is experienced in estrangement, inadequacy and fragmentation.	The systemic de-regulation and loss of unity is the Lacanian thesis that the symptom is an effect (but also cause) of the untying between Real, Symbolic and Imaginary.
Badiou/Laclau	(3) the modality of suffering in the Badiouan subject, which only appears conditioned through the fidelity to an Event - trying to mourn ghosts from the past.	The neomasoquist narrative of the violation of the Symbolic pact of origin, with its phantasmatic return, rescuing the thesis on negation at the Oedipal drama and in the Castration Complex.
Agamben	(4) the condominium suffering emerged from the paranoid state created by sheltered life and propagated on a State of exception in Agambenian terms.	The paranoid narrative of intrusive objects that infiltrate within walls and regulations, the paradoxical satisfaction of jouissance appears here.

What we learned from Dunker's further development is that from all these modalities of literary possibilities, horror is the one which seems to have experienced less alterations and less experimentations in comparison with others (e.g., romance, tragedies and so on) (Dunker 2018, 15). Dunker argues that the horror does not weaken in the face of repetition, that horror establishes a *structural* relationship with its renditions. The horror sustains itself in the face of repetition, the ticklish feeling experienced by children exposed to a horror tale endures, even when told for a second time. Such horror tales evoke *angst* in two series: (1) *threat*, *void*; (2) *realization*, *cut* and *bodily presence* (Dunker 2018, 16). As the analyst argues:

> For Freud there is a distinction between the horror of the return of experiences we deny within ourselves (return of a truth) and horror from the suspension of beliefs or how reality is perceived (return in the Real which de-constructs unity and the identity of our experience. But, in this case, not only the return in the Real of that which was not inscribed or not affirmed in the Symbolic, but also the return in the Real of that which was not inscribed in the Imaginary.
>
> *(Dunker 2018, 16)*

In a sense, Dunker sustains a Lacanian reading of the Imaginary, which does not ignore what returns in the Real for not being Symbolically inscribed; but he also addresses the clinical role of the Imaginary. Of course, Dunker is far from being naïve here, he critically understands the Imaginary participating in alienation and fetishism of lack; nonetheless, he argues the Imaginary role in "inventing new forms of images, new narrative forms, the invention of nonexistent times and nonexistent places, the creation of uncertainty to denounce what surrealists called "this much reality"" (Dunker 2018, 16). So, "imaginarization" as a procedure can support *creation*, which does not (automatically) mean setting Ideals (different than plans, ideals enact imaginary traps important to be avoided[9]), but *alternatives*. Although Dunker does not state this with all the letters, a possible interpretation lies in considering the role of Imaginary in reinventing temporalities *as such* – not only what is at stake in possible "*futures*," but also on the reinvention of the past itself in this process – something symbolically crucial and profoundly monstrous.

For Dunker, horror only occurs in the combination of the corruption of intimacy and critique of reality (Dunker 2018, 16) – which could be easily noticed as crucial ingredients of Freudian uncanny (2003). There is something about the uncertainty between fiction and reality, about the role of fantasy and that none of this should be taken lightly. The conception of well-defined lines separating intimate life and external reality as opposites does not make sense, these are intrinsically intertwined "opposites." Such false dichotomies only explain the intricacies of fantasies they produce. As Dunker remembers, there is a double possibility here: either to "escape *from* reality" or "escape *into* reality" (2018, 17). The first one is rather common in daydreaming, subjective fragmentation, disassociation, dispersion and so on; but the second one, is less common, with "expectant anxiety, its orientation towards action and the externalization of conflicts" (2018, 17). The main questions concerning the imaginary are summarized by Dunker as:

> ...truth as contingency in a fictional structure and the Real as the impossible that does not cease to inscribe itself. This presents itself, historically, in

the case of horror, as narratives that question intimacy and as narratives which question the body.

(17)

In Dunker's (2018), further investigation of *identification types: Zombies, Frankensteins, Ghosts and Vampires*; the elements of their logic, their monstrous grammar, seem much more in consonance with the intricacies of the uncanny than tragedy or comic. And why is that? Because as Dunker states, the monstrous captures the movement in-between, it captures the language of transformation. Take the Freudian uncanny, that which was supposed to have been kept secret but that came to light. It is not strictly external, from far away, from abroad or from other worlds, it is an invasion from within, the alterity within us. Thus, horror and terror are experiences of the transition between familiarity and alterity for Dunker (2018, 24). He explains how each one of them operates and tries to capture something of the expression of subjective suffering aligned with a clinical perspective. Dunker does not present a simple juxtaposition of elements or an aimless theoretical construction – the psychoanalyst argues how this construction always has the clinic at its horizon. Therefore, Dunker argues that uncanniness relates to the experience of dealing with death, glancing into our material mortality, setting an existential examination of time for the subject (with this uncanny affect along the way) and also, demonstrating how horror lies in our willingness to *suture* with a horrific object the very own gap between reality and truth (which is symbolically established).

Although the experience of estrangement and horror do occur, they do not force us to question the value of reality – except for traumatic experiences, these moments tend to have their own temporality and shake our experience with reality. And as Dunker remind us:

> Our attraction for horror, expressed by the compulsion to repeat experiences which horror evokes, does not compose a pathological feature. On the contrary, it works as an antidote for the impoverishment of our fantasies, eventually stuck at conditions and limitations that express our cowardness to cross the standpoint protected by horror, by terror and by uncanniness. At the moment where we face many forms of segregation, intolerance and forcing towards sharing reality and to the same form of truth, it lies in horror a possible critical potential, and a potency to recovering desire. Our attraction to horror denounces that we have not yet totally conformed with what reality places in front of our eyes.
>
> *(2018, 28–29)*

And also:

> Anyone can say that zombies and ghosts *do not exist*, but, at the same time, we have crack houses, systematic murders of black people in the periphery

> of big cities and the bodies of refugees floating in the Mediterranean *do exist*. The central problem here is that between *existence* and *nonexistence* there is something called Real. And its truth can only be accessed through the structure of fiction. The two strategies, combined by weird realism, are forms of creating a conscience of the non-Real, which is, in itself, a space determined by an experience outside of the territory, non-localized or of loss of its place.
>
> *(2018, 33)*

The possibility of considering horror is completely connected with the possibility of understanding the *fictional structure of truth* which sets reality itself, Dunker defends how horror has a potency. The relationship between that which exists and that which does not exist, sets the proper monstrous topos for our subjectivity, where a certain politics of the negative occurs, a certain less than nothing or a more than something, can be symbolically engaged (knowingly that at the limit, it is symbolically impossible to be fully conceived – but even the attempt itself, is *necessary*). More than just a mere theoretical consideration, what becomes clear from the clinical impasses of psychoanalysis here at this level, concerns how these always point out to our negative ontological limits. For instance, the horror points out to a necessity in comprehending dynamics of (in)human *jouissance*, it points out to our inherent difficulties of dealing with our bodies, languages and truths (Badiou 2008), certainly (in)human jouissance translates the monstrous topos of the struggling with indeterminacy and determinacy which shatter our subjective experiences of everyday life.

To consider the investigation of these monsters as a waste of time, because they do materially *exist* is to not understand how language works, these monsters are real abstractions, these monstrous *figurations* (in the Jamesonian sense), are creatures that exist without needing to "consist of": which makes them even more consistent. In a way, our own (in)humanity benefits from this discussion, especially when these monstrous features relate to our inherent condition, our predicament facing language and our shared (social) experiences in a capitalist reality.

Taking a further look at the monstrous traits of identification prescribed by Dunker (2020), it becomes important to notice how the articulation with the uncanny seems to add symbolic potency to its engagement, instead of further confusion or troubles. One could say that in a way, the articulation of welcoming the uncanny within the clinic is a possibility of further engaging with crucial elements of our (in)human anguish (the next scheme is only a way of further separating a bit better what the analyst's explore).

For Dunker's horror in general is the combination of two levels: loss of intimacy and a critique of reality provokes horror. It is a discourse that explores uncertainty between fiction and factual. It is the threshold between traumatic and transgressive, a strange fragment of the truth of our desire and the horror awakened by such grain of the Real, which is the object of our angst. The attitude of fooling ourselves and evading from this truth by "not wanting to know" and escaping this Real by convincing ourselves it is "just our imagination," are its usual responses. Horror collects a large price to be paid in order for us to continue sleeping at night, the price of avoiding any reminder that things can turn for the worst... at any time. He furthers his investigation (Table 5.3):

Horror as a genre, uncannily spreads through the symbolic fabric with its particular images (e.g., the monsters and their figurations), but it also carries with its emissaries from the Real. Each grain of the Real that manifests itself, enacts a shattering remainder of irreversibility, that nothing escapes unprotected by it, and the role of fantasy tries to sustain its grounds in this operation. As Dunker describes, the element of fantasy is fundamental to understand what escaping *into* reality or escaping *from* reality means; in a way, this resonates directly with Zupančič's debate between Sygne and Antigone's grimace (2013, 233), as previously presented.

There is much more to be digested from Dunker's scheme. First, there is the combination of questions of intimacy and the questions of the body in order to produce horror – which for itself, is an uncanny designation of the body through a Lacanian understanding. Not only the questions of truth and of the Real are at stake at this level, but also, the appreciation on how these are bound to one another. Thus, the Real of the body in all its monstrous, and in all its uncanniness, has something to do with the non-symbolical dimension of it and the Imaginary (re)articulations capitalize on these monsters of negativity. So, how to perhaps engage with the negative dimension of the Symbolic and the Imaginary? This provocation points to how the addressing of suffering could follow a certain monstrous predicament, which is a limit between the unbearable traversal of fantasy, but also, as the attempt of localizing a dimension which is Symbolically or Imaginarily dislocated. Therefore, the proposition of a zombified transmission of suffering, or a vampiric one, Frankensteinian one or a ghostly one, certainly does not sound so wild. Obviously, this does not mean to substitute Lacanian discourses or even less, has the capability of obliterating the tragedy endeavours (nor its ethical implications); what the psychoanalyst defends is the possibility of *identification* with these monstrous traits, which seems to be an attempt to localize this "unlocalizable" addressment.

Dunker's attempt at the uncanny, through his Lacanian refinement, paves this monstrous perspective. The modalities of desire portrayed by him are based on uncanny foundations, which invite us (or which it could) to consider the current encounters with horrors in our daily lives. Especially those which we tend to pretend not to be scared by or that we pretend to ourselves that will never happen to us... Couldn't those be (neurotic) defences against the invasions of the Real in its de-articulation with the Symbolic and the Imaginary? The modalities of Ghosts, Vampires, Frankensteins and Zombies, defended by

TABLE 5.3 Dunker's (2018) general development on horror

Fantasy level	*Directions*	*Questions cause by it*	*Key narrative elements*	*Quality of narrative at stake*	*Moral of the history*	*Identification types*
Escape from reality (deregulation of spirit and break of symbolic pacts)	Truth as contingency in a fictional structure	Intimacy (Hawthorne; Poe)	Intrigue, suspense and mystery	Eerie coincidences, superstitions and weirdness. Twist the relationship with the truth – showing something we knew but prefer not to look at. Unrealness evokes Symbolic truth to emerge – setting the score with the dead.	The truth is someplace else, the horror is because we've been mistaken, wronged or betrayed	Ghosts Vampires
Escape into reality (losing your soul and the intrusion of object)	Real as the impossible that does not cease to inscribe itself	Body (Hoffmann; Lovecraft)	Corruption of reality of other possible worlds	A critique of our beliefs concerning the nature of reality. The Horror from the formlessness, from that which has no name or meaning. We do not know if it is a dream, an illusion, an unknown reality, bad omen – the unheard-of....	The Real is someplace else.	Frankensteins Zombies

Dunker, are uncanny derivations of the monstrous topos seen through a psychoanalytic standpoint. Basically, this means that the analytic apparatus can resonate with the monstrous topos and (re)engage with it, taking these figurations much further. Let's look at Dunker's identification traits, in order to map what these figurations designate. Starting with the Ghosts (Table 5.4):

What the psychoanalyst determines, and we can extrapolate, is that psychoanalysis has a great deal to do with *ghosts*. The French psychoanalyst Jacques Lacan had different moments of his quintessential return to Freud, always

TABLE 5.4 Dunker's (2018) psychoanalytic appreciation of ghosts

Identification types	*Main Introductory features*	*Main conceptual feature*	*Element of desire*
Ghosts	The ghost that haunts you was always already there, for example, Hamlet's father.	The horror and terror are experiences between the transition of familiarity and alterity. The missing element from the plot, the hidden image from the object that mandates the spectator to put himself/herself to complete the scene. The intrusive object is missing, and it is built up from the subject's suppositions. The structure of suture operates here. The haunted objects and haunted places are the theme of the violation of the Symbolic agreement between the living and the dead, man and gods, children and adults…	The trait of sexuality, or corporeal estrangement, loneliness and *angst*. Unheimlich. The suture is a perfect marriage (since it is formulated by us) between what we see and what we cannot see. The ghost comes back to collect the debt of the renounced, haunting for the rest of our lives… Ghosts have a certain Symbolic justice to balance the scales between the living and the dead. Haunted relates to the interior of unconscious fantasy, between the function of organizing reality and the function of transmitting desires. Something about reality did not sexualize or symbolize properly – producing a return.

with issues along the way but, in a sense, it is a constant construction site, Lacan's analytic formalizations were taking place while he was constructing most of them. Dunker explains how the "ghostly topic" lies on how Lacan uses the anthropological constructions of Cláude Levi-Strauss and the linguistic inversion of Ferdinand de Saussure (signifier – signified, turned upside down into signified-signifier) managing to revisit the old Freudian motto of "talking cure" (2018, 24).

When Freud was developing the first steps of psychoanalysis, he was dealing with mesmerism, magnetism and the early beginnings of hypnosis, pseudoscientific practices that were a part of psychiatry and neurology at the time (Gay 1989). And his insight on listening instead of hypnotizing their patients in order to cure them, transforms the passive role of the analysand in the transformative process of subjectivization towards emancipation against suffering. Back to our ghostly debate, through Lacanian lenses, Dunker states how ghosts give us the opportunity of addressing the hauntings of our lives. And what is one of the most haunting ghostly feelings one can experience (always remembering that neurotic, perverted and psychotic individuals, will always experience reality in a different fashion)? To *owe*, to be indebted. The ghostly lurking around everything and haunting everybody fits perfectly with global capitalism. The constant feeling of owing, this experience of being dragged around through reality always permeated by a debt is no new topic for psychoanalysis. This is one of the main features of neurosis, the experience that we are not in terms with the Other. The ghostly dimensions of suffering are a monstrous tone of the suffering which comes from Symbolic agreements and how the subject (of the unconscious) deals with it. In this sense, this haunting has everything to do with being able to participate in language and within the Symbolic, respecting its own structural features, but also, highlighting how desire and suffering re-edits this ghostly feature for the subject (Dunker 2018, 25). And even further, how to suffer from this specific trait of symbolic reality is a different kind of suffering than what traverses other identificatory traits (e.g., Zombies, Frankensteins or Vampires). Now for the vampiric identification trait, there is another visual (Table 5.5):

For Dunker, the genre of terror concerns the "experience of *losing one's soul* and the *intrusion of an object* disturbing our relationship of belief in reality" (Dunker 2018, p.28), then terror the accurate genre in order to address "the *deregulation of the spirit* and the *violation of the symbolic pacts* [at] the dimension of knowledge and truth" (Dunker 2018, 28). The peculiarity of vampires is that they encapsulate the ability of becoming *intrusive objects*, managing to manipulate the desire of others, transforming them into soulless slaves, multiplying the desire of the original vampire (Dunker 2018, 28). Basically, vampires "...*violate the pact* of the living in the name of their immortality" (Dunker 2018, 28). The next figure concerns details about the Frankenstein-like Creatures (Table 5.6):

TABLE 5.5 Dunker's (2018) psychoanalytic appreciation of Vampires

Identification types	*Main introductory features*	*Main conceptual feature*	*Element of desire*
Vampires	Product of the return to the medieval, temporal decentring and denied mortality – exponential trait of the desire. You invite the vampire in. Bram Stoker's Dracula. Dracula is bored at an endless life.	A pact which is not maintained or sustained, a part of the bargain which is not held.	Horror narratives combine 4 strategies of articulating the fantasy: (1) the destitution of the soul – melancholic, cold, fixed on an object; (2) intrusive object – a form hard to be captured, which seductively induces, manipulates and co-opts the desire from others; (3) deregulation of the spirit – fruit from the vampiric intrusion, their soul is slaved and multiplies the original will of the original vampire; (4) violation of the pact – they are not where they were supposed to be beyond living, they push towards immortality.

The core dilemma of Frankenstein's Creature is that of an "organs without bodies." The main strategy here concerns the experience of *deregulation of the spirit* (Dunker 2018, 23), where basically, it is all out there in the open, the organs are all out to be seen and yet, a full integration is always shattering. As the analyst defends, "the terror effect comes from the schizoid aspects deriving from fantasy" (Dunker 2018, 23). This argument seems valid in the examination of the theme of the double as well, as Dunker defends, where similarly lies a shattering sentiment, an experience of fragmentation and strangeness of the ego (Dunker 2018, 24). As Dunker explains, Frankenstein's Creature portrays how the body itself becomes uncanny, the "estrangement between ego and the other. A certain kind of possession of desire through the interests of the system takes place, i.e., by the Other" (Dunker 2018, 24). And finally, the analyst addresses zombies (Table 5.7):

TABLE 5.6 Dunker's (2018) psychoanalytic appreciation of Frankensteins

Identification types	*Main introductory features*	*Main conceptual feature*	*Element of desire*
Frankensteins	Is a fabricated doll from human remains, a joyful ride between the set of organs and a body. Mary Shelley's Frankenstein. Blade Runner. Terminator.	The Double, Dr Jekyll and Mr. Hyde, Metamorphosis. The schizoid feeling of the cut, fragmentation and estrangement of itself. Not only for losing your soul, but from the loss of the measures in order to try to recognize it. The body itself becomes uncanny, experiences of disjunction between elements and parts, the estrangement between me and the other.	De-regulation of the spirit. The multiplication or indefinite fragmentation of the I, lacking its own unity and totality. A part becomes the whole, and the feeling where although completely visible, something is not fully recognizable. The schizoid elements in the montage of fantasy. A co-option of the desire by the Other.

The zombie is approached by Dunker as the equivalent figuration of alienation, "an indeterminate creature, autonomous or automata, human or inhuman" (Dunker 2018, 21). The zombie-like creature translates moments where:

> ...one's life has become a mere function which repeats itself, in a senseless way, collective and undifferentiated. Zombies cannot actually die, since what is at stake is precisely their living status. This is why they are killed with impunity, as Agamben's *homo sacer*. In rigor, they are not dead, but defunctionalized by separating their heads from their bodies... these are the workers who cannot sleep, the lumpen dispossessed of themselves, the "*noias*" [drug addicts] and "crackheads", the refugees and immigrants floating in the Mediterranean sea or reduced to crosses at the borders between US and Mexico, the African wandering masses, the old people who weight on the federal pension. These are all the zombies which seem to "disturb" the functioning march of those whose lives are gifted with value against those whose lives obstruct the productive processes... These figures do not want to know, only to act. Here lies one of the most common montages of the unconscious fantasies.

TABLE 5.7 Dunker's (2018) psychoanalytic appreciation of Zombies

Identification types	*Main introductory features*	*Main conceptual feature*	*Element of desire*
Zombies	Repeats endlessly that which knows no discontinuity – knows no act – without reflexivity, knows only desperation and how to survive – therefore, without desire. The indeterminate creature, autonomous, human or inhuman. Zombies do not die because they are not alive to begin with. They are not killed but defunctionalized – usually de-attachment of the head from the body. Much like workers, refugees, drug addicts… the bodies "in the way" of productivity. Creatures that don't want to know, only to do.	Alienation (losing your own soul, your inner most), the pathology of not recognizing our own desire. The alienated is the one who suffers with an excess of determination of its own desire. Hegel's *Entfremdrung* (alienation and incapability of self-recognition in the other) and *Austäusserung* (inability to recognize yourself as consequence of your own acts, desires, thoughts and labour). The alienated consciousness which does not recognize the other, itself or in its objects and actions. Two qualities of madness: to be too much in ourselves and too much out of ourselves.	Fixed orientation towards an object. To resign from your own desire acquiring a tragic and universal dimension. A common montage of unconscious fantasy: to not know and only do. When there is only space for the object and it covers the I, generating hopelessness and melancholia.

> Once at it, there is only space to the object and if the shadow of the object falls onto the ego, only helplessness and melancholy remains.
>
> (*Dunker 2018, 21–22*)

Clearly, Dunker addresses the figuration of the zombie as a crucial point of the monstrous topos, concerning anguish. A very peculiar operation can be perceived by investigating the zombies: "We run away from reality by saying: "I don't want to know," but we avoid the Real convincing ourselves that "it is only imagination" (Dunker 2018, 22). This is a highly nuanced point and rather crucial, in order to dimension the zombie-like impasses.

Following Dunker's investigation on these monstrous strategies and on how identificatory traits can be perceived from them, it seems valid to introduce Žižek's monstrous contours at this point. Žižek's monstrous contours, as well as Zupančič's debate on the monstrous act (between Antigone and Sygne), seem to notice in their approach to tragedy a monstrous dimension which can be traversed as a solution to the very own impasse. Perhaps, the possibility of assuming these monstrous points of identification, their engagement as strategies, could also lead the way towards a proper monstrous grammar that organizes new symptoms and new suffering arrangements in the clinic.

Lacan's psychoanalytic teaching takes a substantial step from Freud's in terms of its ethical and aesthetical conditions of possibility. This does not mean Lacan's efforts are any less clinical, it is actually the opposite: his efforts are *always* clinically oriented (and as any psychoanalytic efforts *should be*). Lacan was focusing on how clinical transformations towards a cure made itself available in the face of suffering. In a way, the overall idea of raising such impasses does concern with the condition of possibility of improving psychoanalysis itself along the way. It is clearly not about making it worse or taking a turn …to the worst. Well, another important point is to be able to approach what a notion of the psychoanalytic science of Real means, not by denying the implications of the logic of the *suture*, but from it. To be informed by the logic of sutures is a way to produce a psychoanalysis oriented against any metaphysical tendencies (Badiou 2005), engaged in a condition of possibility which does not suppress its capabilities towards multiplicity and, does not give in to the *equivocity* of signifiers. If we ought to seriously understand how we invent/create individuals that live in our societies, the monstrous potency must be understood as an operator to question normativity and to allow transformation towards indeterminacy making more room for radical difference instead of less.

The entire debate of the present chapter can be seen as a highly speculative discussion, but the approximation between monstrosity within Lacanian psychoanalysis is not a new point. It seems more than clear now, how Lacanian psychoanalysis is in part, dedicated to try, as best as possible, to *listen* to what the monstrous impasses of the subject (of the unconscious) are about. So, the chapter opens with the investigation of a particular kind of monster, the Brazilian treatment of the *trickster*, as a different kind of monster (Guimarães 2003), which seems to invite an open and highly animistic approach to the theme of monstrosity, circumscribe by the psychoanalytic debate on animism and totemism inside a colonized country. Brazil's colonial and slavery past has left structural wounds and contradictions that are still socially repressed, this past is a ghostly dimension of the country's reality which returns in violence, because it has not been subsumed under proper terms.

The monstrous dimension highlights contradictions and the uncanny informs us of them. Of course, this is not an immediate response, and the

Hegelian argumentation presented by Žižek (2016) on Aesthetics informs the validity of "dealing" with monstrous encounters, with real abstractions. Therefore, more than just the engagement with the imaginary stance of these figurations, the proper symbolic realm which these evoke, seem to present a meaningful and important aspect which can be addressed. When Dunker (2013, 2018) provides his dedicated investigation on these identificatory traits, his cunningness lies precisely at the invitation of the animistic perspective embedded in his psychoanalytic approach, noticing the possibility of addressing the *monstrous topos* in which this suffering comes from. Thus, it is not simply a matter of figurations restricted to the imaginary, but a negative point for symbolic transformation. However, the proper point of transformation seems to be reached, if and only if, such monstrous encounters, emissaries, identificatory traits, are elevated, investigated, dissolved and destituted of their control, brought up the level of becoming the response to the very impasses from which these monstrous emissions were created. Only the traversal of this dialectical monstrosity concerns a monstrous (uncanny) materialism, which seems like to provide the proper way to new symbolic possibilities.

Notes

1 See more in William Shakespeare's "Titus Andronicus."

2 Magalhães finds in Freud's totemic meals and the anthropophagic absorption of the enemy in order to transform it into a totem (Dunker 2018, 77), something heavily present in the Brazilian Modernist writer Oswaldo de Andrade's formulations.

3 The passage commented by Žižek (2016) in Hegel's "Aesthetics" is the following:

> in this self-transcendence art is nevertheless a withdrawal of man into himself, a descent into his own breast, whereby art strips away from itself all fixed restriction to a specific range of content and treatment, and makes Humanus its new holy of holies: i.e. the depths and heights of the human heart as such, mankind in its joys and sorrows, its strivings, deeds, and fates. Herewith the artist acquires his subject-matter in himself and is the human spirit actually self-determining and considering, meditating, and expressing the infinity of its feelings and situations: nothing that can be living in the human breast is alien to that spirit any more. This is a subject-matter which does not remain determined artistically in itself and on its own account; on the contrary, the specific character of the topic and its outward formation is left to capricious invention, yet no interest is excluded – for art does not need any longer to represent only what is absolutely at home at one of its specific stages, but everything in which man as such is capable of being at home.
>
> in Hegel's Aesthetics, 1:607

4 Hegel passage from the Aesthetics examined by Žižek (2016 240):

> …absolute subjective personality moves free in itself and in the spiritual world. Satisfied in itself, it no longer unites itself with anything objective and particularized and it brings the negative side of this dissolution into consciousness in the humour of comedy. Yet on this peak comedy leads at the same time to the dissolution of art altogether. All art aims at the identity, produced by the spirit, in which eternal things, God, and absolute truth are revealed in real appearance

> and shape to our contemplation, to our hearts and minds. But if comedy presents this unity only as its self-destruction because the Absolute, which wants to realize itself, sees its self-actualization destroyed by interests that have now become explicitly free in the real world and are directed only on what is accidental and subjective, then the presence and agency of the Absolute no longer appears positively unified.
>
> (Hegel's "Aesthetics," 2:1236)

5 The philosopher's investigation of the dilemma presented by the film Sophie's Choice (Zupančič 2000, 216), as the philosopher states:

> We must not forget that Sophie finds herself faced with two choices. The first compels her to decide if she agrees to choose between the two children or if she refuses and thus loses them both. It is difficult to say what Kant would have suggested if he had been faced with this dilemma. We might nevertheless have grounds for claiming that he would have agreed with Sophie's choice. Seeing that one life is going to be lost in any case, he might have said that the categorical imperative demands that we save the other.
>
> (Zupančič 2000, 216–217)

6 Zupančič explains the Kantian law in its purest form and Lacan's point, from the dialogue between Sygne and the priest Bailon. In a first moment, Sygne is repulsed by the possibility of marrying Turelure in order to save the Pope. She'd rather die than losing her honour of betraying all she believes in, which could be a way to summarize her initial reaction, as Zupančič explains. Following Zupančič's analysis, Sygne is confronted by Badilon who intervenes reminding her, that Turelure has not only her like and Pope's in his hands, Turelure also has the life of Georges (the only person Sygne cares about). But she does not flinch: she argues that she is ready to die and if Georges dies, so be it. Sygne makes a case for her name and her women's honour which are her own, as Zupančič (219) highlights. Sygne confesses to Badilon that she regrets not having killed Turelure, even if in return, his friends would have killed everybody in the house. Thus, Sygne claims she would have preferred death than to be forced to choose. The paradoxical dimension lies, following Zupančič's discussion, in Sygne's facing the possibility of saving Pope at the cost of her own soul. This leads to the logic of the ethical dilemma debated by Zupančič:

> must I do my duty at the price of my humanity? Must I do my duty even if it implies the loss of that something in me that makes me worthy of duty? Is God able to ask, as the ultimate proof of my faith and my fidelity, that I betray this faith and fidelity, and that, as a consequence, I betray Him Himself? Faced with this attitude of Sygne's, Badilon does not impose a duty on her.
>
> (Zupančič 2000, 220)

Here is the point Zupančič finds

> the Kantian law in its purest form, the law which becomes truly unbearable at the very moment when it wants nothing (from us)? It is to this aspect of the Kantian law that Lacan refers when he says that 'the moral law… looked at more closely, is simply desire in its pure state'.
>
> (Zupančič 2000, 220)

7 Zupančič appreciates this point as follows, there are two key points at stake: first, the presupposition that both Sygne and Georges de Coûfontaine are ready to be sacrificed in the name of honour. While assuming life as a thing amongst others to be given away or not, something you may have, but a *reason* to live configures a different level, basically, honour concerns being (Zupančič 2000, 230). It is the honour of the two characters which determines what they are beyond life and death, as

Zupančič explains. Nonetheless, the drama does discuss 'honour or life', what it actually portrays is a level of choice where the "sacrifice of their lives is no longer relevant" (Zupančič 2000, 230). Basically, where sacrifice is required in order to save their Cause. As Zupančič explains: "the very Cause which determines them at the level of their being – this very being, their honour. In other words, they cannot choose 'the reason for living' without losing it at the same time" (Zupančič 2000, 231). This leads to the second point illustrated by Zupančič, when honour is the only thing left and there is nothing else to give, this is what they will give. Sygne defends her maxim:

> 'Sadder than to lose one's life is it to lose one's reason for living'. This maxim, and the support she finds in it, are all that is left to her, her only link with a world which is about to disappear and to which she belongs with all her being.
>
> (Zupančič 2000, 231)

8 In a brief article (2013) which was later on transformed into a book chapter (2018) Dunker discusses Catherine Malabou, Slavoj Žižek, Alain Badiou and Ernesto Laclau, engaging with four main modes of suffering: (1) the post-traumatic subjectivity that translates its suffering by compulsively repeating in a more "zombie-like" state and not managing to engage with a proper tragic narrative (i.e., a fundamental struggle with naming feelings and unconscious mutism); (2) the monstrous conditioned (inspired by Žižek) which surfaces the inhuman way of experiencing life, emerged in indeterminacy it concerns

> those who cannot inscribe their suffering in a discourse,..., [a] permanent state of systematic failure of naming the cause of their suffering. Trying to locate the reason of their discontent in the world, exploring the strength of estrangement, inadequacy and fragmentation;.
>
> (Dunker 2013)

(3) the modality of suffering in the Baudelairean Heautontimorumenos or in the Badiouian subject, which only appears conditioned through the fidelity to an event – trying to escape of ghosts from the past; (4) the condominial suffering emerged from the paranoid state created by sheltering life and propagating a State of exception in Agambenian terms. This separates them in two subsets:

> Zombies and Frankensteins who suffer from the lack of productive experiences of indetermination, where processes of rationalization appear as an indifferent void... While ghosts and vampires, on the other hand, suffer with the excess of unproductive experiences of determination, i.e., as if they trusted too much in processes of symbolization and subjectivization that regulate different regimes of truths.
>
> (Dunker 2013)

9 Much in line with what Jean-Claude Milner had already prescribed about this matter in *L'Œuvre claire: Lacan, la Science, la philosophie: "L'Ordre philosophique"* [1995]. It becomes clear that the distinction between Ideal of Ego and Ego-Ideal, sets the precedent for the risks one must try to avoid. Not to chase Ideals as fixed constructs and also, not to drop them completely. In a similar sense Dunker finds the answer in China Miéville, stating that the antidote for this interplays goes as follows:

> The experience of the city and its program of recovery depend on two strategies of negating the impossible: the reconstruction of *what never was*, i.e., the reinvention of the past through fantasy, with ghosts, vampires, Frankensteins and, the invention of a new future based on the *not yet possible*, like zombies, mutants and aliens.
>
> (Dunker 2018, 33)

References

Badiou, Alain. *Being and Event. 1998*. London: Continuum, 2005.

Badiou, Alain. *Logics of Worlds.* . London: Continuum, 2008.

Dunker, Christian. *O real e a verdade do sintoma*. São Paulo: In Revista Cult, 2013.

Dunker, Christian. *Mal-Estar, Sofrimento e Sintoma*. São Paulo: Ed. Boitempo, 2015.

Dunker, Christian. Zumbis, fantasmas, vampiros e frankensteins. In *Ensaios Sobre mortos-vivos*, edited by Rodrigo Gonsalves e Diego Penha. São Paulo: Ed. Aller, 2018, 15–35.

Dunker, Christian I. L. and Katz, I. Clínica do cuidado: Estrangeiridade, estrangeiro e estranhamento. *Calibán: Revista Latino Americana de Psicanálise*, Vol. 18, No. 1, 38–59, 2020.

Freud, Sigmund. Totem and Taboo and Other Works. Translation by. James Strachey. In *The Standard Edition of the Complete Works of Sigmund Freud*, Vol. 13. London: The Hogarth Press and the Institute of Psycho-analysis, 1955.

Freud, Sigmund. *The Uncanny. 1919*. London: Penguin Books, 2003.

Gay, Peter. *Freud*. London: W. W. Norton, 1989, 229–230.

Lacan, Jacques. [1959–60] *The Ethics of Psychoanalysis: The Seminar of Jacques Lacan, Book VII*. New York: W. W. Norton & Company, 1992.

Magalhães, Célia. *Os monstros e a questão racial na narrativa modernista brasileira*. Belo Horizonte: Ed. UFGM, 2003.

Milner, Jean-Claude. L'Œuvre claire: Lacan, la Science, la philosophie: "L'Ordre philosophique". In *Champs*, Vol. 454. Paris: Flammarion, 1995.

Žižek, Slavoj. 1989. *The Sublime Object of Ideology*. London: VersoBooks.

Žižek, Slavoj. *Disparities*. London: Bloomsbury, 2016.

Zupančič, Alenka. *Ethics of the Real*. London: VersoBooks, 2000.

Zupančič, Alenka. Reversals of Nothing: the case of the sneezing corpse. *Filozofski vestnik XXVI*, Vol. 2, 173–186, 2005.

Zupančič, Alenka. *What Is Sex?* Cambrige, MA: MIT Press, 2017.

CONCLUSION

Monstrosity and monsters must be taken seriously. Certainly, to come across monsters and monstrous things is an easy topic to be dismissed or to become dismissive about it. The cultural overproduction of TV shows, books and novellas about monsters or monstrosity diminishes the topic all too quickly. Nonetheless, it is not so much about the figures which come to surface, but about the position which these seem to inspire and the debate which can be addressed, if these are assumed with any dignity. The guiding question behind this thesis has always been the pursuit of philosophically appreciating what it could mean to take monstrosity seriously. Throughout the different chapters of the book, there is always a certain concern with adding a further layer, a further argument, another perspective, to try to defend that instead of just another imaginary figment, perhaps another approach to this topic, could provide more meaningful debates concerning our symbolic reality, as well as the ways which this creates seem to populate our own lives (in a more meaningful way). The research has noticed right from the beginning, the difficulties of the heterogeneous aspect involving this topic and instead of shrinking it down, diminishing it, the option was to bring it forward the points of tension which the topic necessarily evokes. One of the necessary points reached in the present examination on this theme is how points of tension need a proper grammar to be addressed, almost as if to address a certain tension a homogenous approach is required, it must be created along its process.

The commitment of philosophically investigating monstrosity comes with the troubles of having to deal with an immense range of lines of investigation, fields, topics, figures, authors and so on. To add to this debate, a framework was required and chosen; this certainly did not shy away from these tensions

DOI: 10.4324/9781003437543-7

(and certainly did not resolve them). Nonetheless, the philosophical engagement presented in this thesis aims at working with monstrosity as a peculiar realm to engage with points of tension deriving from our (in)humanity. The realm of ontological (dis)orientation seems to require a proper monstrous approach to further conceive all its self-relating negativity indications towards the symbolic. This is one of the many possible efforts which this theme permits, and perhaps, an effort which aims at providing a little more dignity to it. Although it is not a very compelling or charming topic within philosophy, it is a fundamental one. Forgotten and dismissively treated, but an important one. To provide dignity to monstrosity is to provide a deeper philosophical approach to the emblematic realm of negativity and the subsequent encounters with it.

Through the approach to the Lacanian psychoanalysis, its field and developments, it has become clear how it certainly provides meaningful endeavours within its dispositive. More importantly, through Lacan's return to Freud and his psychoanalytic engagement lies the crucial (re)insertion of the theme of the subject (of the unconscious), and with it, the proper realm of a (dis)oriented ontology (Zupančič 2017) towards symbolic reality finds its footing. The monstrous dimension is not excluded from psychoanalysis, and it is not *owned* by it. The realm of monstrosity is a priori, and it seems to be the sparkles and fleeting encounters with the Real with which psychoanalysis engages; certainly, not only does psychoanalysis deal with this, but the present text also tries to demonstrate it.

There are a very few emissaries (of the Real) that seem to permit this debate, and uncanny experiences are one of those. Within the uncanny lies a formidable element of negativity, which exposes how uncanny encounters are undeniable encounters with emissaries of the Real (through either the circuit of desire, the circuit of drive or the circuit of fantasy), and which can only be experienced through (dis)orientation, since such encounters can only be at fundamentally "monstrated" (Zupančič 2017, 69). Of course, this point can only be made after the treatment provided by Lacan to the uncanny. There are three crucial remarks on anguish and his unique contribution to psychoanalysis of the *object a*. The present work investigated Lacan's (a) the architecture of *anxiety* and the development of the *object a*; (b) the "extimite" space and (c) the truth of the unconscious for the subject. The Möbius strip torsion introduced by the French psychoanalyst demonstrates how far from being a "discovery," it is more of a *fact* that within *object a*'s "DNA" lies the Freudian *unheimlich*.

The groundwork for monstrous materialism concerns approaching the monstrous grammar of late capitalism *in its own terms*. Uncanniness understood in a dialectical sense sustains the materialistic depths of the foreignness of capital in our daily lives. The self-regulatory loops (Wright 2020) which are operating in capitalism impose their ruling upon us and they sustain a monstrous grammar that forcefully goes beyond its mathematizations. Basically, to approach logically the contradictions of capital is simply not enough to approach its monstrous foreign core, since it is not only mathematical but also monstrous. The *grammar* that enables its operation is disguised as financial mathematics, but this is an effect; its core is a self-regulating one, which operates for itself and by itself. This is why the present elements of this thesis would like to defend that, to approach the proper *topos* of the contradictions of capital, one must "*monstrate*" its grammar by advocating for a new signifier to arrive which denounces such contradictions within this very own grammar. The discussion about the monstrous topos is crucial to approach the conditions of possibility of the many bursts of the Real. This is where extreme formalism and equally extreme subjectivism meet as a fundamental impasse.

The role of the uncanny as a peculiar mediator seems to indicate a site to be further engaged precisely as a surfacing of (dis)orientation which evokes a monstration. The overall experience of the uncanny assumed as a site demands investigation of its infiltrations and manifestations. The uncanny requires an open logic to set dialectical materialism into motion, since it does not obey the regular formalism of classic oppositions. In a way, the uncanny permits inherent contradiction to take place and to reach the level of symbolic reality; it is certainly not an element restricted to the imaginary (as we have seen). The uncanny is the negative operator *par excellence*, it simultaneously approximates subjectivity in its more (in)human possibility, as well as it automatically confirms the excess of symbolic reality as such. Groundwork for monstrous materialism is nothing but the consolidation of efforts of *monstrations*, which do not fall into the impasses of equivocity in language and nor ignore them, which acknowledges multiplicity and how uncanniness addresses something peculiar about it. Far from another effort towards a suture, the overall idea of a monstrous materialism is to approach the power of negativity in dialectics and accommodate a proper grammar to our current impasses.

References

Wright, Ian. *What Is Abstract Labour and Who Does the Abstracting?* 2020. https://ianwrightsite.wordpress.com/2020/06/13/what-is-abstract-labour-and-who-does-the-abstracting/

Zupančič, Alenka. *What Is Sex?* Cambridge, MA: MIT Press, 2017.

INDEX

Pages in **bold** refer to tables.

FSC
www.fsc.org
MIX
Papier | Fördert gute Waldnutzung
FSC® C083411

Kolibri 360 GmbH
Ferdinand-Jühlke-Straße 7
99095 Erfurt, Deutschland
produktsicherheit@kolibri360.de